# GLOBALIZATION

*Edited by Charles Lemert*

CURRENT TITLES

*Globalization: An Introduction to the End of the Known World*
Charles Lemert (2015)
*Searching for the Spirit of American Democracy:
Max Weber's Analysis of a Unique Political
Culture, Past, Present, and Future*
Stephen Kalberg (2014)
*Cities: Unauthorized Resistances and Uncertain
Sovereignty in the Urban World*
Raymond Joshua Scannell (2011)
*Deploying Ourselves: Islamist Violence and the
Responsible Projection of U.S. Force*
David A. Westbrook (2010)

FORTHCOMING TITLES

*On Time and the World-System*
Immanuel Wallerstein
*Black Men: How Does It Feel to Be a "Problem"?*
Al Young

# GLOBALIZATION
An Introduction to the End of the Known World

## CHARLES LEMERT

*Paradigm Publishers*
Boulder • London

All rights reserved. No part of this publication may be transmitted or reproduced in any media or form, including electronic, mechanical, photocopy, recording, or informational storage and retrieval systems, without the express written consent of the publisher.

Copyright © 2015 by Paradigm Publishers

Published in the United States by Paradigm Publishers, 5589 Arapahoe Avenue, Boulder, CO 80303 USA.

Paradigm Publishers is the trade name of Birkenkamp & Company, LLC, Dean Birkenkamp, President and Publisher.

Library of Congress Cataloging-in-Publication Data

Lemert, Charles C., 1937–
    Globalization : an introduction to the end of the known world / Charles Lemert.
        pages cm. — (New world series)
    Includes bibliographical references and index.
    ISBN 978-1-61205-826-9 (hardcover : alk. paper) —
    ISBN 978-1-61205-913-6 (lib. ebook)
    1. Globalization.   2. Globalization—Social aspects.   3. Globalization—Economic aspects.   4. Culture diffusion.   I. Title.
    JZ1318.L446 2014
    303.48'2—dc23

2014033945

Printed and bound in the United States of America on acid-free paper that meets the standards of the American National Standard for Permanence of Paper for Printed Library Materials.

19  18  17  16  15   1  2  3  4  5

*For Michael Lemert, brother along the way
from another world to the ones to come*

# CONTENTS

| | |
|---|---|
| *Text Box Features* | *ix* |
| *Preface: Unknown Worlds* | *xi* |
| *Acknowledgments* | *xvii* |

| | |
|---|---|
| 1 World Under Siege: The Dark Side of Globalization | 1 |
| 2 What Is Globalization? Economic, Political, and Cultural Clashes | 16 |
| 3 When Did Globalization Begin? | 36 |
| 4 Globalization in the Modern World-System, 1500–1914 | 65 |
| 5 Changing Global Structures in the Short Twentieth Century, 1914–1991 | 93 |
| 6 The Globalization Debates: After the Short Twentieth Century and into the Twenty-First | 122 |
| 7 The Future of Globalization: The Unknown Worlds to Come | 142 |

| | |
|---|---|
| *References* | *R-1* |
| *Index* | *I-1* |
| *About the Author* | *AA-1* |

vii

# TEXT BOX FEATURES

Who in the World Is That?   xiii
Not Just a Story   5–6
Hidden but Not Lost   8
No Help for Jane Doe   8–9
A Neighborhood Always on the Move   11
Friends in Fast Global Space   22
*Alone Together*   24
Palestine and Israel: A Continuing Struggle over Land and Security   27–28
Stanley Hoffman, *Clash of Globalizations: A New Paradigm?*   34
Gilgamesh, the Legendary Global Hero   36
The Fear of Floods   37–38
Small Technologies and Big Changes   39–40
Marco Polo's Wonder at China's Coal   41–42
Central Asia as a Global Black Hole   43–44
Toynbee on the Universality and Vulnerability of Empires   47–48
Funeral Oration of Pericles, Thucydides, *History of the Peloponnesian War*
   (431 BCE)   51–52
Winston Churchill on History   52
Max Weber on the Ethic of Capitalism   53–54
Peace Treaty between the Holy Roman Emperor and the King of France and
   Their Respective Allies at Westphalia, 1648   56–57
Global Powers Assassinated Patrice Lumumba   60
Escaping Civilization to Live, Perhaps to Die   65
Martin Luther's Treatise on Christian Liberty/The Words of God
   (1520)   70

x  &#x2295; *Text Box Features*

The Bretton Woods Agreement, 1944/Report from the US Federal
Reserve  74
Karl Marx: The Buying and Selling of Human Labor Power  75–76
Max Weber on Calvinism and Worldly Asceticism  78
René Descartes, *Discourse on Method* (1637)  79
Jeremy Bentham on the Principle of Utility (1789)  80
Charles Darwin, *The Origin of Species* (1859)  82
W. W. Rostow, Questions of the Five Stages of Economic Growth  88
"The Structural Crisis: Middle-Run Imponderables"  90–92
What Is a Structure?  95–96
What Is a Present Time?  97
Henry Luce: The Twentieth Century Is the American Century (1941)  103
The Christmas Truce of 1914  104
F. W. Taylor's *The Principles of Scientific Management* (1911)  106
Adolf Hitler, *Mein Kampf* (1925)  109–110
Winston Churchill, Cold War, and the Iron Curtain (1946)  111
Pig's Feet and Profit  115
Fast Capitalism in China  118
Big Bank/Small Borrowers  119
Strong State/Weak State  129–130
Global Networks in Personal Life  131–132
Between Father and Daughter, Generations of Global Distances  138
Party Lines and Operators  143
The Last Typewriter  144
Junk in the Global Attic?  145–146
The Production of Wasted Lives  147
Thomas Piketty: The Past Devours the Future  150–151
When the Crisis Hit Home  153–154
Global Hunger  156–157
The Hebrew Myth of the Origins of All Things  159–160
Hesiod's Theogony: The Birth of Gaia, Mother Earth (ca. 700 BCE,
Greek)  160–161
*Climate Change: Evidence & Causes*—An Overview from the Royal Society
and the US National Academy of Sciences  164–165
World's Rural Settlements Disappearing  167–168
The Great Revolution of 1789–1848  169
The Global Future at Sea  174

### PREFACE

# UNKNOWN WORLDS

A cherished myth of the early modern North Atlantic peoples was that their world explorers defied the common wisdom that the earth was flat. To sail the seas beyond the known world was to risk falling off the world's edge. As most myths do, this one ignores the fact that early voyagers, like Christopher Columbus late in the fifteenth century, knew very well that the world was a sphere. Otherwise it is unlikely they could have persuaded royal patrons to venture capital against the prospect of access to the riches of Asia. They were curious as to what riches might lay beyond their known world.

Curiosity about our world is natural to most of us, as it was to our global ancestors. The theory that the earth orbited a sun that was the center of all things imaginable goes back to ancient Greek and Islamic cultures, then to Ptolemy in 150 CE—long before 1514, when Copernicus published his mathematically convincing commentary on the round, orbiting earth. Still the idea was known and accepted by the learned well before 1492 when Columbus set sail for the Americas.

It is improbable that any enduring culture—old or recent, near or far—would not have some sort of a received idea about its world. Whether grand or local, ancient, traditional, or modern, worlds are always figments

xii ⊕ *Preface*

of the spatial imagination. The traditional Wotjobaluk world of Australian aboriginal peoples was neatly ordered by the spaces occupied by its totemic clans, themselves organized into two dominant structures. The whole of the original Wotjobaluk world (which still exists) is limited to a smallish region in Northern Australia. The early Christian world was imagined to be on a human plane between, crudely put, heaven and hell. This was the flat-earth theory contested first by Ptolemy and largely put to rest by Copernicus. Today it is hard to say where our earth is in the vastness of the universe, with more stars than can be named. Still, we think of our physical earth as somehow identical to our culturally identified world, as if there were a truly singular "our" to the inhabitants of the place. We are many, but our earth is one, even if our cultural worlds are also many, if not unlimited.

These days it is no longer prudent to speak of worlds and earths. The phenomenon called *globalization* has intruded upon these settled ideas and places. Thus we must ask what is meant by the term *globalization* and the realities to which it is meant to refer. There is a great deal of debate on the question. Some think globalization is the wave of a good future; others believe it to be a disaster of an uncertain kind. Some think it is a cultural notion associated with the worldwide spread of popular music, clothing fads, and the like. Others think it is economic, as in the evident fact that wealth or poverty in one part of the world is caused by events beyond any one region. Others think it is political or military and that the great global powers are particularly hell-bent on controlling, even threatening, the lesser powers that in turn resist and rebel.

The purpose of this book is to sort out questions like these and others that inevitably arise whenever one tries to account for a real but complex historical process. In brief, the view taken here is that globalization is neither good nor bad. Nor is it any one kind of social process. Around 2010 I met a young Chinese man in Beijing who spoke near-perfect English. I asked how he learned the language. He replied with a few lines of early Jay-Z. About the same time in Bishkek, Kyrgyzstan, I heard Rihanna everywhere but not Taylor Swift, which, to me, was a sign of cultural sophistication. Yet it is also very well known that popular music is as much economic as cultural and, in the case of a great deal of hip-hop culture and popular music, explicitly political.

Unknown Worlds  xiii

## WHO IN THE WORLD IS THAT?

Not long ago, while scanning my Facebook notifications (whatever they are), I found one from a friend, David Levy, whom I met in Bishkek when he was living and teaching there. David is an American who did graduate work in Hungary and took a teaching position in Bishkek, where he met his Kyrgyz wife, Aisalkyn Botoeva. Both are fluent in Russian, the Kyrgyz language, and of course English. Today they live, with their baby, in Providence, Rhode Island, while working on their graduate research—which (not surprisingly) involves field work in Kyrgyzstan, from where he wrote me the following note:

> After a long drive from Bishkek to Almaty, during which we had to abandon our taxi and hitchhike after our driver was detained for carrying contraband merchandise (we even got to watch the police take him around behind their post and slap him around a bit—вся слава таможенному союзу), the first thing that greeted me in Almaty was a picture of Peter Dinklage's face indicating the men's room in the bus station. I'm used to the permeation of western popular culture here, but that still made me do a double-take.

As I was surprised to hear Rihanna in Bishkek, David was taken aback to see an image of Peter Dinklage in Almaty, the largest city in Kazakhstan. I was doubly surprised because I had no idea who Peter Dinklage might be. Then I looked him up and discovered that he is a very well known award-winning actor who, among other roles, was the lead in *The Station Agent,* a film I've seen and liked very much.

Is it me? Or is it globalization? I know who Jay-Z and Rihanna, not to mention Beyoncé, are because I have a teenage American daughter. Likely I would have known them without Anna's music. All are popular enough to be famous in Beijing and Bishkek, as around the world. Then too, Peter Dinklage, perhaps not as much the popular icon, is known the world over, even in Almaty, where Beyoncé was once criticized for giving a private concert requested by Kazakhstan's rather authoritarian leader. As things turned out she did *not* give this performance, though it seems that Kanye West may have. Who knows the truth or meaning of these things? Do they matter? If the subject is globalization, they do—at least to the extent of illustrating how different and confusing global networks are these days.

xiv   🌐   *Preface*

So it must be concluded that whatever globalization is, two things are true of it. We don't yet know what it will turn out to be or whether it is good or evil or some unpredictable mix of the two. What we can say is that globalization requires us to rethink space, time, and speed in ways that make Columbus's voyage seem quaintly part of a world we no longer know. Still, to understand globalization as it presents itself today, it is necessary to consider the historical fact that human beings have always migrated around the world, even if slowly and with little sense of their time. Even more, it is reasonably clear that well-organized societies have always, with rare exception, sought to increase their territories, and thus to push the limits of their own local worlds in ever more global directions.

The book's title may seem, depending on taste, a little too clever or overly wordy, if not obscure. Yet I use it to convey an underlying assumption that, so far as I know, cannot be simply put. Whatever, in the long run of global history, this world turns out to be or become, what we now call globalization signals a reality of our times that cannot be known. What we persist in calling *the* world (by which we mean *our* world) is changing in deep structural ways—or so it seems to those in the know. In the second decade of the twenty-first century, what those above a certain age thought they knew about the world is no longer true. Hence the subtitle: *An Introduction to the End of the Known World*. Worlds of all kinds, including those that might exist in stellar space beyond our present knowledge, are known by any who inhabit them.

We who live in this world know only what we allow ourselves to know. Scientists, with no reputable exception, know that the global climate is changing because of human carelessness. Others, for their own reasons, deny or doubt this reality. They or their children will learn the truth of the matter only when (or if, to be fair) the sea floods South Florida, lower Manhattan, coastal Japan, and most of the Pacific islands. Then only the Dutch will be able to build dikes to keep the watery disaster at bay. The point is that we know only what we want to know of our world. We should, therefore, not put climate scientists on too high a pedestal. There is plenty they don't know or want to know. Surely a good many of their lovers are cheating on them while they crunch their data.

But what are we to do when the worlds we think we know undergo, or seem to be undergoing, important structural changes? The last time such a change occurred was about a half millennium ago in the centuries on either side of 1500—a time that included the beginning of the European voyages of world discovery and settlement, of which Columbus's was but one. This was the time taken to be a point of departure from the long medieval period, and the beginning of the modern world.

Yet it is well known that there is no such thing as a single point in time when a world changes. The power of the medieval age held sway well into the late 1700s in even the most modern parts of Europe and North America, and much later in Russia, China, and Japan, where medieval cultures dominated into the early 1900s. Even now there are temples and cathedrals, museums and monuments, music and ideas that endure from their beginnings in premodern times. In fact, there is a book called *The Known World Handbook: Being a Compendium of Information, Traditions and Crafts Practiced in These Current Middle Ages in the Society for Creative Anachronism*. The title alone is mystifying if only because one wonders what "these current middle ages" might mean. It turns out that the book is but one of many products of the Society for Creative Anachronism. Since the 1960s this organization has brought together people from around the world who engage in reenactments of medieval traditions—dances, costumes, heraldry, armor, and the like. It has even organized the world into kingdoms. Arizona is Atenveldt. Europe and Africa are Drachenwald. I live, it happens, in the East Kingdom. One presumes that there are enough people in all the kingdoms to support their fascination with medieval worlds to the extent of making them, for a time, known to them. It may seem odd. But then again, we are all living in worlds that arose from those long gone, as ours will be one day—a day some think is upon us. This will be a day when as little is known of Jay-Z and Rihanna as most of us know about the Wotjobaluk. If it turns out that our world has begun to pass away, globalization is the current name for that supposed reality. In all likelihood none alive today will live to learn the truth of the matter, just as none alive in 1500 knew what was coming upon them.

Globalization is a concept meant to account for a new worldly reality. Like all such concepts there is little likelihood of common agreement as to its meaning. Still, given that, if real, globalization is of unquestionable importance to our lives on this earth, it is important to do what can be done to make sense of its most basic qualities—and that is what I will do here.

# ACKNOWLEDGMENTS

*Globalization: An Introduction to the End of the Known World* bears a direct and dependent relation to an earlier book in which I had a hand: *Globalization: A Reader,* which I edited with Anthony Elliott, Daniel Chaffee, and Eric Hsu (Routledge, 2010). Many of the references in *Globalization: An Introduction to the End of the Known World* are included in that one (for which I have been forced to use the immodest citation "Lemert et al. 2010" to avoid excessive referencing). Plus which, a number of the long section introductions in that book were mostly composed by the author of this one. As a result, it should surprise no one if some of what is said here was said there in different words and ways. Readers who are just beginning to think about globalization may want to consult that earlier book, which collects many of the classic and contemporary texts on the subject. Much of what I do in this book is influenced by my friendship and collaboration with the editors of that one.

Anthony Elliott has been an intellectual companion and friend over many years. Without his always-keen intellectual and administrative gifts, *Globalization: A Reader* would not have come to be. Much the same can be said of the research and writing work done by Daniel Chaffee and Eric Hsu, both of whom I've known and worked with across most of the years of the twenty-first century. Kristin Plys and Vani Kulkarni are among my best Yale colleagues. They have helped immeasurably to clarify my thinking on many aspects of the global situation both general and particular. I

xviii    *Acknowledgments*

have also benefited over some years now from the thinking of friends and colleagues in Yale's Senior Fellowship of retired social scientists. I came late into the group, which for years has been guided by Kai Erikson, who never fails to impose his unique genius for intellectual fellowship. I presented a part of this book to that group, on which occasion Wendell Bell went out of his way to comment in detail and, importantly, to influence the final chapter, on the future of globalization.

In writing *Globalization: An Introduction to the End of the Known World*, at nearly every crucial turn I paused to reconsider what Immanuel Wallerstein (also a member of the Senior Fellows group) had to say on the subject at hand. More often than not I had to agree with him. The truth of the matter was brought home as I was writing one of the sections where I departed from Wallerstein to some slight extent. On a late November afternoon I took time out to attend a lecture he was giving at Yale (Wallerstein 2013a). As on other such occasions, the room was packed a good twenty minutes before the announced start. As often happens for some reason at academic occasions like this one, he was all but alone with his wife in the front row. For reasons beyond the need of a place to sit, I walked down to join them. Both graciously stood as I approached to exchange greetings. He then said, "What are you doing here? You know all this stuff." I said something innocuous to the effect that that wasn't so. Then he gave his lecture with the usual clarity and unassuming wit. I realized that indeed I did know much of it. This was due only partly to the fact that I had played a secondary role in one of his then-recent books (Wallerstein, Lemert, and Rojas 2012), for which I read or reread most of Wallerstein's writings and discussed many of them with him. Still, I realized that I was in an awkward situation. This book was already nearly finished, much of it thought through with his ideas more or less consciously in mind and, as it turns out, on the page. I tell this story on myself only to exonerate him. Authors often profess responsibility for the mistakes they make when relying on the work of others. Never could such a profession be more apt.

Charles Lemert
New Haven, CT
November 4, 2014

# CHAPTER ONE

# WORLD UNDER SIEGE
## *THE DARK SIDE OF GLOBALIZATION*

A small band of boys on a school excursion are lost at sea near a remote island. No adults survived. The boys are on their own. After gathering themselves to face their situation, they decide to elect a leader, Ralph. A rival, Jack, after losing the election, emerges as the organizing force of resistance to Ralph's civilizing leadership. The symbol of order, entrusted to Ralph, is a large seashell. When blown, the conch broadcasts a sound loud enough to call the boys to assemble. This is the disturbing fable of the origins of human society as retold in William Golding's brilliant 1954 novel *Lord of the Flies*.

Fables play on symbolism. Here, Ralph is the representation of civil order. Jack is the symbol of disorder, even evil, in human nature. The "lord of the flies" is of ancient, probably Greek, origin. The flies are the infestation of human society arising from human nature. The general idea is that human society is always under siege by forces within its own nature that threaten social order. In Golding's story, Ralph gradually loses control of the group as Jack becomes the dominant force of aggression. The story turns on a terrifying scene in which Jack leads his hunters to kill a female pig, representing mother nature herself: "Struck down by the heat, the sow fell and the hunters hurled themselves at her. This dreadful eruption from an unknown world made her frantic; she squealed and bucked and the air was full of sweat and noise and blood and terror. Roger ran round the heap, prodding with his spear whenever pigflesh appeared. Jack was on top of

2    CHAPTER ONE

the sow, stabbing downward with his knife. Roger found the lodgment for his point and began to push till he was leaning with his whole weight. The spear moved forward inch by inch and the terrified squealing became a high-pitched scream. Then Jack found the throat and the hot blood spouted over his hands." Thereafter, all is violence. The symbolic death of mother nature unleashes human rage among the boys. The hunters attack Ralph and his few remaining companions. Piggy, his friend, is murdered. The conch shatters into pieces. The primitive society is destroyed. In the end, Ralph is rescued. He has no idea what happened or why. He sobs uncontrollably.

As for the philosophy behind the story, many would deny that human nature is so deeply destructive. Yet there is more than enough evidence to suggest it may be. Versions of this fable have been told and retold since the earliest times, certainly from Sophocles to Shakespeare and Freud, then to Golding and a very great deal of popular as well as high fiction. When my then-fifteen-year-old daughter left her middle school, she volunteered that *Lord of the Flies* was her favorite book because, as she put it: "It reminded me of my school. We were left alone to destroy each other." Humans of all ages and conditions seem to recognize that their better natures are regularly under siege.

## WORLD UNDER SIEGE

Usually, to speak of a siege is to refer to an alien attack upon a settled village, city, or larger political entity. In the sixteenth century, for example, the British colony in Roanoke, Virginia, was lost sometime after 1590. An earlier settlement presumed that the native peoples would feed them. Soon the Indians lost patience and destroyed the white people. A few years later the British sent another band of settlers who were largely abandoned by the Royal Navy, which was preoccupied with raiding Spanish and French ships in the Atlantic. When, finally, one ship stopped to look for the second Roanoke colony they found the site deserted. To this day no one knows what happened to the settlers. Perhaps it was the primitive conditions or the weather or the failure of the crown to resupply them. If not that, perhaps native peoples laid siege on the small band of aliens. Long before the Roanoke colony disappeared, in 410 CE, the then-dominant global civilization, Rome, fell to Alaric and the Goths. Closer to our day, in 1944, when Germany's almost 900-day siege on Leningrad in World War II failed, Hitler's regime began its rapid decline. A siege on any scale is violent and destructive of social order.

Normally, unlike the *Lord of the Flies* fable, a siege is thought to be from an external force against a given settlement of any number of sizes. Usually a siege is strategic. When Osama bin Laden's Al Qaeda movement attacked the World Trade Center in New York City and the Pentagon in the District of Columbia, the attacks were tactical assaults drawn from a long-standing terrorist strategy of laying siege on a symbolic aspect of the enemy to demoralize its people or cripple its economic or military power. September 11, 2001, failed tactically, but the continuing siege succeeded in mobilizing Euro-American powers to engage a war against terrorism that eventually resulted in the destruction of Osama bin Laden in 2011. "To lay siege" means, originally, to attack in order to seize the seat of power, as the Nazis tried but failed in Leningrad and as the Goths did in Rome.

What might a *siege on the world* mean? Rome thought of itself as the center of the world and Hitler wanted to rule the world, but neither Rome in its day nor Hitler's delusion of a world under his boots were worlds—not even in their dreams. The world, as we think of it in our day, may not be the world pure and simple. At least in our time it might be better to speak of *worlds* comprising regions, states, and subcultures. Many of them are at least marginal to *the* world order and some are all but outside of it—Antarctica is one example; parts of the Australian outback and Siberia are others. At the very least, a siege on the world is different from Alaric's siege on Rome in that "the world" has no single, all-powerful seat or center—not even when Britannia ruled the seas; not even in the days after World War II when the United States stood alone as the global economic power. Never has it been possible for a lesser power to attack the world as such.

Still, we can speak of the world under siege, if it is understood that the world as we have known it is one that must pay the piper for the destruction its greatest powers have wrought. Individuals may, from time to time, get away with their crimes. But large political powers never do; certainly not when their crimes are against the nature of worldly things. The settlers in the lost Roanoke colony did no more than common human evil themselves, but, like all colonizers, Britain did. In the long run Britannia collapsed in due course when it overreached in its desire to control the world. The very fact of colonizing is, at least, evil. Whatever good may be done is never purely good for the colonized. It always spoils the land and the resources of the subjugated.

Sooner or later the dominated reject their dominators, usually not for an abstract value like freedom but for the real-life right to their own piece

# 4 ⊕ CHAPTER ONE

of the earth—its wealth, its food, or its wood. In 1930, colonial India rebelled against the British for its right to salt, as in 1773 the colonized in North America began their revolution over rights to tea. Decolonizing struggles may have material symbols like salt and tea but in the long run they are about throwing off the colonizers. Political domination hurts the dominated, who in time reject the system, whether by force or withdrawal of cooperation. Still, no matter how awful the world may be it is impossible to imagine how its inhabitants can express their outrage by attacking *it*—the world as such. Worlds do not have seats of power. Whatever else they are, and regardless of how many there may be in the wider universe, worlds are primarily environments for lesser entities, some of which are indeed powerful and evil.

Powerful states could not do what they do, good or bad, were they not grounded in a world. A world, bigger by far than a kingdom, is not as encompassing as an earth. Our local earth is land, sand, sea, and rocks. Our worlds, however, are a coming together of political, economic, social, and cultural forces distributed unevenly among a variety of worldly powers—some grand, some tiny, but all with a definite relation to the others. They may be dominators or dominated. They may be everywhere at once on the seas, in the air, or across the lands. They may be so remote and beside the point that no one notices them until their oil or timber is discovered.

Worlds, therefore, are mysterious spheres of human and natural life. Whether there are worlds on any earthlike body in the known universe is not known. Thus, we must speak of *this* world, without supposing other worlds of a divine or material sort. It may be that this or that set of beliefs common to various human cultures insist on the existence of other worlds ruled by gods or monsters. Such beliefs are common enough to seem necessary. They are not unappealing. In fact, gods, even monsters, serve to explain why believers are where they are in the scheme of things. Famously, these are concerns for which there are no easy or certain answers. This alone may be one reason human beings do so much damage to each other and to the world on which they depend. Since we don't really know why we are here now, there is a natural tendency to think *What the hell! I should take what I can while I'm here.* Not all humanoids are selfish in this way, but even the saintly are taking something for themselves out of the good deeds they do or think they are doing. In either case they do what they do.

This is why the world is always at risk—under siege from those who most depend on it. Grass withers, beasts die, sands blow, but without the burden of wondering why. We die and in some sense it makes us anxious if not downright mad. This may be why the vast majority of us ultimately don't deeply care about remote others or the world we share with them. It sounds harsh. But it cannot be ruled out, if only because our siege on the world is so absurdly illogical.

## THE HUMAN ANIMAL

One day, while walking my dogs in the woods, I came upon a mother, her daughter, and their family dog. Their dog was recently adopted, young, and frisky. As we dog walkers do, especially when breaking the leash laws, we both apologized for our dogs, whereupon she launched into a way-too-long explanation that her dog was new to her and lacked *manners*. Everyone uses metaphors, but to expect manners of a domesticated animal is, I think, strange. Dogs may be obedient, even charming. They surely have a healthy set of animal instincts, including those drawing them into packs. Our dogs sleep in the same room with one or another or with us. Still, whatever instincts are, they are not manners. We humanoids have manners and may have had them in the earliest times. Whenever humanoids evolved from the beasts of the jungle, they no doubt had instincts, as did their phylogenetic ancestors. But real manners are overlaid upon and beyond instincts.

> ### NOT JUST A STORY
>
> In 1845 Captain Sir John Franklin set off by sea from England for the Arctic. His mission was to discover a Northwest Passage from the Atlantic to the Pacific. He was not the first of the Arctic explorers, or the last. Then as now, the Northwest Passage was a much-valued prize—one that would drastically shorten the travel time from Europe to Asia, where most colonial powers since Columbus traded for riches valued in European capital markets.
>
> The venture was dangerous. Well into their navigation across the Arctic, Franklin and his company were lost. Some years later, after a number of searches, stone markers and the remains of three crewmen were found at Beechey Island. Local Inuit were found to have artifacts they could only have come upon by trading with the English crew. There the Franklin expedition had ended. Lives were lost. Still, it was not clear how a well-supplied expedition had lost its way. They were not

# 6 ⊕ CHAPTER ONE

abandoned as had been the Roanoke colony, which was lost in a far more hospitable climate. Then again, while the English in Virginia may have been destroyed by native peoples, those found on Beechey Island clearly had established good enough relations with local Inuits who, apparently, spoke well of them—perhaps even to the extent of helping them. No one knows. Then too, they may have been victims of the inadequacy of their own modern technologies. One theory is that they suffered food poisoning from leaks in the tin containers meant to preserve their food.

It was not until a good century later, early in the 1980s, that a forensic scientist studied the remains of the Franklin crew to discover that their bones bore cuts that could only have been inflicted for the purpose of cannibalism. Some who had remained were willing to eat their shipmates to survive.

Cannibalism usually shocks human beings, especially so-called modern ones. This is why *Lord of the Flies* can be such a shocking story. Piggy was killed but not eaten. Still, the story is one of the extent to which human nature is willing to kill for just or evil reasons. Franklin's crew was not evil. They formed, it seems, human enough relations with the Inuit people. Yet when they came to their end they did what other animals do. They struggled to survive to the extent of killing and eating their kind.

The disturbing truth of the story of Franklin's crew is that normally subhuman animals do not eat their own. Though humans may not be the only cannibals among vertebrates or mammals, they are creatures who will eat each other. If this, then how far will we go in destroying our own world?

We are animals. We are human. We would not be the latter were we not also the former. We must be both. Were it the case, which it is not, that we had to choose one or the other, we humans would be foolish to choose to be nothing but human. This would be choosing nothing or little at all. Whatever is good about human cultures, manners included, without our animal nature we would succumb to the forces of nature, including most likely the revenge of dogs and wolves and other creatures our species has taken advantage of. Though it is hard to imagine, one supposes that if they could, buffaloes, especially, would stomp us out for what we did to their ancestors on the American plains and the whales would rise up against our greedy harvesting of the sea animals.

Left to their own natural devices, lesser animals seem to get along quite well without us. Even parakeets and poodles came from a genetic line that knew nothing of cages and foolish groomings. So far as we can tell, they don't long for an afterlife or, for that matter, any kind of life in this world that does not come naturally to them. They may starve in droughts or be eaten by their local predators, but for the most part the so-called lesser animal species figure out how to get by in the long run. Dinosaurs are the exception. Cockroaches are the animal normal.

Yet if cockroaches are closer to the animal normal, this prospect presents a moral challenge to our species, which thinks of itself as higher, more evolved, than bugs and dogs. Dogs, even wild ones, do not seem to make quite the mess of our shared world as we domesticated people have. As wonderful as so very much human ingenuity has been, the genius of our inventions has been bought at the price of a terrible devastation we have visited on each other and on the world we must share.

## THE DARK SIDE OF GLOBALIZATION

Today, still early in the twenty-first century, the aftereffects of our long-standing siege on our own world are of acute concern and pose particularly urgent problems in our time.

Today few deny that we have degraded our natural environment. For centuries, petroleum fuel, including coal, was considered nothing but a miraculous gift that lent heat and light to homes and ran the engines of modern industry and technology. Now it is plainly foolish not to consider its dangers. Burning oil sends gases into the atmosphere that choke the air, warm the planet, melt the ice caps that will flood our coastal cities sooner than we dare to know. Just when the global human community ought to be set on saving our planet and each other, violence of all kinds, including against the seas and atmosphere, tear at what natural social bonds we have and need. We think of ourselves as somehow special, but whatever cockroaches may do to the world, they do not degrade it as we do. Most modern cultures do not take seriously the fact that, whatever humans are, we are first and foremost natural beings. Human social life begins as animal life. Yet we pretend this is not so. Lions roam the Serengeti. They hunt antelope to survive, but they are not as preoccupied as we are with destroying each other.

You might suppose that to the extent that globalization has increased the prospects for global communications and visual awareness of each other, it would have already begun to make us more aware of the urgency with

# CHAPTER ONE

> **HIDDEN BUT NOT LOST**
>
> In my town, just over the hill pushed up in the Jurassic period, is a park I enjoy for long hikes with my dog. Several years ago, I came across a small, neatly kept camp site—a tent, a few provisions for cooking, other signs of regular occupation. It was off the beaten path, hidden in summer by bushes and tall grass. One day it was gone, cleared, I supposed, by the park rangers. I never saw anyone there, but I was sure that it had been if not a home, at least a shelter for someone who needed a place to rest or, perhaps, for an occasional sexual encounter. I never knew and never will. But my idea was confirmed on a walk deeper into the woods, when I found a similarly tidy settlement well hidden from public view. Shanty shelters like these are domestic settlements for people without access to a private dwelling. To be homeless is far from being lost. In fact, people without an address may well be among the world's most inventive in finding or making shelter—in getting by.

which we require a healthy natural and social environment. Instead, sadly, so far globalization seems to have cast a dark shadow over human prospects.

Homelessness is on the darker side of globalization. Whatever may be the promised benefits of globalization, it has led to a sharp increase in the numbers of human individuals and families with no place to go or be. Whether in isolated encampments like the ones near my home, or refugee camps, or assemblages of squatters outside many of the world's burgeoning urban sprawls, or abandoned grates in deep pockets of urban abandonment, the people living on the margins of organized society are an uncountable number who defy the odds of an otherwise-affluent world. Their number has been estimated to be at least a billion, perhaps more. If you were to include those who are sheltered, however inadequately, but are living with scant hope of doing better, the number rises.

> **NO HELP FOR JANE DOE**
>
> The horrors of abandonment in a cruel world very often present themselves just around the corner. Nicholas Kristof (2014), as he does so often, tells a story so gut-wrenching as to be almost impossible to read.
>
> Jane Doe (obviously not her name) was abandoned by her father (in prison) and her mother (an addict). She was placed in a relative's home.

World Under Siege  9

> When she was but eight years old, she was raped so severely by a cousin that the anal penetrations tore her bowels. Unable to control them, she often defecated about the house. Her vile grandfather told her, Kristof reports, "only animals do that, and if you don't stop I'll treat you like one." She was often forced to sleep outside.
>
> In time she was removed by the state and placed in a public institution for children, where staff repeatedly raped her as her cousin had. She was twelve, Hispanic, brown, and transgender. At fifteen she was homeless. Jane made what way she could by prostitution. She was sent to prison, eventually released. Since the state could find no better place, she was then placed in a youth-detention facility, where she remained confined for want of a place to go. Today she is somewhere in the state where I live, close by in an otherwise elite college town.

The World Hunger Education Service (2013) reports that no fewer than 1.3 billion people (22.4 percent of the global population) live on less than US$1.25 a day. This is considered progress since in 1990 the number was 1.9 billion (43 percent of the global population). The number is shocking because, over the thirty years prior to 2013, the number living in deepest poverty had declined by 30 percent. Yet when examined more closely, the World Hunger report reveals that 80 percent of the world's population in *developing* countries is living on less than $10 a day and the actual number does *not* include those living on so scant an income in the *developed* world. Since those among the poorest—living as squatters or homeless—cannot really be counted (and the difference between $1 and $10 a day is real statistically but appalling humanly), all we really know is that the world is very poor in spite of the marvels of globalization. The very, very rich are fewer in number and richer than ever. The vast majority of the world's population below the top 5 percent in terms of wealth live at risk of losing what they have or without hope of having anything at all.

A related consequence of global poverty is the sharp increase in human migration—aggravated by global crises that force the poor to flee hopelessness for not much more hope. According to the Population Division of the Economic and Social Affairs Department of the United Nations (2013), international migrations have increased from 155 million in 1990 to 190 million in 2005, and to 250 million in 2013—and still growing. This does not include the millions who migrate within countries—as from the impoverished rural villages in China to the factory centers, from the

10 CHAPTER ONE

depleted rural regions to the urban agglomerations in African cities like Nairobi and Lagos, from the closed-down factory towns to New Haven and Hartford in Connecticut. Migrants are nearly as uncountable as the global poor, especially when they are unregistered workers from the rural villages in China, from below the border of the United States, or beggars and peddlers in Kinshasa and Mumbai.

In one basic sense, globalization is about migration. People move often in their lives. This has been perhaps the principal defining characteristic of the modern world. Since about the middle of the nineteenth century, the factory system came to dominate the world of work. Rural people moved to factory towns and cities. As they left behind the life of farming, food production in the world's bread baskets became factories of a sort themselves. Monsanto chemicals control Indian seed resources. Iowa land is bought as an investment commodity. The Australian outback is a mining region dominated by Chinese interests. The Amazon is being clear-cut for timber shipped to Japan. The already barren Arctic is populated by pipeline workers and oil producers in Canada, the United States, and Russia. The iron law of modernization is migration to ever-larger cities from ever-shrinking villages. Few remain where their ancestors lived. Their places are taken, when they are, by agents of international capital who cut the forests, mine the land, and suck up the gas and oil—until they are depleted. Then they move on. Everyone moves. The better off have a place to go. The poorest have no place.

If one wants to be a bit clever, it could be said that the globalized world is one in which all are homeless in one way or another. For some this is part of the adventure of the fast life. For others it is a bitter metaphor for the reality that less and less does the meaning of life have to do with relations with the family and friends of childhood. Home in a globalized world is a figment. My depressed father was "home" every day, but in my experience he was never there. In my home today we hang out a lot with each other—when, that is, we are not answering email or checking social media. That is something, but nothing like the old days when families would sit around the fire as the sun set, reading Shakespeare to each other or knitting or listening to the radio. Is one better than the other? Maybe not. But in the long run of most lives globalization draws us away from whatever hearth we may have had. Kids move on and out, as most of us have or will. Some become famous. Most don't. But nearly all move.

World Under Siege  11

> **A NEIGHBORHOOD ALWAYS ON THE MOVE**
>
> On the block where I live, there are, as best I can tell, no more than two households with individuals over eighty years old. There were four, but two died last winter. There are another few, myself included, who are still in their seventies. None of us was born on the block, though one youngish woman lives in the house she grew up in. Most of the homes are owned by people who have been here for a good many years. But many of them have rented out attic apartments to students or young faculty at Yale. Several years ago a Yale student was murdered on campus. That was terrible, made worse by the news reporters who rang our bells to ask for news. Soon enough they went away. The wound healed over. But there will always be a tear in the flesh of our apparently normal neighborhood. Every year when leases expire there are moving trucks. Someone next door moved yesterday. I think it was the young teacher who is getting married to a guy in North Carolina, but she didn't say goodbye. It may have been the Chinese couple who came just last year. Mike owns this property. He grew up across the street, but he now lives somewhere in the suburbs. The other day I offered to haul his trash cans out for him. He said thanks, but he liked coming by once a week. Steve grew up a few blocks over. He now lives in the suburbs but still owns his childhood home, which is occupied by a member of his extended family, her wife, and their son. Her parents live a few blocks over, but they grew up in Brooklyn. Steve married their other daughter, whose children went to school with my daughter before the kids moved on to different high schools. That is what we call rootedness in a globalized world. As these things go, this is far from the worst. Still, no one is quite home and many are soon gone. Then too, there are the homeless camped in the woods on the other side of East Rock, the hill where dinosaurs saw but surely did not understand the night lights that sped to them from long-dead distant stars.

What is dark about global migration is that so many move out of desperation, pushed from their homes because of hunger, disease, civil strife, or just plain poverty. Had I stayed in the home of my sad father and confused but kind mother, I would not have starved after they died. Nor, it seems, did the cancers and heart troubles they suffered afflict me. I have outlived them by

## 12 ⊕ CHAPTER ONE

far. But in my mind's eye, had I stayed I likely would have died in a moral sense for having fallen into the sad lives they lived. But the fact remains, whether there in that one-dimensional suburb of a very dull Midwestern city or here in allegedly progressive New England, I was not forced to flee. I chose to. But the choice was not mine alone to make.

The kids I played with in Cincinnati all went to college, against the norm of the wider neighborhood. In those days we were a flawed sort of elite. A few of them came back to that city. Most moved on. Nearly all of us moved up. The one of my high-school friends who went to an Ivy League college was very successful. He settled in retirement in Vermont. By accident I found his phone number and called him to propose a visit. He said no. You can take some kids out of Cincinnati, but its conservative habits often remain.

In my school days, it was normal for college graduates to do well, often better than their parents. Today it isn't. According to the *Washington Post* (January 25, 2012), a report by Georgetown University's Center on Education and the Workforce stated that 8.2 percent of new college graduates in math and computer science will be unemployed. This was 2012 in the United States, where math and computer science are crucial to the nation's economic future but the American economy suffered nearly 8 percent unemployment. In the wealthiest economy in the world, the rich get richer, the poor get poorer, and the shrinking number between get by in a middling sort of way. This is not poverty, but it is related to the facts of global poverty. Not long ago I had dinner with a student at the self-appointed elite college where I taught. I asked her what had been special about her college experience. She said that for the first time in her life she got to sleep in a bed. Today some years later she has a job, but for two years upon graduation she was living back in the projects, sleeping on the sofa of her childhood.

One might well wonder what anecdotes about individuals and tent settlements, suburbs in the old days and slums in these days, and migrants in Nigeria and Cameroon really have to do with globalization. Weren't there always poor people, migrating here and there around the world? There were. But there is an important difference in respect to poverty in a globalized world.

Today everyone, with rare exception, knows that out there in the wider world forces push and pull at them. Whether they are the not-so-apparently benign forces of corporate jobs in glamorous cities abroad or the armed militia that raid one's village, rape the women, and shoot the men and boys, people cannot avoid the experience of forces bigger than they are. If they are on the very bottom rung of global poverty, they may not fully understand what these forces are, which would not be surprising since the average kid in a fancy prep school may not either. But the very poor know, if only because they are migrants camped along the highways and dirt roads leading to major urban centers. They cannot help but see the walled establishments of the well-off. If they must beg, they beg on the streets along which the better off travel. If they are homeless, they know to find what shelter they can find on the margins, away from the police and other guardians of the righteous. If they are temporarily settled in a refugee camp or squatter village, they encounter agents of the well-intentioned who offer kind but insufficient ministry to their suffering. If they are sold into the global sex trade, they are, literally, slaves, screwed by clients with cash in hand. If their water is foul or their land depleted they must walk as best they can for relief—which, if found at all, is given by international agents who are themselves swimming upstream against the global flood of indifference. Along their migratory ways, the very poor may even spot a billboard or, in a settlement, come upon a sole television run by pirated electricity in compensation for the open sewage by the side of dirt roads. Whatever their affliction, the very poor sooner or later come upon the harsh exclusions or exceptional kindness of the wider world.

The traditional poor of an earlier time lived in a smaller, less well connected world. What news they had of the wider global realities came to them from mendicant monks across the Alps from Rome, caravans of merchants along the Silk Road from China, or nomadic tribes across the deserts stopping at a common oasis. Neither poverty nor migration is new to the globalized world. But news as we get it today is. In the 1770s news of battles in the American Revolution would slowly pass to Europe in reports and mail carried across the Atlantic by ship. When I was a child in the 1940s, news of the war in Europe was available daily in newspaper and radio reports sent along by wire or radio by reporters in the trenches. When I had become an adult, reports in the 1960s of the war in Vietnam came taped on the nightly TV news. As I have grown old, I have watched revolutions and massacres around this sad world as they happen, reported often by ordinary people crouching from the fire while posting the scenes on YouTube. My daughter will grow up, as her older brother has, in a world where, even more than now, the practical problems of daily life will be how to screen out all the global information that now, when she is barely a teenager, sneaks into her Facebook world: who is dating or defriending

## 14 CHAPTER ONE

whom and why. True, the young who are poor are not likely to be wired, but as cell phones saturate the globe, they will be one day.

In 2012 there were 5.6 billion mobile phones, one for roughly 80 percent of the global population. The phones are not, of course, evenly distributed. In the United States there are more cell phones than people. There are four working mobile phones in my three-person household. No one uses the fourth. There are another five I know of that are abandoned somewhere in our messy attic. That makes nine. Not everyone in town has one, but I know for a fact that a good many of those temporarily sheltered and a few unsheltered do. Around the world, the University of Oxford Poverty and Human Development Institute (2012) estimates that by multiple measures of poverty 54 percent of India's population is poor. Yet 75 percent of Indians own and use cell phones. Plus which, there is an increasing number of programs providing the global poor free cell phones with prepaid minutes. Still, the point is made. News of the world is increasingly available to the many if not the all, and for some—like the kids in my daughter's school—a mobile phone is an appendage they use as much to narrow as to widen the field of global information. Globalized technologies are but one aspect of globalization, but perhaps the one that brings globalization closest to home.

It helps to put globalization in perspective to realize that the word "global" has two meanings. One is the meaning behind "globalization"—roughly, something powerful and important that is changing the world. The other, closely related, is "global" in the sense of everything in a given sphere. To say that oxygen is a global necessity is to say that every living thing on the planet depends on it. To say that poverty is a global problem is to say both that it is everywhere on the globe *and* that the extent of global poverty sooner or later affects everyone in the world because the cost of human suffering eventually touches everyone.

Though there are a few maniacs who would consider poverty a failure of the poor, the sane understand that as the number of poor grows, the less the better off can avoid them. For some of the have-mores this may mean, in the short run, not having to see the have-nots. In the long run, the poor cannot be ignored even though those who built cities did their best to hide the realities. Most modern cities are constructed so that the better off can get from place to place without encountering more than a few of the worse off. Highways skirt the poor sections. Subways do not extend deep into the poorest neighborhoods, whose people travel by bus. But globally the problem of poverty is that in the long run when the public declines to help the poor, the poor catch up with them. They use the city hospitals and schools. They are more inclined to illness, and thus their diseases spread across social borders. HIV and drug addiction are borderless afflictions. In the extreme, the poor rebel against political tyrants and social injustices alike.

When a good half of the global population lives either in poverty or at the risk of falling into poverty, the poverty problem is global in both senses of the word—everywhere and across the globe. The latter is a global fact. Just look at the maps of income distribution. Poverty creeps steadily onto the agenda of the policy makers and their bankers. Of all the global forces that change global relations, it is not speedy technologies so much as morbid impoverishment that is the most powerful and most insidious. If some 20 percent of the world lives on barely a dollar a day, it can hardly be said to be *their* fault. Human beings screw up, whether rich or poor. Surely when the very poor screw up it is because they have already been screwed by the global system. This may be a crude way to put it, but there is a sense in which the very poor have been economically violated by the indifference of the well-off and the failure of the well intentioned to solve the problem. Indifference and failure are not the same, but when it comes to the plight of the poor they might as well be.

Poverty, violence, environmental degradation—these are among the gloomier aspects of the dark side of globalization. One might suppose that to one degree or another the world has always suffered from the troubles people visit upon themselves. What makes for a more urgent concern today is that the more the world globalizes, the darker it gets. This is in large part due to the great hope modern peoples have long put in their abilities to achieve meaningful progress toward the good society. They have, of course. Few today would prefer life among the Wotjobaluk to life in the splendors of Sydney or Shanghai. Even the poor in global cities today are better off materially, even if, as some would argue, the simpler well-defined world of totemic villages offers a sense of order and purpose cities may not.

Yet it would be silly to suggest that the globalizing world is somehow nothing but misery. It is not. Still, in the larger historical sense it is at least a huge disappointment. At a time when we know better and, collectively, have the wealth and know-how to make the world better all around, it isn't. Not even close. Just the same, it is right, I think, to seriously consider what globalization is by at least calling attention to this one glaring aspect of what it is not.

## CHAPTER TWO

# WHAT IS GLOBALIZATION?

## *ECONOMIC, POLITICAL, AND CULTURAL CLASHES*

Globalization is as old as the hills—literally. Before there was a world populated by plants and animals, there was a physical thing hung out in space. It was and remains roughly the shape of a globe, covered with sea and bits of land, thus with hills.

At the same time, and weirdly, globalization is as new as new can be. Globalization today refers usually (not always correctly) to the speed with which many (not all) people on the planet can send and receive information—including money, nasty notes, mistaken identities, pictures, entire books, pirated movies, ear-defying music, orders to destroy buildings, and much more. Today, whatever else globalization is about, it is about speed and technology. For those who can afford such things, it is possible to carry about a small device through which one sends and receives information to and from anywhere in the world. Stuff gets there and comes back to us with unfathomable speed.

Globalization is surely about speed, yet speed is hardly new to the hill I can see from my study window. East Rock in New Haven was pushed up some 200 million years ago in the early Jurassic period. If then there were dinosaurs here they certainly saw the light of the stars and moons and comets above. That light, then as now, sped through the then-unknowable universe at 299,792,458 miles per second. Nothing manmade, not even a cybertext, is anywhere near as fast as that. Speed is not new, even if the dinosaurs had no idea what was going on above.

What is new in our time are advanced technologies of many marvelous kinds—including a huge subatomic particle accelerator in Switzerland, where physicists are trying to get subatomic particles to go faster than light. So far they have not quite succeeded. Still, fast is as fast does. What speed does in our time is make the connections among all human and natural things more available, even visible, to the imagination. We like the idea that we can send messages at many times warp speed, but there is little evidence that this ability makes our daily lives better, especially when we send foolish remarks around the world while under the influence of some intoxicating experience.

Technologies of all kinds make things faster. In many ways increased speed has always been a compelling quality of new technologies. Hard metal spears made hunting more efficient, as the wheel made work faster. In due course, steam engines led to faster ships and trains as jet engines made long-haul air travel faster. Of course, electronic devices replaced the typewriter, making postal services antiquated. Even books are at risk. Still, technologies don't make the fastest things faster. They create the illusion that the speed of communications makes us closer to people and things around the world. It doesn't. Distances are immutable. Still, information technologies promote the feeling that we are in a world where our relations with others are closer than we think. If you are late finishing work—too late to submit in person—it is usually possible to send it in by email attachment. Even teachers or bosses to whom we send our tardy work have come to appreciate the advantage of getting it electronically, especially when they are secretly away from their offices doing what they don't want us to know they are doing. One seldom sends late work without a personal note of some kind, often anything but the truth. "Thanks for a great semester." "I really enjoyed working on this project." Niceties aside, this kind of thing is a blessing of sorts. On the other hand, when banks and other financial institutions send our money across the world or sell our mortgages and car loans to a faraway capitalist shark, we can be screwed by the ease with which our friendly loan officer disappears and our debt or credit is in the ruthless hands of strangers.

Nothing in this life is a pure blessing. Whether speedy technologies make life better depends on who one is and where in the social scheme of things one is located. Usually, the better off and otherwise privileged benefit more from the speed of some global transactions. The most poor rarely

## 18 ⊕ CHAPTER TWO

have access to such things as e-trading or even computers connected to the Internet. The somewhat less poor may have this access, but then they are more likely to be trapped by the unscrupulous who use the Internet to prey on people. Think of it. Who actually opens those emails from strangely familiar nobodies asking that we take their millions of dollars for safekeeping? This stuff is only for the desperate and lonely who can't buy their way out of their troubles.

Still, globalization has much to do with technologically enhanced speed. It is neither good nor bad, but it can be both and usually is. The physical globe is our most important environment. To have a better sense that it is there is good. That the global environment is damaged by what we have done to it is bad. Yet it still hangs there in space. The hills are much as they were in the long ago. Speed is still what it always was, and still faster than we can go. But technologies are different in ways that change how individuals and global populations live.

Globalization, thus, is about *speed, technologies,* and the *relations* we have with our fellow beings and the material things on the planet. The combination of these three is powerful enough to change the world itself. Still, the worlds of living creatures cling to the surface of the globe. Globalization is at one and the same time both very new and very old. If this is so, what is the reason that in our time so many people talk about globalization whereas before they never did?

The word "globalization" is itself new. The first really public use of the word was in 1961, in the *Economist.* The reference was to the beginnings of the European Economic Community—obviously an early version of the international institution that opened borders among European nations and their economies. The common use of the word began in earnest in the 1990s. Why the 1990s? As in all questions of the history of relatively recent times, it is hard to say for certain. But one thing is clear: In the 1990s many began to think that the world, if not the physical globe, was changing into something unfamiliar. At the time there emerged a good many not-entirely-compatible ideas about the world being radically different or, at least, importantly altered.

One of the first ideas of globalization was primarily political. It took seriously the collapse of communism in Eastern Europe and Russia between 1989 and 1991 as a sign that the values of Western capitalism had triumphed over what President Ronald Reagan had earlier called the Evil Empire. One of the more notable, if high-minded, books on the historical implications of the collapse of communism was Francis Fukuyama's *The End of History and the Last Man* (1992). The book clearly took advantage of the collapse of state socialism in Eastern Europe to argue that Western history itself had triumphed by clearing the way for Man (with an ideological capital *M*) to fulfill human destiny. Needless to say, this theory of globalization was optimistic to the point of naiveté. It was founded on assumptions, not evidence. When facts are few, the imagination soars.

A second idea of globalization appeared in 1992 as a widely read article, and later as a book, *Clash of Civilizations*. It was even more theoretical and only slightly more empirical, but vastly more pessimistic. It was in some part a response to the optimism of Fukuyama's claim. This idea was that the West was challenged by a variety of other global cultures. In 1996, Samuel Huntington's book *Clash of Civilizations* popularized the phrase "the West and the Rest." Huntington's idea was that Western world dominance was threatened by the rising hostility and economic power of the Islamic and East Asian parts of the world, among others. The markedly different cultures of the Islamic world were, as they still are today, mysterious to Western cultures. At the same time, Japan, South Korea, China, and other Asian economies gave every indication of becoming true economic powers and serious rivals to Western Europe and the United States. Then too, already in the 1990s Russia, freed from communist rule but with its geographic reach and a seemingly limitless supply of resources, remained a force to be reckoned with. Even those who could not follow Huntington's rather grandiose theory realized that the global economy was transformed such that no one power could dominate with impunity. Within a short decade, the events of September 11, 2001, lent considerable support to Huntington's idea, as did the still-growing evidence that China and India were emerging as major economic powers in the global economy.

Relatedly, also in the 1990s, a third even more theoretical view of global change was postmodernism—a largely philosophical (as opposed to historical or economic) idea that the modern world had run its course and was giving way to something completely different. Postmodernism, as it was belatedly known in the United States, was, for some, falsely associated with a then-new and controversial group of thinkers, most of whom were French, Italian, or otherwise European. Names like Michel Foucault, Jacques Derrida, Jacques Lacan, Slavoj Žižek, and Claude Lévi-Strauss were being dropped by intellectual elites at conferences and cocktail parties in New York and San Francisco.

20 ⊕ CHAPTER TWO

A growing number of academics (myself among them) read their works seriously while others, even the popular media, would make jokes about postmodernists they barely knew. In truth, the ideas thought of as post-modern were various and not particularly close to one another in kind. Still, they were alarming to more traditional thinkers because, in their different ways, the new European social theorists systematically attacked classical ideas that modern culture thought of as immutable.

Those defending the old ways imagined this new wave of European thinkers to be a flood that would drown their own beliefs. Thus, without reading them, opponents would reject their ideas by distorting what little they took from them, most famously Derrida's term "deconstruction," which to them was a method for rejecting everything that for so long had mattered—science, truth, and morality, among other master ideals. This, of course, was an extreme example of sophisticated ignorance. Yet postmod-ernism stood for something not too different from theories like those of Fukuyama and Huntington. Eventually postmodernism, having sounded the alarm that the modern world was in deep need of a rethinking, began to fade, giving way to a wide variety of theories and claims about the nature and importance of globalization.

Thus "globalization"—the word and the idea—came to be a key word in the vocabulary of serious policy makers and common folk who accepted that, like it or not, something about the world at large was shifting—and shifting at a rate faster than any geological eruption, if slower than the speed of light. Between the hills and light there is ample room for change. Time will tell if the 1990s were what in the 2010s they seem to have been. For the time being it is enough to say that globalization is a big theory that has entered the global conversation. At the least it is a question important to anyone who wants to understand what she is likely to be facing in the years to come.

## FAST TIME/FIXED SPACES: GLOBALIZATION AND CONFLICT

My Facebook friends are mostly people from Kyrgyzstan, China, Australia, and Mongolia, and there's one grade-school classmate who somehow found me and friended (what a verb!) me. Some of my closest real-life friends live thousands of miles away. One just moved to Singapore. Three others are now living in Australia. Another one, who is Chinese, hosted me in Beijing after we met in Seoul at meetings organized by a longtime Korean friend.

*What Is Globalization?* 21

Once, oddly, my Chinese friend and I bumped into each other in Taiwan. She is truly global. Her family lives in Queens, so we normally see each other when she is able to come to her other home. I see her and other global friends in person once or so a year. I am surely closer in some sense to people near at hand, especially my family. Would my life be empty without those at great distances who in today's language are called friends, whether they are or not? No, but still they matter, often in a strange kind of way.

The Facebook "friend" from Mongolia I met in Istanbul. He had known my Kyrgyzstan friends. We all went out drinking and dancing after an evening on the Bosporus, where Asia and Europe meet and part ways. My friendship (if that is what it is) with a lovely person from Mongolia is based on a chance meeting in a city alien to us both. It continues through an occasional greeting or posted photo. What these kinds of relations are when measured against traditional friendships is hard to say. But they are not nothing. They certainly enrich my life, if only because when they pop up on Facebook, I remember them as I almost never do the nearer-by "real" friends from years ago in school days. Friends and family, near and far, keep connections alive. Some of these may not be friendships, but there is nothing wrong with calling them that.

In the wealthier regions of the world, thousands, perhaps millions, of people live electronically—constantly on their cell phones; their computers logged in all day and night; music or television playing in the background; minds uprooted, drifting somewhere in cyberspace. This kind of thing may not be good; nor is it necessarily bad. In either case, whichever it may turn out to be, it seems to be the coming reality. Whatever the threat to life of living online, there is much good that comes to us from cyberspace. Yes, I still occasionally hear from improbable strangers offering me riches in exchange for my bank routing numbers. From time to time I also hear from people more likely to be real strangers. One claimed to be a prisoner in Iran. He said he "needed" a copy of one of my books. I sent it along, and heard again from him a few years later. He needed another copy of the same book. Who knows what that was? I also once heard by email from a friend of an inmate I taught in prison. I met her for coffee a few times and encouraged her efforts to get through high school. Several years later, I got a note saying she had graduated at the top of her class and was off to college. Her friend in prison is there for life. He's quite a good man. She's a good person too, but she is beginning a better life on the outside. And so on. I can't really say that any of the many stray relations that come to me from

## CHAPTER TWO

cyberspace are necessarily more than probes from afar; some go to trash, others hover out there over my inbox, and a rare few come to something.

The connections we make in cyberspace are formed at unfathomable speeds over great distances where time is almost nothing (*almost*). That being said, the real-world spaces separating actual people who move about on (or above) the ground or seas are what they have almost always been. Air travel makes Australia only metaphorically closer than when the first British prisoners were sent by ship to Botany Bay in 1786. The space of physical travel is the same even if the conveyances are somewhat faster. But cyber travel is time travel and it is very much faster. So when I speak of a Facebook "friend" I met once a few years ago I am speaking of a "real" person in the sense that I know, until I hear otherwise, that he is a physical being somewhere on the planet. The guy from Iran and others who come

---

### FRIENDS IN FAST GLOBAL SPACE

I will never meet the guy from Iran who periodically asks me for books. He might or might not be who he claims he is. I know the guy in a prison that is two towns away and can see him on visiting days. I never get email from him because inmates are not permitted access to the Internet. Hence, an important difference. The friend in Mongolia and the friend in prison are, in a sense, equally nearby. It took many hours to get to Istanbul, and many more than that to go to Bishkek, then Adelaide by way of Dubai, as I did on the trip when I met the Mongolian friend—who has a PhD from Cambridge University and teaches history at a university in Ulan Bator. It takes no time to send and receive word from any of these email acquaintances or friends, wherever they are. But my friend in a nearby prison is just about as far away as Ulan Bator or Adelaide or, for that matter, from the guy who might be in prison in Iran. Hence, a fact of the globalized world. "We" (so to speak) can travel around the world in no time in cyberspace. But if we want to go to any of these places it takes a long time, if just because there can be only so many real document checkers and wait spaces. It would take at least three days to arrange a visit to the prison nearby, and about two hours to drive there, to check in, and to be escorted to the visitor room. When all is said and done, it takes about that long to get to Adelaide or Ulan Bator when travel to the airport, waiting for planes, making transfers, waiting more, and finding the way to a hotel are taken into account.

## What Is Globalization?  23

from nowhere asking or offering tricks of a kind, I just don't know. They are figments until I hear or see otherwise. But since getting an email from someone is not really hearing from them, any more than a photo sent by attachment would be seeing them, they remain essentially unreal. All the many images and words sent across cyberspace are surely not nothing, but neither are they what humans in the flesh would normally call real.

The problem here is that heavy users of the Internet tend to think of all those messages as real when they would do better to apply the pragmatist test—are they real in experience? If so, what is the experience—or *where* is it? Is it even possible to think when one is in cyber-timespace? If so, then what is thinking when there are no specific objects available to this life? And so on. Questions like these about cyberspace can go on forever.

When all is said and done, the basic fact about cyberspace is that it is fast because everything in it is decomposed into a digital language—a pure field of nothing but zeros and ones organized by very complicated codes. The simplest of signals can travel very fast, but when they arrive at a destination they must be recomposed or decoded. All this happens with extraordinary speed and it happens because things in cyberspace, as opposed to a friend in Ulan Bator, are codes and digits. This, in our world, is what time travel amounts to—not quite science fiction, but not actually what on the ground of life is considered real.

Speed, this fundamental aspect of a globalized world, comes at a rate and in a form new to human experience. At the same time, the very presence of cyber time travel creates a most confusing contradiction associated with globalization by altering how humans who live with cyberspeed experience their relations with others. The globe itself still hangs out there in space, itself a mostly unchanged spatial thing. The time of its revolutions and orbits remains much as it always has been, just as the space of settlements on earth remains within relatively stable fixed borders and distances that separate. In and across space we can only travel so fast. Yet the speed of what is bloodlessly called "information transfer" alters its senders and recipients in ways they may not fully realize.

Sherry Turkle, psychoanalyst and social-science professor at MIT, has for many years studied the social and psychological effects on human behavior of computers, cell phones, and other information-transfer tools. She explains what those who use these things will recognize as true: We use them without being aware of their effects on us, and after a while they are irresistible. We check our email too often. We text during meetings, while driving, in class,

## 24 CHAPTER TWO

and in churches if not mosques. We get the idea that these *connections* are real. We may call digital interlocutors "friends" when they are not. We say that we "talk" to them when in fact what we may be doing is texting them and in a barely intelligible code. "TDTM" (talk dirty to me) is juiceless precisely because it is overcoded. Without a real other available for physical or, at least, audible contact, TDTM is certainly not talk, much less erotic. Erotic proposals imply a figurative if not literal *coming together*. Any actual coming together may not be orgasmic, but it surely involves something more than a connection. Coitus is not fucking, which can be anonymous or paid for but still is more than information transfer.

Sherry Turkle argues in *Alone Together: Why We Expect More from Technology and Less from Each Other* (2011) that there is a world of difference between being linked or connected to someone and being a friend or a companion. Friendship, she reminds, requires an ability to keep a

---

### *ALONE TOGETHER* (TURKLE 2011, 23)

Technology is seductive when what it offers meets our human vulnerabilities. And as it turns out, we are very vulnerable indeed. We are lonely but fearful of intimacy. Digital connections and the sociable robot may offer the illusion of companionship without the demands of friendship. Our networked life allows us to hide from each other, even as we are tethered to each other. We'd rather text than talk. A simple story makes this last point, told in her own words by a harried mother in her late forties:

> I needed to find a new nanny. When I interview nannies, I like to go to where they live, so that I can see them in their environment, not just in mine. So, I made an appointment to interview Ronnie, who had applied for the job. I show up at her apartment and her housemate answers the door. She is a young woman, around twenty-one, texting on her BlackBerry. Her thumbs are bandaged. I look at them, pained at the tiny thumb splints, and I try to be sympathetic. "That must hurt." But she just shrugs. She explains that she is still able to text. I tell her I am here to speak with Ronnie; this is her job interview. Could she please knock on Ronnie's bedroom door? The girl with the bandaged thumbs looks surprised. "Oh no," she says, "I would never do that. That would be intrusive. I'll text her." And so she sent a text message to Ronnie, no more than fifteen feet away.

## What Is Globalization? 🌐 25

conversation going, to listen to what may or may not make complete sense, to endure patiently a friend's sufferings or ecstasies that may not be yours, and enough personal experience with solitude to be able simply to sit with someone or, literally, to be a companion. Friendships demand, above all, knowing oneself well enough not to have to talk too much. Digital connections are all about saying things, often in unintelligible codes, the meaning of which do not ultimately matter.

For a good many years I worked with a group of people who enjoyed real if not deep friendships. We had lunches together regularly, we occasionally had parties, we observed sad or happy events in each other's lives. Then, when computers entered our lives, almost everything was done on email. The luncheons were abandoned. Meetings were strictly according to business. We seldom saw each other except in the hallways. We almost never thanked one another for deeds of generosity or kindness. The friendships waned. As time went by, we knew almost nothing about each other. We even forgot some of the most intimate details of each other's losses and hopes. In the end we went our own ways into other more real friendships, leaving our work relations empty, barely even linked. Though I don't really have a friendship with the friend in Mongolia, I feel I know more about him from one night of drinking in a Turkish club than I do about these people I had known for years. He at least never forgets my birthday, nor I his. Even if his well wishes are prompted by Facebook, they matter somehow.

The startling thing to realize about fast, technological connections is that they get under our skin, become habits, sneak below the surface of consciousness. Last night I woke in mid-sleep to pee. Afterward, still not really awake, I grabbed my cell phone to check on an email from a real friend in Australia about the time of our Skype meeting in the morning. It wasn't there. If it had been, I wouldn't have done anything about it. But still I checked before dozing away to pick up another strange dream. Fast global relations are many times dreamlike. They feel real but may not be. The characters in them seem familiar but more often they are projections of a psychic movie turning deep inside the unconscious mind.

What globalization does, among other things, is dramatically change our concepts of time and space, and thus also our suppositions about what is and is not real. On margin, most users of cybertools, if they stop to think about it, think of them as wonderful conveniences. Some suppose they are a necessity. Disillusioning though it may be, one better understands

## 26 CHAPTER TWO

globalization by being clear about the evil fast technologies spawn. "Evil" may be too strong a word, but at least it is possible to say that a great deal that goes on in this world is ugly.

Where there is evil or ugliness, whatever we call it, it arises because actual people must live in a hard, enveloping, nourishing, but sometimes harsh space. This is a law that applies globally (in the sense of always and everywhere) and it is just as true for astronauts living in the International Space Station as for us who live on the ground. Living together in or on real spaces creates trouble. When people in any number have to share the same or proximate spaces, eventually there is trouble that under dire circumstances can turn ugly, even evil.

The world populated by human beings has always been an amalgam of good and evil, or intermittent beauty and ugliness. Whenever once-local worlds became global in the sense of venturing into each other's places, conflict soon followed. The clash of cultures was a fact of life on the planet eons before globalization. When people come to the limits of their known worlds, they encounter places and perhaps people stranger than words can say. Conflict arises on territorial borders where local cultures can no longer speak.

When there is conflict between individuals, the differences normally are settled or they part ways. Only rarely do they break into violence, though this happens and is always a possibility. But between and among states or civilizations conflict is a given. In relatively modern times, kingdoms or states may attempt to resolve differences diplomatically, peaceably. Sometimes they succeed. But one thing they cannot do is part ways. An organized social group of any settled kind cannot relinquish its territory—even if it is no more than a small nomadic tribe that travels fixed routes across deserts or plains, along coastal fishing grounds or up and down mountains. Enduring human groups must have a territory with limits and borders, pathways and water sources, assured spaces in which they can hunt and fish, gather or grow food. Defense of a territory is a defense of a way of life and its habits. Without a productive territory, states and empires, tribes and villages will die. The Lakota were nomads of the Great Plains. When white people ruthlessly conquered the plains, the Lakota civilization died, forced to retreat to barren Dakota reservations.

Wherever aboriginal people have lost their native territory, they are lost. So too great civilizations. Where now are the Romans or, for that matter, the Persians and Babylonians and Silla kings? Descendants survive and traces of

## What Is Globalization?

their cultures endure, but the civilizations were doomed the moment their territorial borders were definitively breached. Between robustly structured human groups, conflict almost always turns violent. A popular theory is that the Roman and British empires simply declined by some inexplicable natural cycle of rise and fall. Whatever may be the generic truth of this idea, somewhere along the path to oblivion there is always a conflict that does violence to the collective will and imperial authority—whether Alaric and the Goths sacking Rome or Gandhi's Salt March in India or Eisenhower's Normandy invasion, empires or aggressor states sooner or later encounter resistance—hence conflict and violence.

When talking about such a thing as globalization, one must always talk about the soft or hard conflicts that inevitably arise because states and empires are territorial. When they come up against a rival for their spaces, states cannot walk away from each other. One will soon enough encroach on the other. Few who have lost their original land survive long enough to reclaim it. This is why today Israel is such a fierce defender of its territory in the face of considerable global dismay. For the better part of three millennia the Jewish people were without title to their holy lands. Unlike the Lakota, who also suffered wicked abuse by a conquering power, the Jewish people returned to their native lands. People will fight ferociously, if they can, to defend their territories. If they lose them they will long to regain them, but most do not. Ancient Israel was little compared to the Roman Empire, but the Romans are gone and Israel survives, ready for any and all attacks. To be sure, they have enemies who think of them as evil, but on the point of conflict and violence between states no example better illustrates how and why states, whether weak or imperial, cannot walk away from a fight.

### PALESTINE AND ISRAEL: A CONTINUING STRUGGLE OVER LAND AND SECURITY

Most people, myself included, are confused over the whys and wherefores of the very long struggle between Israel and Palestinians. On June 16, 2014, there were two funerals at nearly the same hour. One was in the West Bank, the other in Israel—but miles apart. Both mourned and honored persons killed in the latest of many conflicts, violent and political, over nearly a century. Both sides treasure the relatively small parcels of land they call their own. One side, Israel, has vastly more military, political, and economic power than the other. The other, the

CHAPTER TWO

Palestinians, are poor but have many powerful supporters in the Middle East. Peace is hard to make. Both think they are right in claiming what territories they have. Even the best informed see little but gloom ahead. For example, the following commentary appeared in the *Huffington Post*:

> Once again, a conflict breaks out between Israel and one of its neighbors; this time, as in 2008, against Hamas, which still governs Gaza.
>
> The downward spiral appears to be unstoppable: The killing of three Israeli teens. The abhorrent murder of a Palestinian teen. Missiles launched from Gaza by Hamas on Israeli cities and at Ben Gurion International Airport, without provoking a catastrophe for the time being, because of the extraordinary efficiency of the Israeli anti-missile shield. And the deadly Israeli bombing raids in Gaza to halt the rocket strikes.
>
> The result of this downward spiral is clear: Thousands of victims from Palestine's coastal strip, which will weaken Fatah, accused of "collaboration" with Israel. And other victims on the Israeli side, which will nourish a desire for vengeance.
>
> In both countries, those in power [are] increasingly weak.
>
> In Palestine, a discrediting of all leaders; so much so that, if elections were to be held today, Hamas would win in the West Bank, and Fatah in Gaza, leaving the country, or its equivalent, totally ungovernable.
>
> In Israel, a ramshackle coalition between the extremists of Mr. Lieberman and those of Mr. Netanyahu, losing ground. As President Peres prepares to step down from the presidency.
>
> Not far, an already convalescent Egypt who fights against both the Muslim Brotherhood at home and Hamas in Gaza. Lebanon paralyzed by Hezbollah, that is to say: Iran. A martyred Syria, whose tyrant, and enemies alike, are supporting Hamas. Iraq in full meltdown in which two new States are emerging. One is a Kurdish state and peaceful, the other is a Sunni Islamic state, spearhead of a war of creeds between the two branches of Islam. (Attali 2014)

Globalization takes place on the ground where different people live and where, it seems, conflict is seldom far off and far too often near at hand.

This fact of global realities in any and all times may seem to be just another aspect of globalization's dark side. It is better, however, to consider it a fact of geopolitical life through human history. Few would vote for violence. But in and of itself, violence is a deep structural inclination of all animals, including the human ones. Violence is the raw energy by which living things fight to survive. What makes human violence different is that humans have developed cultures that introduce the idea that killing can be evil and ugly if done for reasons other than basic survival. The line is porous, making violence a uniquely human impulse.

## GLOBAL SPACES AND CHANGING HUMAN RELATIONS

All living things live off other living things. Most of them kill what food comes along—whether rival cells in a bloodstream or plankton in the sea or vulnerable plants and animals in the wild. They are all territorial in the sense that they can only kill what they find in a space they know—bloodstreams, atmospheres, waters, forests, or open plains. Where there is violence, there too is the intransigence of space. Life occurs on and in spaces that are necessarily limited in one or another way.

Globalization, therefore, is about *speed, technologies,* and transformed *relations* among people and things, but it is also about fixed *spaces*—territories that are friction against the ability of speedy technologies to change relations for the better. Catch a lover cheating, you can instantaneously change your relationship entry on Facebook or otherwise announce to the world of those who might care that he, if a he, is a louse. But he or she will still be around somewhere, occupying the places to avoid in order to avoid the contact.

*Speed, technologies, new relations,* and fixed *spaces* are the basic categories necessary to understand (or at least form a good enough theory of) globalization. Ever since some living creature improvised a tool to move a rock in search of food to carry on life, some version of these four have always been elements around which life revolves. All that globalization has done is to alter the dynamics among them.

In the wake of September 11, 2001, and a good decade after the early optimistic, pessimistic, or just plain speculative theories of globalization came to public attention in the 1990s, Stanley Hoffman's influential essay "Clash of Globalizations" appeared in *Foreign Affairs* (Hoffman 2002). The title makes it clear that Hoffman meant to reject Huntington's earlier "clash of civilizations" argument as much as he dismissed Fukuyama's "end of history" thesis (while just plain ignoring the by-then-fading talk of postmodernism). Obviously, Hoffman dramatically shifted the focus to the concept itself by using the plural form "globalizations." He meant to say

## 30 ⊕ CHAPTER TWO

that the underlying clash in the new world order is among the conflicting elements of the phenomenon itself. Where the ideas of a thing are many, so too must we consider that the thing itself is many.

Hoffman, thus, identified three basic kinds of clashing globalizations—economic, cultural, and political—and went on to explain that each refers to a different set of realities and that none has the same *type* of effect as the others. In other words, each is good in some ways, ugly in others, and none is perfectly one or the other.

As new as globalization seems to be in some ways, even the newest of new things comes from *somewhere*. There is always a *before* that explains the *now*. In history, as in some religions, new testaments must have old ones. In history some enormous changes appear to have come from nowhere. They did not. Once the railroad became a well-established system for land travel, stagecoaches, you would think, became obsolete. They did, but only after a time. You can still ride stagecoaches in theme parks here and there. Once the telephone spread across the globe, one would suppose that radio signaling would have disappeared. In time it did, except for the fact that communications we get from far outer space are decoded through an advanced type of radio technology. And so on, including cell phones and the rest. The new comes upon the old, which lingers on, occasionally to return in some fresh form.

When the question concerns an immense global change, the historical question is all the more important. Nothing in this world changes in a single instant. The historical question soon enough becomes a question of when the change began and why then. Strangely, this is important in very practical ways. If there is reason to believe that the ways we have lived and thought until now are changing, then we really need to know how those changes will alter the future for us. If, as it seems, telecommunications change how we relate to others and to the world at large, then it follows that if we are smart we will want to know what we must do to get by. Eventually, a question like this leads back to where this transformation came from and why. If *it* (whatever the *it* might be) was there from the beginning of history, even if only as a possibility, then that makes a difference.

When it concerns such a thing as globalization, it makes quite a serious difference to know, or at least to try to figure out, when the world became global. Consider the example of global climate change. It is well known that in all times there were floods, sandstorms, fires, ice ages, and droughts. We

*What Is Globalization?* 🌐 31

see them on Mars. It is reasonable to conclude that the dinosaurs must not have thought the climate change that killed them was their fault (if, that is, they were able to think anything in particular). But we may be able to do something about climate change today—a certified global phenomenon. Globalization in general may or may not be a threat to human life. But the now-rapid melting of the Arctic ice is. Those willing to face facts know when—it was 1956—greenhouse gases first rose to the heavens to warm the earth's surfaces. It remains to be seen whether we will do what needs to be done to keep this planet from becoming another Mars. Globalization, whatever it is, is another big but related matter—one that surely began well before 1956. But when, and why? Tough questions.

It is easier to say when globalization did *not* begin than to settle the question of when it did. It did not begin with the hills on a global sphere hung out in space at the dawn of this earth. Nor did it begin with the spread of the word "globalization" in the 1990s. Yet these two incongruous points before and immediately in human time help to settle why the question is both difficult to answer and important to consider.

There can hardly be any doubt that if one were forced to select one and only one reason why globalization caught the public fancy in 1990, it would be the startling effects of fast technologies that, as I said, created the impression that global things not only had changed but changed more than any other fundamental change in human history. This idea remains an impression bearing some (but not very much) truth. Still, it is a cardinal feature of globalization theory. The wild innovations of information technologies are at the core of today's *cultural globalization*—information, plain and not so simple, became a new cultural form that changed global economics and politics, as well as culture.

But cultural globalization itself is anything but new. Habits, fads, styles, and ideas flowing around the world is at least as old as the earliest of global explorations. Europeans were captivated by Marco Polo's account of his travels to Asia in the thirteenth century. In the late fifteenth century the early European explorers of the Atlantic, including Columbus, were inspired by Polo's narrative of the riches and mysteries of Asia. They crossed the seas in search of a route to Asia's imagined wealth. They found a new world. Once the New World was settled, coffee, spices, and tobacco were traded back and forth—none a life's necessity. Jazz and blue jeans were fads in Europe in the twentieth century. Bruce Springsteen, Bono, and Bob Dylan are today global figures. Muhammad Ali was in his day

## 32 ✦ CHAPTER TWO

the most famous person on the planet. Still, the cyberworld of electronic sounds and images has spread the word of the latest hits, but also of the most current science, political movements, and much more, including, of course, economic markets and bargains. If cultural globalization in the form of fast information transfers is the most stunningly new aspect of the changed world in the late twentieth century, then the irony is that the most *important* type of globalization is the one that causes deeper changes while being less visibly new.

*Economic globalization* was always *the* fundamental dynamic arising from the clash of empires, states, and tribes at the limits of their territories. In a broad sense, the most elemental aspect of economic action is the ability of a people, however they are organized, to adapt to their environment. This, roughly, is the way Talcott Parsons, one of the founders of contemporary social science after World War II, described what he called the adaptive function of all human societies. It is a little out of date to put it this way, but Parsons had an important point. Whatever else economic behavior is about, it starts with survival and survival is always territorial. Through the ages people, from the most primitive to the most postmodern, venture beyond their ill-marked local borders in order to survive. A few very traditional groups are known to have survived very well for incalculably long times in their corners of resource-rich rain forests in deepest Amazonia. Once discovered, they are doomed. Once their territories are breached, their timber and waters are soon cut and drained by intruders from the global economy; they can no longer adapt their traditional economies to the new invasive ways. At the other end of the historical trajectory, we today could not survive for long in the forests and caves that were once homes to our ancestors. Instead, faced with a need, we shop.

The magnetic pull of economic globalization sucks both the poor and the well-provided-for out of their local habitats and into inhospitably sleek stucco apartments where the collapse of the human into the space of dead things approaches maximum entropy. Poverty is the ugliest of the names for the way economic globalization today sweeps away the hinterlands of once-thriving villages and yurts. At the other end of timespace, the barrio is no more than a poorly appointed Grand Hyatt—a temporary place of shelter and ill-cooked comfort for those looking to scratch what coin they can from someone's else territory. As cultural globalization, in its glittering aspects, may be as new as the 1990s, so economic globalization, in its most empty territorial features, is as old as the hills. Whether it is a clash of globalizations or a clash of territorial cultures, when the very new comes up against the very old something must give in the breach. In the wider societal sense, it is the task of politics to manage breaches—to fill what can be filled with the trash of the old, to build bridges over the chasms with structural shards of the new. Since whenever what today we call globalization began, cultures and economies have simultaneously been wed one to the other. Cultures function to motivate and justify the risks and labors necessary to survival. Whether it is an adolescent brave sent into the wild on a vision quest or a young business-school graduate sent off to sell the lie-laden services her corporate employers offer foreign markets, both are sent away in service to their tribe. The risks they take are taught them in childhood. Venturing forth in the name of the Cockatoo clan is no more than a dimly lit precursor of the Capitalist clan's avaricious appetite for young ones who believe it their duty to prove themselves and bring home material proof of their worth.

Politics reconciles, when it can, the absurdity of the intimate contradictions between cultures and economies. The Romans sent their armies to remote places, as did the Greeks and the Han. They brought with them the Eternal City, the Hellenic civilization, and other legends of an *axis mundi*—of a cosmic axis at the center of the world in order to conquer new lands meant to enrich the empires. No less, the modern state, with all its professions of democratic virtue, secures its hold on domestic power by building vast naval forces to protect the sea lanes along which merchant ships and colonizers travel. State politics are caught in an impossible double bind. Unable to deny allegiance to corporate greed, they must claim as their virtue faithfulness to the will of people from whom they extract taxes and loyalty. The function of politics is to reconcile economic greed and cultural virtue. The people are not long fooled. Greed takes its toll. Today, politics are cast into an international contradiction.

*Political globalization,* like state politics, is torn by the clash between cultures and economies. As information technologies speed up the flow of capital accumulation, the appropriation of global resources, and the flow of labor toward higher profits and cheaper production costs, modern states are left borderless. People still live in nations, where they cling precariously to the right of legitimate citizens. When today they pledge allegiance to a local flag it is as likely to be the icon of an ethnic past as of a global promise of a proud nation. Political globalization concerns the weakening of a given state's grip on its citizens.

CHAPTER TWO

> ## STANLEY HOFFMAN, *CLASH OF GLOBALIZATIONS: A NEW PARADIGM?*
>
> Nearly a decade after publishing his famous essay "The Clash of Globalizations" Stanley Hoffman reviewed the global 1990s—to a particularly pessimistic conclusion: globalization itself is a question of tensions between the traditional political, cultural, and economic norms and the new conflicts promoted by globalization.
>
>> What is the state of international relations today? In the 1990s, specialists concentrated on the partial disintegration of the global order's traditional foundations: states. During that decade, many countries, often those born of decolonization, revealed themselves to be no more than pseudostates, without solid institutions, internal cohesion, or national consciousness. The end of communist coercion in the former Soviet Union and in the former Yugoslavia also revealed long-hidden ethnic tensions. Minorities that were or considered themselves oppressed demanded independence. In Iraq, Sudan, Afghanistan, and Haiti, rulers waged open warfare against their subjects. These wars increased the importance of humanitarian interventions, which came at the expense of the hallowed principles of national sovereignty and nonintervention. Thus the dominant tension of the decade was the clash between the fragmentation of states (and the state system) and the progress of economic, cultural, and political integration—in others words, globalization. (Hoffman 2002, 9)
>
> Not everyone, even now, would agree with Hoffman, but those who want to understand what is going on in the world today must at least consider the historical facts of global change.

As Hoffman points out, today there are fewer wars between states and very many more among political and ethnic fractions within them. The Americans and their ever-shrinking number of allies may enter national territories to protect a thin collective interest in democratic freedoms by controlling internal conflicts—as they did with scant success in Vietnam and Iraq and tried a while longer in Afghanistan. As the Soviet imperium collapsed, in some measure due to its own failure to dominate Afghanistan, and the British Empire failed to defend its South Asian colonies against global forces, so today's technological otherworldly military machine fails time and again. Drones slaughter innocents, provoking political wrath against the United States. The underlying reason for military might is the same as it was for the ancient empires—loss of a strategic port or base of operations; of, that is, access to territorial wealth.

Where there are cultural pronouncements there will be economic motives pressing up against the high-minded virtues, putting stress on national political authorities to enter a local fray or to join other nations to create new global institutions meant to fill the empty space left by the states shrunken before global forces they cannot control.

It has been a practice since the earliest days of modern philosophy to posit what the political philosopher John Rawls called a people in the original position—that is to say a people outside history, to whom are attributed the elemental features of the ideal social arrangement. Globalization in our time is too raw to begin with an imagined community of first peoples. It entails clashes and conflicts too far gone to be imaginably reduced to some primitive possibility. Cultures, economics, and politics today clash. Peace, survival, and order remain good, even necessary, aspects of global life. History may not be reversible any more than it is moving inexorably toward a triumphant state of common good. But if you grant these premises, they do not give cause for out-and-out alarm. There is much good in this world, and every reason to trust that wherever globalization leads the world, the next stage after the current uncertainties is as likely to be a new form of order in which decent values might prevail and sufficient means are available to most if not all.

Still, the systemic study of globalization, such as it is, must be pursued by those who recognize the need to be alert to whatever lies ahead. That study cannot return to an ideal past any more than its outcome can be supposed to be the liberal paradise of not so long ago. But it can take account of a beginning in history when the structural form of a global order was already well in place—the Age of Empires.

CHAPTER THREE

# WHEN DID GLOBALIZATION BEGIN?

Some believe that globalization began in relatively recent times when the word "globalization" came into play. Yet we know very well that a word does not a thing make. What the thing might be is not necessarily what those living with it think it is. One of the better ways around a problem like this is to ask when the thing began. The backwards glance allows one to trace the sometimes-slow emergence of a grand historical change. Thus, in asking what globalization is, it makes good sense to ask—with a healthy dose of skepticism—when it began. Were there not global realities before the telephone, the radio, the television, the Internet, and jet travel? There were, of course.

Legends from the oldest of times tell of heroic figures who strode across the world. One was Gilgamesh, who is believed to have represented a hero-king who may have dated from as early as 2800 BCE.

> **GILGAMESH, THE LEGENDARY GLOBAL HERO**
> Gilgamesh the tall, magnificent and terrible,
>   who opened passes in the mountains,
> who dug wells on the slopes of the uplands,
>   and crossed the ocean, the wide sea to the sunrise;
> Who scoured the world ever searching for life,
>   and reached through sheer force Uta-napishti the Distant;
> who restored the cult-centres destroyed by the Deluge,
>   and set in place for the people the rites of the cosmos.
>         —*Epic of Gilgamesh* (in Lemert et al. 2010, 15)

The Gilgamesh legend, as we know it today, was written down centuries after its probable origins in oral tradition. This version is from sometime between 1300 and 1000 BCE in Mesopotamia. It is apparent—even from this short excerpt of the version passed down much later—that the Gilgamesh story bears a strong resemblance to the Noah legend of ancient Israel that was circulating about the same time in the same region. Gilgamesh, like Noah, saved his people from a great flood covering the world, over which he too roamed—Gilgamesh by giant steps, and Noah by sail. In an unthinkable long-ago time, human communities, thus, imagined if not a global sphere, then a cosmos "set in place for the people."

## THE FEAR OF FLOODS

I was born just months after the great 1937 flood of the Ohio River, which drenched the bottoms of Cincinnati, Ohio. At the time, we lived in a low-lying neighborhood a good several miles from the river, near the hospital where my father cared for his patients. I was a newborn. I had no experience of the flood itself. Yet I was told so much about it over the years that when I was old enough to visit that low-lying neighborhood from the house on a hill to which my parents fled, I realized that no story of my earliest years impressed me more. It remains the single most powerful story of the year of my birth. Today many, many years later, I live in a comparably low-lying neighborhood, some miles from Long Island Sound—one that could well be flooded under the right circumstances. We've endured a good many hurricanes that ravaged nearby coastal towns. Our street has been flooded by heavy rains, but it never occurred to us until recently that we have reason for fearing a real flood. But now that the Western Antarctic Ice Shelf is about to break off, global sea levels will rise much sooner than anyone thought.

Fear of floods and of the vast oceans that feed many of them is quite ancient. The waters that Gilgamesh and Noah's ark crossed were but two of many in ancient Mesopotamia, not to mention the Greco-Roman and Middle Eastern cultures of old. In fact, worldwide it is difficult to find any ancient civilization without a myth about either floods as a cleansing threat or the seas as the deep waters of creation. Those myths of original waters are not so much mythic illusion as scientific fact. All life, so far as we know, came from the seas—a biological fact confirmed by the evidence that, at least among mammalians, our blood and other

## 38 CHAPTER THREE

> bodily fluids are mostly water, with nearly the same percentage of saline as sea water.
>
> Did my parents repeat and repeat the story of the flood of 1937 because I was born out of it or because they held a primordial fear of floods? Probably neither, but who knows? Then again, somewhere in nearly all there is a thirst for, if not a fear of, the deep waters from which human being came and to which we might return in some final flood. Too extreme in our time of scientific wisdom? Perhaps not in this precise moment when the fresh water we require to survive is diminishing very nearly at the same rate as melting ice caps free salt water that could flood all communities settled on the banks and shores of the world's waters.

Like many other early stories, whether fact or imagination, Gilgamesh and Noah illustrate the iron law of beginnings. Nothing in this world begins in an isolated historical moment—not the creation of worlds, not floods, not great heroic figures, not gods, not a people, nor least of all the worlds invented by people. Historical beginnings are imperceptible stirrings in the foundations of a world yet to be.

The uncertainties as to the beginning of the modern world are a case in point. Some say, with good reason, it began around 1500 when European explorers set out across oceans to settle the New World, an event made possible by modern methods of navigation and cartography. Others would say that these early centuries of a modern people were not firmly established until modern ideas of the more or less rational nation-state took hold in the 1600s; for others, not until the Enlightenment in the 1700s; and for still others, not until industrial capitalism took shape in the 1800s. Yet even reasonable claims like these are trumped by much earlier dates. One medieval historian, Lynn White (who died in 1987), proposed that fourteenth-century agricultural technologies, including the stirrup and the heavy plow, made possible large-scale efficiencies in agriculture that made capital surpluses available to new modernizing economies—which in turn made possible, if not necessary, global explorations. Each theory has its reasons. Together they are similar to early ideas of gods controlling the world that began in the legends of Gilgamesh and others. Nothing begins in an instant, not even, so far as we can tell, the cosmic big bang that made the stars that light the night sky.

When Did Globalization Begin?

## SMALL TECHNOLOGIES AND BIG CHANGES

In our time, we tend to think of global changes as the result (and sometimes the cause) of comparably big and important technologies. The steam engine greatly increased the speed of travel on land and water. The technology of relatively inexpensive steel production made railroads and trains possible. The telephone and radio changed human communication. The automobile required the highway system, which changed how personal travel and commercial shipping work. Rocketry changed warfare. The Internet, some think, changed everything. And so on. But all of this does not begin to consider small changes in the long-ago world that made any of this possible. To think about the history of technologies is to plunge into a stream of possible facts leading back who knows where and how far. Lynn White's influential theory that first the heavy plow, then the stirrup were small changes in the fourteenth century is perhaps the most controversial and therefore well-examined theory of small technological change. The plough, for example, has been around since ancient times. For centuries, ploughs were constructed by individual farmers as simple tools for pushing earth from side to side. This worked well enough in southern climates, where the soil was light and easily broken. Northern Europe, however, lay on heavier, clay soil that required a heavier plough, eventually one made of metal and designed to turn the resistant soil over. This advance, however, required not only the use of powerful horses for pulling power, but more sophisticated ways of gliding the plough—eventually the wheel. It is easy enough to imagine small farmers tilling the soil to eke out a living. Little did they, thousands upon thousands, suppose where their most practical local inventions would lead. The heavy plough greatly increased the amount of land that could be put to agricultural use. Somewhere along the way, as the size of farm lands grew, the stirrup was another small technological change that made possible the use of horses to allow land holders to supervise ever-growing and more efficient agricultural production. In turn, fewer and fewer farmers were needed to produce more and more food, which, in further turn, not only fed a population but yielded a profit. And all this line of development, started perhaps by the heavy plough and the stirrup, led to surplus capital able to fund world exploration and the exploitation of colonial wealth, then more mature forms of capitalism, then the industrial age, from which came the larger technologies we more often think of. Did the heavy plough *cause*

40 CHAPTER THREE

> the modern age? Nothing is that simple. But surely something like it was necessary for the changes that transformed a local agricultural economy into a global postindustrial one.

Globalization, again, is about speed, technologies, new relations, and fixed spaces. By this measure the medieval stirrup could be said to have been a beginning of a kind of globalization. It was a technology that lent speed to agricultural production, which led to new relations among peasants and landholders, and of both to the land—and thus, in time, to surplus wealth that later made world exploration possible, and so forth. A skeptic might say that ancient legends are not the same as arguable facts of modern beginnings. Still, Gilgamesh and Noah had the technical skills to dig wells and build ships. They closed cosmic distances, then united their people in new relations after the floods. Noah in particular is today considered a father of sorts of a fixed place settled by a people in a land flowing with milk and honey, and there was built a nation and a state that endures today.

Of course, this can go too far. Globalization is not, surely, a universal condition of human life on the earth. Probably, the vast majority of settled social groups did not have the technical means to expand their very local, often-isolated worlds. Even today in Mongolia, one of the world's fastest-growing economies, there are rural people living on the remote steppes in yurts. For them, the very idea of leaving their traditional ways of life is seldom more than a figment of the cultural imagination, even if they have and use cell phones. Still, in those figments there is an element of a universal human impulse that is somewhere in the mix of early forms of globalization. Those who preserved and passed on the Gilgamesh legend somehow had the idea that a people is meant to have a world, even to dream of it, sometimes to seek it.

Thus, we can speak of an *imperial disposition*—a native human attitude that lies in waiting for the technologies that may allow a people to move beyond their local settlements to enter new relations in new spaces. In the lands where the ancient legends of Gilgamesh and Noah took hold, there had long been very real wars and struggles over rights to territories. The ancient Persian Epic of Zarathustra (said to be the oldest source of what became monotheistic religions) spoke of this imperial disposition. "I want freedom of movement and freedom of dwelling for those with homesteads, to those who dwell upon the earth with their cattle." Wars are known to have been fought for freedoms like these that can be had only in newly expanded territories. These accounts took place a good three millennia ago, before even familiar Western beliefs in gods ruling the cosmos.

To suggest that most, if not all, human groups hold a disposition toward territorial expansion—toward, that is, the beginnings of empire building—is not, of course, the same thing as saying they all built and controlled empires. Yet some did.

In China in the fourth and third centuries BCE, when China itself was a loose federation of rival groups struggling over territorial claims, Mencius, a Confucian leader, successor in stature to Confucius himself, spoke of discontent arising from the turmoil:

> The rulers of States rob their people of their time, so that they cannot plough and weed their fields, in order to support their parents. Brothers, wives, and children are separated and scattered abroad. (Mencius [in Lemert et al. 2010, 18–19])

Mencius taught during early China's Warring States period, which was brought to an end by the rise of the Han Dynasty (206 BCE–290 CE), one of history's greatest empires. Still today, the Han people are the largest ethnic population in China. Under them, a vast territory was united—from the Gobi Desert in the north to the Indo-China peninsula in the south, and from the Korean Peninsula in the east to the far western mountains. Under the Han Dynasty, China flourished economically. This was the period when the Silk Road was established across China through the western deserts to the highlands of Central Asia, then to Turkey and Europe.

### MARCO POLO'S WONDER AT CHINA'S COAL

In a journey between 1276 and 1291, Marco Polo traveled by land over the Silk Road to China. His wonder at what he saw is recorded in *The Travels of Marco Polo,* based on stories he told upon his return to Venice. Among the wonders he discovered was one not then exploited in the Europe still forming. The text as it has been passed down and translated is a mixture of reports, notes, and commentaries:

> It is a fact that all over the country of Cathay there is a kind of black stones existing in beds in the mountains, which they dig out and burn like firewood. If you supply the fire with them at night, and see that they are well kindled, you will find them still alight in the morning; and they

## CHAPTER THREE

make such capital fuel that no other is used throughout the country. It is true that they have plenty of wood also, but they do not burn it, because those stones burn better and cost less.

Moreover with that vast number of people, and the number of hot baths that they maintain—for every one has such a bath at least three times a week, and in winter if possible every day, whilst every nobleman and man of wealth has a private bath for his own use—the wood would not suffice for the purpose.

There is a great consumption of coal in Northern China, especially in the brick stoves, which are universal, even in poor houses. Coal seems to exist in every one of the eighteen provinces of China, which in this respect is justly pronounced to be one of the most favoured countries in the world. Near the capital coal is mined at Yuen-ming-yuen, and in a variety of isolated deposits among the hills in the direction of the Kalgan road, and in the district round Siuen-hwa-fu. (Sindachu of Polo, ante ch. lix.) But the most important coal-fields in relation to the future are those of Shan-tung Hu-nan, Ho-nan, and Shan-si. The last is eminently the coal and iron province of China, and its coal-field, as described by Baron Richthofen, combines, in an extraordinary manner, all the advantages that can enhance the value of such a field except (at present) that of facile export; whilst the quantity available is so great that from Southern Shan-si alone he estimates the whole world could be supplied, at the present rate of consumption, for several thousand years. "Adits, miles in length, could be driven within the body of the coal. . . . These extraordinary conditions . . . will eventually give rise to some curious features in mining . . . if a railroad should ever be built from the plain to this region . . . branches of it will be constructed within the body of one or other of these beds of anthracite." Baron Richthofen, in the paper which we quote from, indicates the revolution in the deposit of the world's wealth and power, to which such facts, combined with other characteristics of China, point as probable; a revolution so vast that its contemplation seems like that of a planetary catastrophe.

In the coal-fields of Hunan the mines are chiefly opened where the rivers intersect the inclined strata of the coal-measures and allow the coal-beds to be attacked by the miner immediately at their out croppings.

It can well be said that the very idea of global trade and expansion arose from the Han Empire, which established the territorial basis for the Silk Road Marco Polo traveled more than a millennium later. Polo's accounts of

China's treasures inspired later Europeans to dream of finding a sea route to Asia, which led to the fifteenth-century world explorers—Columbus, Magellan, and others—who opened the way to the New World and thus to worldwide exploitation of the Americas and of a good bit of Asia, not to mention Africa. One famous theory, owing to Andre Gunder Frank (Frank 1998), holds that this vast and enduring Asian economic system was the first and the only true world-system, greater even than Europe's would become.

## CENTRAL ASIA AS A GLOBAL BLACK HOLE

Along with Immanuel Wallerstein, Andre Gunder Frank (who died in 2005) was one of the most influential scholars in the early history of world-systems analysis, a movement that drew a great deal of its inspiration from Latin American schools working on the history of their region in the global system. Early in 1992, Frank began to shift his emphasis as a world-systems analyst to Asia. By 1998, in a famously controversial book, he openly disagreed with Wallerstein's emphasis on Europe as the core of the modern world-system. Frank's claim was that the Mongol Empire in the twelfth century under the warrior king Genghis Khan was responsible for history's most important world-system based in East and Northeast China to India, and across Central Asia by the Silk Road to the margins of Europe. This, of course, was not a capitalist system but it was, argued Frank, a world economic system more important than Europe's.

Today it is normal in theories of outer space to speak of black holes filled with dark matter that is all density and no mass, impossible to penetrate by the customary laws of time and space. The earth has long had its black holes. In the early days of colonization Europe thought of Africa this way. Not much later, first the Arctic then Antarctica were black holes from the point of view of their impenetrability. Many, like Sir John Franklin in 1845 and his crew, died trying to find the Northwest Passage through the Arctic ice cap, as the crew of Ernest Shackleton's ship, the *Endurance,* almost did in 1911–1914 in their attempt to explore Antarctica. Andre Gunder Frank, writing as an economic historian, argued that Central Asia since the days of Genghis Khan has been the most enduring of global black holes. Why? Because, in his opinion, the site of the Silk Road of Central Asia connects the world's great economic regions, yet remains poorly and prejudicially understood as a backward region, which it is not. On this, as on other issues, Frank was vividly clear:

## 44 ⊕ CHAPTER THREE

> Central Asia is . . . a black hole in the astronomical sense: It is hugely dark or darkly huge. Central Asia is also central to the civilizations of the outlying peoples, whose life space is sucked into the black hole in the center. It is not clear where civilized peoples and spaces end, and where they interpenetrate with those of Central Asia. None of the civilizations are pristine. All of them were formed and even defined through interaction with Central Asia. . . . Central Asia appears as a sort of black hole in the middle of the world. Little is known or said about it by those who focus on the geographically outlying civilizations of China, India, Persia, Islam, and Europe including Russia. Even world historians only see some migrants or invaders who periodically emerge from Central Asia to impinge on these civilizations and the world history they make. . . . Historians of art and religion view Central Asia as a sort of dark space through which these world cultural achievements moved from one civilization to another. At best, they see Central Asia itself as a dark tabula rasa on which itinerant monks, mullahs and artists from these civilized areas left their marks. Now their remains can be admired in 1000 Buddha caves and mosques spread through Central Asia. Or they have been deposited in museums spread through the cultural capitals of the West and Japan after their "discoverers" unearthed them, crated them up, and carted them away.
>
> Central Asia is also central to any attempt at systematic or systemic analysis of the history of the world system. Central Asia is a black hole that must attract the attention and even the enthusiasm of any analyst of world system history. Yet Central Asia is perhaps both the most important and the most neglected part of the world and its history. Among the reasons for this neglect are the following: History is mostly written by the victors for their own purposes, especially to legitimize their victory. While Central Asia was home to many victors for a long time, they either wrote or left few histories of their accomplishments. Then, since the 15th century, Central Asian peoples have been mostly losers in two ways. They have lost out to others on their home ground, and their Central Asian home lands ceased to be so central to world history. Moreover, these two losses were intimately related to each other: The world historical center of gravity shifted outward, sea-ward, and Westward. (Frank 1992, 46–47)

Neither the early Han Dynasty nor the great Mongol Empire was the first or the last of the ancient empires; the Persian, the Egyptian, the Greco-Roman, and the Ottoman are other familiar examples. Each in its way arose on a desire for territorial expansion—a desire founded in large part, as Mencius remarked, on the troubles associated with rivals seeking desirable territories, rivalries that led states to abuse and oppress their own people.

## FROM ANCIENT EMPIRES TO A RATIONAL WORLD-SYSTEM

Where the empires of history differ from the modern global system is that without exception ancient empires were built and defended by violence. War and the control of conquered people and their lands required superior military force or the threat of force.

Violence as a tool of statecraft and colonization did not, of course, disappear in the modern era, with its superficial allegiance to human rights and reasonable government. But in earlier times, violence was the principal instrument of social control and therefore more salient. Just the same, the violent conquest of lands and peoples is seldom outright violence. There is always some important degree of a cultural idea that stands behind the disposition for empire. Though ancient Israel was never a successful colonizer, still, as is obvious from the story of David and Goliath, they were prepared for war. Civilizational empires go back to well before Israel, at least to the very ancient Sumerians, a settled and cultured people in Mesopotamia as long ago as the fifth millennium BCE who passed forward fragments of their language and legends. Much later, the comparatively less ancient Persian story of Zarathustra was part of the deep background of the first great empire of ancient times—the Persian empire of Cyrus the Great (590–520 BCE). Cyrus's empire was centered in today's Iran but covered the whole of the Near East to the Indian Ocean. Only the imperial conquests of Alexander the Great (356–323 BCE) were more substantial, though not by far.

The conquests of Cyrus were driven by a somewhat diluted version of the much earlier idea that the cosmos had been formed in a struggle between forces of good and evil. This is known as Manichean belief, which was pervasive throughout early Persia. One or another version of this cosmic dualism between good and evil continued through the centuries to influence Roman and Christian cultures. Crude versions of it are evident today in political ideologies as well as various religious cults. Still, with Cyrus this very rigid ideology was modified in remarkably humane ways, as is evident in his justification for the conquest of the Babylonians:

## 46 CHAPTER THREE

> When I entered Babylon as a friend and when I established the seat of government in the palace of the ruler under jubilation and rejoicing, Marduk, the great lord induced the magnanimous inhabitants of Babylon to love me, and I was daily endeavoring to worship him. My numerous troops walked around in Babylon in peace, I did not allow anybody to terrorize any place of the country of Sumer and Akkad. I strove for peace in Babylon and in all the sacred cities. As to the inhabitants of Babylon ... I abolished forced labor. . . . I brought relief to their dilapidated housing, putting any end to their complaints. (The Cyrus Cylinder [in Lemert et al. 2010, 28])

Even conquerors who justify their imperial power as defenders of the good are capable of delusions of their own grandeur, gained not by virtue but by overwhelming military force.

Cyrus is, thus, widely considered to have been a dividing line in the history of empires. The peace Cyrus claims to have brought to Babylon may not have been peace as we moderns think of it, but the very idea that he meant to achieve something like a fair and generous rule of an alien people introduced a strong element of what today we would call reasonable and peaceful order into the ancient imperial impulse. Alexander the Great, who two centuries later conquered the remains of the Persian empire, was not viewed as reasonable by the Persians but he was by the Egyptians he liberated from them. His was the truer version of the emperor. Yet the legend of Alexander the Great plays on the fact that he had been, it is thought, a pupil of Aristotle and, thus, a kind of Hellenic genius who reflected the philosophical culture of the Golden Age of Greek learning.

Somewhere in the time between Cyrus in the sixth century BCE and Alexander in the fourth, the ancient worlds shifted well beyond their rural past to gather into great cities. Emergent centers of culture, politics, and economic trade came to rule more primitive rural, even barbaric, regions of their own plus those of the people they conquered. Thus it was with Athens and Sparta, as well as Rome, but also today's Beijing and other Asian centers that would dazzle Marco Polo and inspire the later Western explorers to uncover the wealth of the Orient.

As the Babylonians fell to Persia, the Persians to Alexander, Greece to the Romans, the Romans to Alaric, and later the Ottomans to the Europeans, it is evident that even the most cultured of empires, like the

## When Did Globalization Begin?  47

Han and the Roman, however long they endured, eventually collapsed. Edward Gibbon's famous theory of the rise and fall of civilizations (in *The Decline and Fall of the Roman Empire*) certified an already long-held idea that empires and their civilizations are locked in historical cycles that cannot be avoided. Gibbon's classic, written in the revolutionary period in France, introduced to the modern era the theory of rise and fall (a theory rewritten just as famously for later times in, among many books, Arnold Toynbee's twelve-volume *A Study of History* (1961 [1934–1961]). Even now there are those who eagerly look for the decline of the American global hegemony and assume that it will follow the pattern of collapse of the British Empire early in World War II. The truth of the inevitability of rises and falls cannot, of course, be known, but the facts of history lend seriousness to the idea.

> ### TOYNBEE ON THE UNIVERSALITY AND VULNERABILITY OF EMPIRES
>
> Arnold Toynbee's *A Study of History* was, at the time, a near miraculous historical and theoretical work of twelve volumes. The following passage is an example of his well-documented history of great global states. He claimed with good evidence that at their height of power, empires considered themselves universal, in large part because they had achieved dominance out of a prior period of decline and warfare. But he adds, also with good evidence, that they are bound to a cycle that leads them to authoritarian rule, which in turn eventually leads to their decline:
>
>> After the breakdown of a civilization, a number of parochial communities are fused together into a universal state, the process of political unification is apt to be accompanied, on the religious plane of ritual and theology, by an incorporation of the diverse parochial divinities into a single pantheon which reflects, and is reflected in, the concomitant change in the order of human life on Earth. As the internecine warfare between conflicting parochial states results in the supremacy of a single victor and in the subjugation of all the rest, so the parochial god of the victorious human community an Amon-Re of Thebes or a Marduk-Bel of Babylon becomes the high god of a pantheon into which the gods of the defeated human communities are marshaled in order that henceforth they may fetch and carry or stand and wait at the pleasure of their new master. It will be seen,

# 48 ⊕ CHAPTER THREE

> however, that the condition of human affairs which finds its superhuman reflexion in a pantheon of this kind is the situation immediately after the genesis of a universal state, and not the constitution into which a polity of that type eventually settles down in the course of the age that follows its establishment; for the ultimate constitution of a universal state is not a hierarchy which preserves its constituent parts intact and merely converts their former equality as sovereign independent states in a hegemony of one of them over the rest. A political structure which, on the morrow of its establishment, may have been accurately described as "the Kingdom of the Lands" solidifies in the course of time into a unitary empire articulated into standardized provinces; and a corresponding process of concentration concurrently transforms the Padishah or King of Kings in fact, if not in name into a solitary autocrat who delegates his plenary authority to creatures of his own instead of simply keeping his foot upon the necks of kinglets whose forefathers had been his own forefathers' peers. (Vol. VI, 15)

Still, the question remains: Why today do we so seldom speak of empires in the sense that was common until not that long ago, when Britain's global reach, while vast, was not the same as ancient Rome's more military dominance of its then-known world? Today the word "empire" is usually reserved for various metaphoric uses as in American president Ronald Reagan's famous 1983 allusion to the Soviet Union as an evil empire; or, alternatively, as the name of a once-popular rap-metal album; or even as a slur against the continuing military and geopolitical authority of the United States.

Why not empires today? The best answer in my view is offered by Immanuel Wallerstein (1974 and 2006), who argues at great length in many books that the empires of old were not really world-systems. One might say, to the contrary, that ancient Greece, though never a global empire, enjoyed the beginnings of a systematic culture of the Hellenic idea. Rome, even more, clearly expanded its empire systematically, especially to the west and around the Mediterranean, which it ruled with a degree of respect for the civil rights of those conquered.

Still, the modern world surely, if slowly, developed since 1500—from the earliest explorers, through the centuries to modern democratic states today. It is evident enough that the role of reasoned calculation in the governing of peoples took on greater and greater importance. Modern states have been, in their own ingenious ways, capable of terrible violence, yet the overriding

## When Did Globalization Begin?  49

fact is that as they matured modern democratic states, at least in principle, favored rational calculation—even diplomacy—over brute force.

Wallerstein's main idea, however, goes beyond a modern culture of rationality and science. The more significant feature of his modern world-system idea is that it was a world-*system* because, first and foremost, it was driven by a rational calculation of economic profit and the purposeful accumulation of wealth. The system's wealth, that is, is a system-sustaining end in itself as opposed to an adornment of an empire's power. The Ming Dynasty's imperial palace, the Forbidden City in Beijing, is today an enduring museum to a long-gone empire's display of its grandiosity. The Twin Towers in New York City, utterly without adornment, were, to be sure, attacked as a symbol of capitalist wealth, but they housed offices wherein the work of capitalism went on. Thus, to put it too simply, the idea is that though all empires of old were driven by economic motives in their quest for new territories, even in the case of the Han Dynasty's Silk Road, where the purpose was trade and wealth, the system was not so much planned and calculated as a perceived necessity arising from need and opportunity. Zarathustra, we saw, spoke of the need for land for a people and their cattle. Cyrus conquered the evil forces in Babylon; thus Babylonians were added to his empire. Still, Cyrus meant to repair the land and the homes to serve his new adherents.

All social forms that strive to fulfill an imperial disposition are surely, above all, economic. The differences in modern systems are how the economic pursuit is organized and the goals toward which it aims. In our time, the United States is far from being the largest nation-state in the world and, technically, it claims no right to rule foreign regions—at least it no longer does, with the possible exception of a few places such as Puerto Rico, the District of Columbia, and island territories scattered across the Pacific, none of which is endowed with full membership in the American state system. After 1991 it was thought that the Russian Federation had given up its claims to nations that asserted their independence from the Soviet Union, but as time goes by, that has become more a wish than a hard reality. Still, in Ukraine, for example, the Russians felt the need to present their invasions as somehow postimperial. Even China, with the exception of its brutal taking of Tibet, has relented by backing down from its once-insistent claim to Taiwan. But again, as time passed, Beijing—in spite of its interests in economically robust Hong Kong—seems unable to keep itself from what might be called a soft imperialism. Still, there are no empires

## 50 ⊕ CHAPTER THREE

as once there were, even if there are modern states, like Russia and China, and corporations, like Monsanto, that act imperiously.

But there is a massive global system—what Wallerstein calls the modern world-system—that asserts itself in all, or nearly all, corners of the earth. Wallerstein holds the view that the world-empires, even those that did not span the globe entirely (as even Britain did not), are no longer at play as empires in the modern global economy. This is not to say that the vestiges of older empires do not linger in former colonies that depend on their former colonizers in many ways. The origins of the British Empire were in its sixteenth-century colonial settlements in North America, India and other parts of Asia, and Africa. Now only a few island outposts are considered British territory. Yet Great Britain still is considered the head of a commonwealth of some fifty nations, most former colonies—most prominently Canada, Australia, South Africa, India. Each will invite members of the royal family for ceremonial visits. Each speaks a version of British English, with the exception of Canada, which has been corrupted by America's television and other of its cultural intrusions. Still even this shadow of a commonwealth is not anything like the British Empire except that it serves to give member nations a certain trade advantage with the UK, as well as relatively easy access to migration rights. Otherwise what remains are the cultural and political vestiges of a colonizing past.

What stands in the stead of empires is a global capitalist system that is widely considered not just the only economic game in town, but the longest-lasting and most powerful global economic system in history. Some of the ancient empires, like the Roman, had longer histories. Yet Rome's colonial world fractured time and again, notably in 26 BCE, when the imperial republic gave way to the formal Roman Empire under Caesar Augustus. Some version of the Roman Empire lasted a millennium plus, from Romulus in the eighth century BCE until the sack of Rome by the Goths early in the fifth century CE. By contrast, the modern system has lasted, in one form or another, from about 1500 CE down into our times, a scant half millennium. The importance, thus, of the modern system is not in its duration or in its geographic reach, but in the degree to which its economic influence and thus its power have spread around the known world.

The idea of a modern world-system is not universally accepted. As I noted, Andre Gunder Frank (1998) argued strongly, but not convincingly, that the ancient Asian global system centered in China and along the Silk Road was the only truly global economic system. Immanuel Wallerstein's

### When Did Globalization Begin?

simple counterargument is, roughly, *Perhaps, but it was not capitalist.* That might sound like an abstract or even a political retort. It is anything but.

Academic social scientists have known at least since Max Weber's great book *The Protestant Ethic and the Spirit of Capitalism* (1992 [1904–1905]) that capitalism became fully what it is today only by the acquisition of a very specific kind of cultural and economic ethic. Whereas the ancient empires were, in their way, rational (Confucian teachings, for example), economically they were, in technical terms, tradition-oriented. Neither the Chinese nor the Greeks had a strong theory of history in the modern sense. For moderns, human history moves ever forward. In traditional cultures there were histories (the writings of Thucydides on the Peloponnesian Wars, for example) that were brilliant narratives of events, but their narrative qualities were often crowded by time-bound chronologies—presentations of events as they happened or were thought to have happened.

> **FUNERAL ORATION OF PERICLES, THUCYDIDES,** ***HISTORY OF THE PELOPONNESIAN WAR*** **(431 BCE)**
>
> Thucydides and his somewhat older contemporary, Herodotus, were Greek historians who have been considered the fathers of modern history. Thucydides's long *History of the Peloponnesian War* in 431 BCE is typical of these masters of fifth-century historical narrative. In contrast to modern historiography, ancient writers viewed history as storytelling rather than analysis. The most famous illustration of their method is the funeral oration of Pericles. Pericles was an Athenian statesman who offered his oration for the Athenians killed in the war with Sparta. *History of the Peloponnesian War,* as this funeral oration illustrates, when not a chronicle of events, was a collection of stories loosely brought together by the author.
>
> > So died these men as became Athenians. You, their survivors, must determine to have as unfaltering a resolution in the field, though you may pray that it may have a happier issue. And not contented with ideas derived only from words of the advantages which are bound up with the defense of your country, though these would furnish a valuable text to a speaker even before an audience so alive to them as the present, you must yourselves realize the power of Athens, and feed your eyes upon her from day to day, till love of her fills your hearts; and then, when all her greatness shall break upon you,

## CHAPTER THREE

you must reflect that it was by courage, sense of duty, and a keen feeling of honor in action that men were enabled to win all this, and that no personal failure in an enterprise could make them consent to deprive their country of their valor, but they laid it at her feet as the most glorious contribution that they could offer. For this offering of their lives made in common by them all they each of them individually received that renown which never grows old, and for a sepulcher, not so much that in which their bones have been deposited, but that noblest of shrines wherein their glory is laid up to be eternally remembered upon every occasion on which deed or story shall call for its commemoration. For heroes have the whole earth for their tomb; and in lands far from their own, where the column with its epitaph declares it, there is enshrined in every breast a record unwritten with no tablet to preserve it, except that of the heart. These take as your model and, judging happiness to be the fruit of freedom and freedom of valor, never decline the dangers of war. For it is not the miserable that would most justly be unsparing of their lives; these have nothing to hope for: it is rather they to whom continued life may bring reverses as yet unknown, and to whom a fall, if it came, would be most tremendous in its consequences. And surely, to a man of spirit, the degradation of cowardice must be immeasurably more grievous than the unfelt death which strikes him in the midst of his strength and patriotism!

Ancient histories, such as they were, were closer to epic poems like Homer's *Iliad* than to modern histories like Winston Churchill's four-volume *A History of the English-Speaking Peoples* (1956–1958). To be sure, modern histories are not free of storytelling or even legend making. Yet Churchill's book, more or less a celebration of Britain's history, was both impeccable scholarship and fine literary nonfiction—fine enough to earn him a Nobel Prize in literature.

## WINSTON CHURCHILL ON HISTORY

No one can understand history without continually relating the long periods which are constantly mentioned to the experiences of our own short lives. Five years is a lot. Twenty years is the horizon to most people. Fifty years is antiquity. To understand how the impact of destiny fell upon any generation of men one must first imagine their position and then apply the time-scale of our own lives.

*When Did Globalization Begin?*  53

Apart from all else Churchill was one of the most eloquent speakers of the twentieth century, at least as much so as Pericles in his day. And he was a magnificent teller of stories. But Churchill's four-volume history was also modern history. Even this short passage imposed an unmistakable analytic order on the story. In the lines quoted from the first volume, *The Birth of Britain*, Churchill begins his magisterial work with a story about history itself. That opens an early chapter entitled, poetically, "The Lost Island." His poetic imagination pervades a very analytic modern history not just of England, but of its language and culture as it passed from an early lost island into a global commonwealth, and to, as he puts it, the great democracies, notably the United States. Modern histories are judged as disciplined accounts of how things unfolded in the past down to a present moment.

This may sound like a small distinction between modern history and ancient chronology; and it would be were it not that modern histories, in the literary sense, were themselves embedded in and defined by a much broader cultural idea. In a sense histories of the modern are themselves modern. Modern cultures, in the West at least, held firm to the principle that mankind was evolving out of a past into a future. Traditional cultures were, as Max Weber put it, inclined toward the eternal yesterday. Modern cultures were imbued with a broader cultural ethic, one that teaches that life is meant to be lived always toward a future goal. Thus, if something is true of the lives of individuals, then it also is true of their cultures, economies, and politics. One cannot live for long outside her culture and all that goes with it.

Weber's contribution in *The Protestant Ethic and the Spirit of Capitalism* was to give evidence that this future-oriented ethic—or spirit of capitalism— necessarily came before full-blown industrial capitalism in the nineteenth century. Without the ethic, no capitalists; without capitalist entrepreneurs, no capitalism.

> **MAX WEBER ON THE ETHIC OF CAPITALISM**
>
> A product of modern European civilization, studying any problem of universal history, is bound to ask himself to what combination of circumstances the fact should be attributed that in Western civilization, and in Western civilization only, cultural phenomena have appeared which (as we like to think) lie in a line of development having universal significance and value. . . .

## 54 ⊕ CHAPTER THREE

> The most fateful force in our modern life [is] capitalism. The impulse to acquisition, pursuit of gain, of money, of the greatest possible amount of money, has in itself nothing to do with capitalism. This impulse exists and has existed among waiters, physicians, coachmen, artists, prostitutes, dishonest officials, soldiers, nobles, crusaders, gamblers, and beggars. One may say that it has been common to all sorts and conditions of men at all times and in all countries of the earth, wherever the objective possibility of it is or has been given. It should be taught in the kindergarten of cultural history that this naïve idea of capitalism must be given up once and for all. Unlimited greed for gain is not in the least identical with capitalism, and is still less its spirit. Capitalism may even be identical with the restraint, or at least a rational tempering, of this irrational impulse. But capitalism is identical with the pursuit of profit, and forever renewed profit, by means of continuous, rational, capitalistic enterprise. For it must be so: in a wholly capitalistic order of society, an individual capitalistic enterprise which did not take advantage of its opportunities for profit-making would be doomed to extinction. (Weber 1992 [1904–1905], xxxi–xxxii)

Naturally, Weber's argument is not without its critics. Just the same, he alerted the new social sciences to the fact that the modern world as it came to be in industrial capitalism depended on a deep cultural revolution long before. Without Protestantism and Calvinism, he said, the Western world might well have remained traditionalist in the sense that religion, culture in general, even economic practices would still serve the interests of maintaining the world as it was, without seeking some future world meant to be better and one day, even, perfectly good.

Thus, goes the theory, modern history is rational in the sense that moderns were from the beginning, and are now, entrepreneurs—always calculating the odds that a next step in life is a venture justified by the prospect of improving one's situation in life. As a capitalist ventures time and what cash she can raise against the chances that, say, a new business venture will pay off, so all moderns are entrepreneurs in their choice of life companions, where to live, whether to go to school (and which school), and so forth. Not all, but most. Modern culture is thus rational in the sense that it puts at risk what parents hold dear in the expectation that their children will leave home to find a purportedly new and better life. Parents whose kids never leave are, in effect, bigger failures than their children who never leave the childhood home. Capitalism is rationalism in this sense. It is not

## When Did Globalization Begin?

merely reasonable, but it reasons that everything (or most things) presents risks worth taking if there is a reasonable chance those risks will pay off.

Wallerstein, who knows Weber's ideas very well, is not preoccupied with theories of modern culture. But his idea of a modern world-system does probe the histories of the economies that arise from this sort of entrepreneurial spirit. As a result, he dates the beginning of that modern system in the sixteenth century after capitalist agriculture made possible sufficient capital surplus for the crowns of Iberia, then the Netherlands, then Britain and France, to invest in transatlantic voyages meant to discover new wealth in a new world; or, as the then-prevailing mistaken assumption was, an Asia thought to be across the seas. This is why we speak today of the *West* Indies originally confused with India itself. Columbus and his sponsors may have been intrigued by the adventure of it all, but theirs was an entrepreneurial investment, a risk for a hoped-for payoff.

Genghis Khan established the great Mongol Empire that stretched from North Asia to the western outposts of the Silk Road. He, or his empire, thereby appropriated wealth, which in turn allowed for these territorial expansions. But in modern terms, he and even Alexander and others of ancient times, were not engaged so much in rational calculation as sheer hoarding.

Capitalism, by contrast, aims to accumulate wealth for future purposes. Along with capital wealth comes power and, to be sure, a new kind of imperial impulse. Hitler was a tyrant in a very old-fashioned way, but he had a theory of history that led him to invest—albeit by the most despicable methods—in the conquest and extermination of peoples who stood in the way of his pure Aryan world power. Emperors, like capitalists, are ethically neutral. They may do good or evil, but the ethics that guide them are judged not by their inherent merit but by results—whether a territory is expanded to serve the empire's traditional needs or whether a product is made that not only produces wealth but also accumulates capital. Thus it is that capital accumulation, whether of lands and spices in a new world or of obscene corporate profits, always looks to the growth of a bottom line.

Today's capitalist manager has a very short time to show a profit, in part because the average investor holds stock for about eight months. Corporate boards will get rid of a CEO who allows the value of a company to slip, in part because they themselves are judged only by bottom lines. Genghis Khan and his successors had centuries to accumulate wealth and no one to judge whether the outcomes had been a good investment—no one, that is, but the next conqueror, whether Tatars or Goths or some other. Even

## 56 CHAPTER THREE

Hitler, who lost his war, was in the end destroyed less by the horror of his deeds than by the fact that he ran out of men and engineers to invent ever-more-aggressive armies and weapons. By the same token, the Soviet Union collapsed less because of Stalin's Gulag than because his socialist state was unable in the long run to produce consumer goods in the face of a costly military misadventure in Afghanistan.

Capital accumulation, thereby, is the fundamental structural feature of a modern world-system; and accumulation is rational, if not always reasonable, according to the degree to which it contributes to some kind of new, presumably better, future—whether for stockholders or voters or ordinary citizens.

In this sense, capitalism is necessarily global. If Columbus's new world was not Asia, then Asia still had to be sought. If any new world when discovered is not obviously wealthy, then its wealth must be found, cultivated, exploited—first spices and tobacco, then cotton and, if these, then the slaughter of native peoples, then slavery, then an oppressed working class. Capitalism is not a bed of roses except for the top 5 percent who control 66 percent or more of its wealth; but it is rational in its own relentless way. Winston Churchill did not write a capitalist history of the English-speaking people, but the kind of history he wrote was governed in the broader sense by the same cultural ethic that allowed him to lead Great Britain in its war against Hitler—to produce an outcome good for the future.

## GLOBAL CAPITALISM

When did globalization begin? Not in the 1990s when the word came into play. The European Community, as some then thought, was not the first coming together of states for a common economic purpose. Such a common state system had long before been settled, at least since the seventeenth century.

---

### PEACE TREATY BETWEEN THE HOLY ROMAN EMPEROR AND THE KING OF FRANCE AND THEIR RESPECTIVE ALLIES AT WESTPHALIA, 1648

That there shall be a Christian and Universal Peace, and a perpetual, true, and sincere Amity, between his Sacred Imperial Majesty, and his most Christian Majesty; as also, between all and each of the Allies, and

> Adherents of his said Imperial Majesty, the House of Austria, and its Heirs, and Successors; but chiefly between the Electors, Princes, and States of the Empire on the one side; and all and each of the Allies of his said Christian Majesty, and all their Heirs and Successors, chiefly between the most Serene Queen and Kingdom of Swedeland, the Electors respectively, the Princes and States of the Empire, on the other part. That this Peace and Amity be observed and cultivated with such a Sincerity and Zeal, that each Party shall endeavor to procure the Benefit, Honor and Advantage of the other; that thus on all sides they may see this Peace and Friendship in the Roman Empire, and the Kingdom of France flourish, by entertaining a good and faithful Neighborhood.

To read the 1648 Treaty of Westphalia is to struggle through a seventeenth-century legal document, filled by seventy-eight articles enumerating all manner of terms and conditions whereby countless dukes and dukedoms and other sovereign parties grand and tiny agreed to establish a peace across the Europe of that day. Most of the places no longer exist. The names in general make little sense. We know what France is and have some idea what the Holy Roman Empire was, but many of the allies and parties mentioned make little sense today (the Fiefs of Rocheveran, for example). Yet though Europe obviously has not since been at continuous peace, the treaty did establish the principle whereby independent states gained the right of respect for their territories only by participating in an interstate system. The treaty, thus, was the first legal document that stood behind the globalization that was then taking shape in the worldwide colonial system.

It is surely not by accident that all of the major European States were, by then, already heavily invested in worldwide global colonial systems. Their interest in peace at home was due not only to war weariness but also to a wider economic interest in asserting their rights to various global colonies. Naturally, a peace treaty does not make for a long-term peace, but it did support an important early idea of globalization.

States cannot long neglect their competitors. Least of all they cannot run roughshod over their rights and claims of costly wars at home or abroad. Thus Portugal more or less settled with Spain its rights to Brazil while ceding claims to the remainder of Latin America. Likewise, the British gave up their claims to the American colonies in part because they were already losing the revolution when the French entered the war on the side of the Americans. In turn, the French ceded most of their interests in North

## 58 ⊕ CHAPTER THREE

America in return for rights to Quebec and Martinique, among lesser New World outposts. And so on.

As the centuries went on, the New World colonizers, just as ruthless in their ways as was Hitler, eventually put their economic interests first or were limited in their ability to accumulate capital wealth by the restrictions of their economies. Spain, once the world's greatest power, fell apart when its armada was defeated and demoralized by the British in a failed attempt to invade Britain in 1588. The Dutch, in the seventeenth century, had built the world's then-greatest navy to protect its overseas investments, especially in Indonesia. Their fleet was in effect privately owned by the Dutch East India Company, which had won a charter for profiteering in Indonesia. It has been said that this was the world's first international corporation. If so, then it suffered the flaws of most large corporations: corruption that led to its collapse in 1800. The French Revolution in 1789 was in large part caused by the crown's overinvestment in blocking the British control of the American colonies. Portugal did not invade Spain. Spain failed to invade England, as the Americans never thought to invade Britain. Hitler tried to conquer all of Europe, including the Soviet Union, but lost everything.

The shifting global fortunes of the core states of the modern world-systems did, of course, involve great military expense and more than a few terrible wars, including at least two world wars—after which, down into our time, even regional wars (especially those in the Middle East, Indochina, and Afghanistan) have tended to become world wars in fact if not by definition. But even after Hitler, the remaining powers did not aim for total conquest. The Soviets demanded and won rights to East Germany and East Europe. But the price of a long Cold War when joined with foolish invasions like those of the Americans in Vietnam or the Soviets in Afghanistan held the interstate system more or less together. As for Germany and Japan, after World War II they were in due course returned nearly entirely to their prior geographic order. The Americans occupied Japan and kept military bases in Germany, but they also invested heavily in the economic reconstruction of both. Why? It was not sheer altruism, but economic necessity.

After World War II, the American economy was by far the largest and most productive in the world. But the nation's postwar power elite, both corporate and governmental, understood very well that without other world markets for their goods, the American economy could not continue to grow. The United States had no choice but to reinvent Asian and European economies after the devastation of a long world war. Hence, a basic fact of capitalist economies: they must always grow. If their internal markets are saturated (or even if they lack future growth opportunities) capitalist markets, with the protection of their state militaries and diplomatic corps, will expand abroad even to the extent of making costly investments. Corporations in collusion with their state elites will create factories where labor is relatively cheap, control foreign states by inducements (usually in the form of loans) to allow capital entrepreneurs to do business, or, when the foreign markets are in shambles, they will pay the price of building them up so that the wealthier (hence, not incidentally, more powerful) capitalist states and their corporations can thrive in the long run.

America's economic reconstruction of Japan and Germany illustrates this law of capital—always look ahead, and find or make the next market. The United States in the 1940s was not the first or the last to do this. Today China is investing heavily in Latin America, Australia, and Africa, not to find cheap labor (of which it has plenty) but to assure its access to resources, especially oil and gas, as well as scarce industrial minerals like bauxite. Likewise, the northernmost nations with borders on the Arctic Circle—Canada, Russia, Denmark, the United States, Sweden, Norway, and Iceland, in particular—are joined competitively to assure access to the north's oil reserves and to shipping lanes opened by the melting of the ice cap. To this end they have formed an Arctic Council alongside other more or less formal arrangements to assure that the competition is, so to speak, fair. Here again is the big difference between a capitalist world-system and a world-empire. Not even the Han Dynasty, with all its glorious learning and culture, thought to expand by, say, entering into treaties with the dynasties in Korea. Before the modern era, the Chinese trespassed on the Korean border from the north. Nor, of course, did Rome seek diplomatic approval to invade Britain. They did what they did because that is what empires did.

Capitalists, to repeat, are not obviously of a better nature than the emperors of old, nor are they any less able to use power to ruthless effect. The American CIA has furtively participated in the murder of popular leaders in, for example, Congo and Chile. The goal was to install terrible people who could be counted upon to serve American interests. Even in these cases, they did what they did in secret and did not admit to their crimes until the evidence was plain to see.

# CHAPTER THREE

> **GLOBAL POWERS ASSASSINATED PATRICE LUMUMBA**
>
> The British intelligence services may have just had one of their best-kept secrets blown: their role in the abduction and assassination of Patrice Lumumba, Congo's first democratically elected prime minister whose Pan-African nationalism and pro-Moscow leanings alarmed the West.
>
> For more than 50 years, rumors have swirled over allegations of British involvement in Lumumba's brutal murder in 1961, but nothing has ever been proved—leaving the CIA and its Belgian peers alone to take the rap for what a Belgian writer has described as "the most important assassination of the 20th century." Now, in a dramatic revelation, a senior British politician has claimed that he got it from the horse's mouth that it was MI6 that "did" it.
>
> In a little noticed letter to the editor in the latest issue of the *London Review of Books* (*LRB*), Lord David Edward Lea responded to the claim in a new book on British intelligence, *Empire of Secrets: British intelligence, the Cold War and the Twilight of Empire* by Calder Walton, that the jury is still out on Britain's role in Lumumba's death. "The question remains whether British plots to assassinate Lumumba ... ever amounted to anything. At present, we do not know," writes Walton.
>
> Lord Lea retorted: "Actually, in this particular case, I can report that we do. It so happens that I was having a cup of tea with Daphne Park. . . . She had been consul and first secretary in Leopoldville, now Kinshasa, from 1959 to 1961, which in practice (this was subsequently acknowledged) meant head of MI6 there. I mentioned the uproar surrounding Lumumba's abduction and murder, and recalled the theory that MI6 might have had something to do with it. 'We did,' she replied, 'I organized it.'" ...
>
> Lumumba, hailed as "the hero of Congolese independence" from Belgium in 1960, was shot dead on January 17, 1961 after being toppled in a US-Belgian backed military coup barely two months after being in office. Lumumba had been sheltered by Rajeshwar Dayal—the Indian diplomat who was the UN Secretary General's representative in the Congo—for several days but was captured and killed soon after he chose to leave the compound. (Suroor 2013)

When in the modern era great modern powers invade without good and sufficient rationale, they usually fall on their faces as, again, the Americans did in Vietnam in the 1960s and in Iraq and Afghanistan in the 2000s.

*When Did Globalization Begin?* 🌐 61

In all cases, including the killing of the Congo's independence leader, they claimed they were acting in defense of worldwide principles of freedom. Global powers paid a very high price for not doing what they thought of as necessary to protect America's global interests in controlling strategic regions with access to valuable resources.

Neither empires nor capitalist systems exist to do good in the world, even if inadvertently they do it. The difference is that empires do what they do without embarrassment by conquering regions they covet. Violence is in their nature. Capitalist systems may do violence but typically, or so they claim, as a last resort required of an alleged good. Both have goals that could well be said, at least in retrospect, to have been rational, but capitalists and their global systems have a good reason for avoiding war and violence. Violence is bad for business and wars are costly. Capitalism already costs the world's states good money. Corporations demand and get military protection, lower taxes, and freedom from unprofitable costs like environmental cleanup. When Exxon or British Petroleum spill oil off Alaska or in the Gulf of Mexico they avoid paying the full cost of the cleanup because governments allow them to lie or otherwise get around what safety regulations apply. Even worse, as they navigate the seas they spoil, they are protected by American naval power.

Ancient Rome, like Alexander's Hellenic Empire before it, had its reasons for its imperial conquests. Those reasons were surely determined by assumptions of rights handed down through imperial predecessors, even from ancient gods on high. But these rights, such as they were, even if divine, were not about economic profit and progress. By contrast, the Dutch East India Company in the seventeenth century, like international oil companies in the twenty-first, could do what it did in large part because its corporate pursuits were chartered by national authorities who in turn relied on the business interests of companies for their political support. If you are concerned with full disclosure, then empires are your thing. They make no secrets as to what they do. Capitalism does because it must conduct business in a modern political environment that assures certain rights to states and citizens. In exchange for vaguely respecting those rights, corporations are paid with direct or indirect military support, lower taxes, and freedom from many of the costs of production and business.

Is globalization pure and simply about business? If for some reason one had to choose one among the many types of globalizations Stanley Hoffman identified in his "Clash of Globalizations" essay, it might be prudent to

## 62 CHAPTER THREE

choose economic globalization as the most fundamental. But globalization, like the world in which it occurs, is never all that simple. Capitalism, as we have seen, is keenly interested in both politics and culture. Modern states, with all their rhetoric about human freedoms, nonetheless give large and global corporations real advantages that are unavailable to your local deli or pub (unless they are franchises of larger companies). No less, corporations profiting from the cultural ideas of free markets and democratic societies are able to move about as they wish, freed of constraints; to hire and fire as their interests demand; to set, even to fix, prices; and much else of this kind. Such a system could not exist as it does without governments and cultures that lend them freedom to do as they think they must in the name of free people and allegedly democratic markets.

### AGAIN, WHY THE 1990s?

Why, still, was it the 1990s when the idea of globalization took off as a way of referring to global things? One of the reasons is certainly then that miraculous information technologies came down to earth as tools available to mass populations. None was particularly new just then. Radio, telephones, and television had been around for a good while, but in retrospect it must be said that these were by definition public in nature. What was new were still more refined forms of information transfer that, before the 1990s, had been reserved for military purposes. The satellite systems that allowed rapid global communications were built not by today's cell-phone companies but by military interests, and they were built well before ordinary people knew about them; so too were the earliest computers.

It may well be that the unique place of information technologies in globalization is not that they exist, but that, after technologies reach a certain point of development, profit-seeking corporations find it very difficult to resist refashioning them as public consumption goods. It is not that ordinary people have become so very smart that they discern that things are out there and they want them. It is more likely that, just as television and radio became public media not long after their technologies were invented and tested, so too will cell phones, computers, and other information technology media. It may be too simple to say that capitalism will always get its dirty hands on something that can be sold, but it does, surely, exercise a pressure in the direction of finding things that exist (or can be made to exist) and turning them into commodities for sale. This, if so, is not necessarily a bad feature of capitalism or, for that matter, of globalization, but it seems to be a motive for the rapid migration of technologies from high to low—from, that is, remotely complex to a simple (if inscrutable) cell phone. This inevitability is economic rationality at its best. Capitalism searches endlessly for markets, then for new commodities to market—thus for ways to simplify high technologies so they can be applied to low (which is to say, popular) consumption.

Thus it is important to recognize that information technologies are, at least, a revolutionary force in culture. It is nearly impossible for cultures to adhere to classically high forms once radio, television, cinema, and all the rest send out music, art, and images of all kinds, as well as ideas and much else according to nearly perfect democratic rules. If people tune in it sells, and if it sells in the cultural sense, then profits can be made. It is not uncommon for tickets to popular music concerts or sports events to cost hundreds of dollars, even before the scalpers get into the game. In turn, the music or sports stars become commodities able to advertise and sell other commodities. It may have been that, in his day, Shakespeare's plays were popular entertainment. But in his day the number of people sufficiently literate to enjoy them was small. In our day, fine but not necessarily great talents play to the world and are fabulously wealthy.

Somewhere along this historical trajectory, information technologies spread cultural forms to more and more people, and more and more people became literate as to their values. Some still call this low culture, but the more accurate term is "mass culture." It is not the number of people that counts in mass culture, but the ability of technologies to create the masses. London in Shakespeare's day was, for the times, a large global city of 200,000, only a few of whom were among the high cultural elite. The population was great, but there was no mass audience because there were no mass media. Shakespeare himself was not a star. If there was an iconic figure then it was Queen Elizabeth, and her only because it is a queen's business to make herself visible to her people.

Globalization as it has come to be is a powerful fusion of a capitalist economic system, politics at all levels of states and interstate relations, and cultural products diffused across borders. Mass-culture icons today are known—even revered—the world over. Information technologies, thus, determine the speed with which financial markets absorb capital in an instant, just as the latest gossip about a star's new baby is broadcast to Beijing and Kinshasa. Along those lines, political careers can collapse in a flash after some claim, true or not, as to a youthful error in judgment.

## 64 CHAPTER THREE

## TIME, TECHNOLOGY, NEW RELATIONS, AND FIXED SPACE

Globalization is about time, technology, new relations, and fixed space. Even empires worked on these four elements—new forms of mobility shortened the time needed to travel great distances, thus to expand imperial territories, which in turn changed the relations among conquerors and the conquered.

It makes little sense to suggest, therefore, that globalization has always been a factor in human societies. Better to say that early transformations such as those in the Han and Roman empires were the result of an imperial impulse—normal in a sense, if grand in their outcomes in these cases. If so, then a question remains: *When did globalization begin?* Is it to be dated from the sensational global changes that were undeniable by the 1990s? Some say yes. But the wiser course is to acknowledge that as brilliant, if terrifying, as the 1990s were, they too were the outcome of a longer historical process. How long? There's the problem. Was it the industrial economics of the nineteenth century? Or the cultural innovations of the Enlightenment? Or the political revolutions in the eighteenth century? Or, as Weber and others say, in the early modern religious and philosophical cultures of the sixteenth century? Each, in its way, was a moment in which what came before took on new structural features promoting new relations.

Some see it differently, but I recommend that the strongest theory is that what we have come to call globalization required, first, an ethic of future progress and, second, the capitalist economic culture that grew from that ethic to beyond a global system. The debate continues, but until someone makes a better argument, it seems to me that Immanuel Wallerstein's claims are the strongest. Even though it is difficult indeed to say when capitalism began, surely its roots in later medieval agricultural practices made it possible. Though that may be, the fact remains that the years on either side of 1500 represented a coming together of new technologies, surplus capital, new cultural and scientific ideas—all of which, and more, were behind the daring ventures of European power and wealth to find a new world—thus, in time, to create first an Atlantic economy, then a global one.

CHAPTER FOUR

# GLOBALIZATION IN THE MODERN WORLD-SYSTEM, 1500–1914

> **ESCAPING CIVILIZATION TO LIVE, PERHAPS TO DIE**
>
> In 1992 an unsettling story appeared in the news. A brilliant young man from a happy family and with an excellent college degree was found dead in the ruins of a long-abandoned bus in a remote wilderness of Alaska. He was Chris McCandles. He had left home in a Virginia suburb of Washington, DC, to travel. He came to call himself Alex Supertramp. Alex had starved to death. He had not wanted to die. A note found with his body said that he walked and hitched his way "to the Great White North No Longer to be Poisoned by Civilization He Flees, and Walks Alone Upon the Land to Become Lost in the Wild." I have told this story before, found it hard to forget. It became the subject of a best-selling book, *Into the Wild* (1996), and later a popular film. Years after Alex lost himself in the wilderness some were still trying to understand how and why he did this. Eventually a biochemist from Fairbanks learned that, as some thought, he had inadvertently died of a natural poison that destroys the body's ability to process food. Alex Supertramp wanted to live.

Why would Alex Supertramp want to escape civilization? Had he somehow lost his mind, as the strange phrasing of his last words suggests? Disgust at modern civilization is not in itself an illness. But to leave it to walk deep

## 66 ⊕ CHAPTER FOUR

into a fatal wilderness is, at the least, strange. Whatever Alex Supertramp was looking for beyond the known world, the fact that he was searching for something is no more than a deep abiding quality of human life that has been lost, for the most part, in the modern world. Today parents often feel that there is always a chance a child will lose her way, stray off the path society defines as normal. If you've lost a child, as I have, you know what I mean. Or if you ever thought about getting out of the rat race or otherwise dropping out, then you may be touched, as Alex was.

On the other hand, if there is a tragic element in modern culture it is that we who are reasonably well settled have lost the ability to wander, to leave all that is familiar. The poor, however, have not. They often must leave to survive famine, disease, civil war, and worse. In his sense, the very poor who move to find some possible better world are closer to human nature than the well established who travel only on business or holiday. For the long history of human society—at least, so far as we know, a good million years—people have left home to search for food and security, never knowing where, or if, they would find them.

Nearly from the beginnings of their organized social life human beings have been voyagers, usually out of necessity and sometimes for the purpose of exploration. Jared Diamond, in *Guns, Germs, and Steel* (1997, 35), the modern-classic study on the history of human societies, wrote,

> A distinctive starting point from which to compare historical developments on the different continents is around 11,000 BC. This date corresponds approximately to the beginnings of village life in a few parts of the world, the first undisputed peopling of the Americas, the end of the Pleistocene Era and the last Ice Age, and the start of what geologists term the Recent Era. Plant and animal domestications began in at least one part of the world within a few thousand years of that date.

Even before that long-ago date, the species migrated east from its origins in Africa, into today's China (about 1,000,000 BCE), then north to Europe (500,000 BCE), then east again across the seas to the Australian continent (40,000 BCE), then north toward Russia (20,000 BCE). By 12,000 BCE hunters had crossed the ice bridge at what is today the Bering Sea to descend in the subsequent 2,000 years to the tip of South America. Along all these very distinct ways they hunted for food, settled villages, and grew grains and other foods they carried farther on.

*Globalization in the Modern World-System, 1500–1914* 67

In this sense America was discovered long before the first Europeans came to this New World from Norway around 1,000 CE. The "Saga of Erik the Red" tells of Leif Ericson coming upon this distant place: "Leif ... was tossed about a long time at sea, and lighted upon lands of which he had no expectation." The lands were rich in wheat and fruit. Leif and his company came upon people who had already settled the lands. Whether these were earlier European explorers or descendants of indigenous people who themselves had migrated from the west some 3,000 years before is hard to say for certain. This was, after all, a legend. Still, what is indisputable is that America, as it came to be, played a part in the European imagination at least 2,500 years before the voyages of discovery around 1,500 CE.

By 1690, the great British political theorist John Locke said, remarkably, "In the beginning all the world was America, and more so than it is now ..."—to which he added, presciently, "for no such thing as money was anywhere known." Locke's idea, though uttered well after the first of England's transatlantic settlements, nonetheless illustrates the extent to which Europeans had come—no doubt since well before the voyages of the early 1500s—to associate this distant place with wealth as the material dream of an original human world. Like Leif Ericson a good half millennium before, Locke imagined America to be a land flowing with a new source of milk and honey—of natural, but commodifiable, wealth.

As idealized as the early legends and sayings were, they also suggest the extent to which America was sought after, even if explorers knew not what to call it. Or, if it was not America in the beginning, as Locke put it, it may have been a deep original human urge to move on, whether out of survival instinct or animal curiosity. Our dogs are well taken care of, yet on walks, they will poke their noses into the (to me) most improbable trace of dirt or whatever. Curiosity is not always economic. It may also be natural.

The first Atlantic voyages early in the sixteenth century were surely economic. They were paid-for ventures for wealth. They were also embarked upon out of curiosity, just as centuries before Marco Polo traveled to the east to find whatever he might find. They were also clumsy and sometimes foolish. Columbus may have come upon Hispaniola in 1492 only because he wildly miscalculated the distance to his hoped-for Asia and found something where his calculations put it. Had he known the true distance to his original goal he might never have set out on what in reality would have been a 10,000-plus-mile voyage. Hispaniola was a third of that distance. Magellan in 1519 set out to circumnavigate the world. His ship's company made

## 68 ⊕ CHAPTER FOUR

it, thus providing the first true reckoning of global time. Magellan did not because he stupidly engaged 3,000 hostiles on a Pacific island, assuming that they would yield to him. They killed him instead. In 1583 Sir Walter Raleigh was sent by Queen Elizabeth to establish a colony in Virginia. When British ships returned, they discovered the colony was lost without a trace.

The British did better in Jamestown and Massachusetts, where their settlements were secure enough to flourish. By 1650 New England was English and reasonably well settled within borders similar to today's. But the British colonizers were slackers. By 1550 the Spanish already controlled most of the Caribbean as well as Central and South America and were well on their way to colonizing North America in the South and West, as the French were active in Canada and the Mississippi Valley, south to New Orleans. It hardly need be said that the scientific exploration of the Americas was not the principal purpose of these early sixteenth-century voyages of discovery. Soon European powers had, as today's world makes evident, settled the world over. Magellan was killed in the Philippines, but soon enough the Spanish and Portuguese had interests not only in the Americas but also in Africa, South and Southeast Asia, as well as East Asia. By 1498 Vasco da Gama had discovered India. Portugal, in particular, settled colonies in all these global regions and soon became wealthy beyond imagination. Already in 1494, in the Treaty of Tordesillas, Portugal and Spain had settled on a division of the Christian world, a bold act of early modern arrogance. Portugal, for example, famously won the right to Brazil, ceding most of the remainder of South America to Spain. Spain's empire was not as well extended around the world, but in the Americas it was far the more substantial. Some argue that Portugal's global empire was the first. Had it not been for its inability to defend its interests, Portugal might even have resisted the challenges of the Dutch and the British, who in their times developed better naval forces and technologies that allowed them to control their interests and produce even greater wealth. The key to the earliest system was, as it still is, naval superiority. Today the Americans control and police the global seas, thus exerting their military power by the threat of a mobile navy that is able to launch air strikes anywhere in the world. Then too, they use the menace of drones to the same effect.

Even in the 1500s, naval power was not simply a matter of the number of ships and marines that could be deployed. In 1588 the Spanish Armada was dealt its crushing defeat by the English because they were outmaneuvered by a smaller but tactically smarter British fleet deploying fire attacks. A similar lesson is taught by Magellan's foolishness, which did not prevent the success of his primary goal of sailing around the world. When Magellan, born in Portugal, began his voyage in 1519 he had become a loyal subject of the Spanish throne. His global mission in the name of Spain was motivated by Spain's need to discover an alternate route to Asia that would avoid Portugal's Brazil—the great protrusion into the South Atlantic seas that stood in the way of a direct passage from Iberia around the southern tip of the Americas.

## GLOBAL TIME AND NEW SCIENCES OF NAVIGATION

Magellan himself failed to complete the voyage around the world. One ship of but 18 men (out of the original five ships with 237 men) found its way back to Spain. The voyage in itself was remarkable in the day. But even more important was that the ship's company kept scrupulous logs of their geographic progress according to dates. Their data were crude of necessity. Navigational sciences were primitive at best. Celestial navigation based on lunar and stellar observations was fraught with problems, not the least of which was that cloud-laden skies made it impossible. Since the Greeks, there had been strong theories of both latitudes and longitudes. In fact, the earliest maps of the known world were surprisingly accurate—at least in respect to which Mediterranean and proto-European lands were where relative to others.

Still, prior to the modern era navigation on the seas was mostly limited to coastal shipping lanes that permitted sightings of approximate locations. How the first settlers around 40,000 BCE found their ways from the South Asian islands (like today's New Guinea) to Australia is hard to imagine. Theirs had to have been a hit-or-miss process, much as millennia later early Scandinavians deployed in the northern seas happened upon today's Canada. They thought they more or less knew where they were going, or at least hoped they did.

The ship's logs kept by Magellan's crew led to important navigational knowledge. Time, they discovered, varied according to global location. Thus, these logs (available today for examination) revealed that Magellan's ship returned to Spain but one day after departure—not one clock day, of course, but one solar calendrical day. This was, in that era, a surprising quirk of global time. Time and space on the earth must be determined, as we now know very well, by global positioning relative to the sun. The world not only was round and *not* the center of the universe, but it orbited the

## 70 CHAPTER FOUR

sun in a regular manner as it rotated on an axis. Those logs were not high science, but they were rational in the sense of having been systematically kept. They made longitudinal reckoning possible. Latitude was an easier calculation—a direct measure of the location, so to speak, of the sun relative to a ship. But longitude is a measure of a position relative to an imaginary line from the North Pole to the South Pole. Only when longitude could be calculated could a true science of open sea navigation become possible. The new science of navigation would come well after Magellan's day, but the very possibility of such a thing was opened by those simple logs.

Magellan's logs were not, strictly speaking, what began the modern navigational era. Still, Magellan's expedition from 1519 to 1522 was certainly part of a conjuncture—including the other voyages of discovery, Gutenberg's movable-type printing process (1439), the Protestant Reformation (after 1517), and later Copernicus's stellar proofs (1543)—that were part of the force field around 1500 that gave rise to the capitalist world-system.

In our secular age, it may seem odd, at the least, to suggest that the impassioned theological debate in the sixteenth century was a key event in the evolution of modern rational thinking. Yet even before Calvin's ideas on rationality, Martin Luther, actually a generally traditional thinker, challenged the papacy of the Roman Church on the grounds that the priests cannot assure or withhold salvation. One is saved, he said, by faith alone—by which he meant the individual's personal faith. Crucial to Luther's affirmation of personal faith was his corollary doctrine that faith is attained by Scripture alone. This is to assume that the Scriptures are translated and reproduced in the language of ordinary people, which

---

### MARTIN LUTHER'S TREATISE ON CHRISTIAN LIBERTY/THE WORDS OF GOD (1520)

Let us therefore hold it for certain and firmly established that the soul can do without everything except the word of God, without which none at all of its wants are provided for. But, having the word, it is rich and wants for nothing, since that is the word of life, of truth, of light, of peace, of justification, of salvation, of joy, of liberty, of wisdom, of virtue, of grace, of glory, and of every good thing. It is on this account that the prophet in a whole Psalm (Psalm 114) and in many other places, sighs for and calls upon the word of God with so many groanings and words.

*Globalization in the Modern World-System, 1500–1914*    71

in turn assumes an advance in the popular ability to read. Thus, in one seemingly irrelevant move, Luther advanced the three most fundamental values of modern culture—the thinking individual, the printed word in common languages, and reading (thus learning). All three are implicit in the above passage from his 1520 *A Treatise on Christian Liberty*—a work that appeared early in the century after Gutenberg's invention of the movable-type press and the first voyages of discovery and, importantly, a century before Descartes's *cogito ergo sum,* the secular doctrine of modern thinking as rooted in rational consciousness.

Capitalism as it came to be in our day is, of course, a very different creature from its global beginnings early in the 1500s. Still, the important point is that the modern capitalist world-system was part and parcel of both the early modern era and its dominant economic practices. It is clear enough that along the way both came forward because of key technological innovations that cumulatively transformed the speed with which people could travel across spaces and thereby the relations individuals and societies had to one another. If, with respect to the early traces of globalization in a global world economy, there was one crucial factor, it was technologies that opened the way for deep global changes.

The stirrup and the plow transformed medieval agriculture by speeding up farming practices, thus allowing landholders to put more and more land under production—thus, in time, to increase food supplies with fewer and fewer workers required in the fields. Then clearly the older system of peasants pressed to hard labor gave way as capitalist agriculture won surplus values while also putting former peasants out of the life's work they and their ancestors had known. This took considerable time, of course, but still the social relations of workers to the land changed their relations to each other. Centuries later they were forced in large numbers to leave the countryside to find what work they could in cities and factory towns where their traditionally rural relations declined to be replaced by what were, and for many still are, strange urban ways.

So too it could be said that Magellan's log book, by establishing the arithmetic that made possible the calculation of longitude, was an important first step in the new science of navigation. The underlying fact of longitudinal reckoning is that time changes as one moves across what today we call time zones. Today's jet lag is apparently a physiological symptom caused by moving "too fast" through time zones; hence we speak of biological time being at some odds with clock time. This was not a problem

## 72 ⊕ CHAPTER FOUR

in Magellan's day because their voyage took so long. Still, what their logs caused to be discovered was that while time, in the long run, changes with global position, when navigating the world around, global time in the end returns to the zero degree of longitude. Thus, when one arrives back to the starting line (so to speak), longitudinal time starts over. It took until late in the nineteenth century, as Dava Sobel explains in *Longitude* (1995), for the international community to agree that this zero degree would be Greenwich, England. The famous world clock on the Thames River is the zero degree of Greenwich Mean Time. The zero degree could be any particular location. This one no doubt won out because, through the nineteenth century, Britain was the world's maritime power.

The very idea of a zero-time global clock meant that the world could be measured. Latitude was a relatively easy measurement for which there was a technology: the astrolabe. The equator is naturally discerned by the north-south point where the angle of the sun relative to the earth changes. Yet when the weather is bad and the sun occluded, latitude is hard to calculate; even so, over the course of a voyage it can be. Yet without a precise measure of longitude, east-west positions are at best informed guesses. Once the basic fact of globe time was discovered on the basis of Magellan's log book, longitude could be reckoned before radio and other truly modern technologies with sufficient precision to prevent ships on transoceanic voyages from wandering off course. Of course setting a global mean time at Greenwich or anywhere else is an arbitrary matter arising from a social contract among those navigating by sea. So one can say that latitude is natural and longitude is social. Yet the two together serve to measure the world—thus to calculate global position, which is a measure of location in global space at a given time. Therefore a fundamental requirement not only of navigation but of the modern economic world was established: measurement.

## GLOBAL MEASURES OF SPEED, WEIGHT, AND MONETARY VALUE

Crudely put, global trade is impossible without standard measures. Merchants in different parts of the world must be able to come to agreement as to the relative value of commodities bought and sold. This fact alone begins to account for the decline of imperial plunder and the rise of allegedly rational capitalist markets. Advances in navigational technologies were but one of the important measurements necessary for capitalism.

Another was standard units for distances in global space. The British (like the Americans) had used (still do) their own now-quaint Imperial system for measuring distances, from which evolved the mile as opposed to the kilometer. During the French Revolution, in spite of the bitter hostilities, the National Assembly gave safe passage to Pierre Méchain and Jean-Baptiste Delambre, who were assigned the task of visually measuring the distance from Dunkirk in the north to Barcelona in the south. From systematic observations, often taken from church steeples or trees, they were able to calculate the distance between the North and South poles; and therefrom to invent the meter as the standard unit of a line of longitude (and then, by consequence, as the unit of all measured distances). The revolutionary regime sought thereby to replace the measures of the *ancien régime* they had overthrown with a new, more rationally determined, system of distances—but also, of course, of speed and eventually weights and values, hence of money. These were times of Enlightenment rationality; hence the idea was to use perfectly rational units of measure—in the case of the meter a measured unit of global space. Though versions of the British imperial system of measures endure today, soon enough the more rational metric system became the global system of nearly all kinds of measures.

The metric system eventually became the global standard—as travelers accustomed to speed limits defined as miles per hour realize when they misjudge their speed when driving in a country with kilometers per hour. Time in general, however, seems to have resisted units measured by multiples of ten. An hour is, of course, sixty minutes and one twenty-fourth of a day even though in some circumstances (like scientific measures) a bastard unit like milliseconds is common. Then too, money also has more or less refused to bow to common global standards. A bewildering number of currencies seem to share for the most part denomination into tens and on a regional basis to share common names like dollars, pesos, and pounds. But what a Canadian dollar is actually worth relative to the Australian or American one is a day-to-day calculation. Hence the need for a global exchange standard. Once gold fell away as that standard, the American dollar (after the Bretton Woods Conference in 1944) became the international unit of monetary exchange. Surely one day it too will be replaced. Still, among many other aspects, one of the most important contributions of the Bretton Woods Conference, convening in a time of world war, was for major global economies to agree to join together to form global institutions that would use the dollar as a global currency to attempt to stabilize global economies.

## 74 CHAPTER FOUR

> ### THE BRETTON WOODS AGREEMENT, 1944/
> ### REPORT FROM THE US FEDERAL RESERVE
>
> In July of this year there was held in Bretton Woods, New Hampshire, a United Nations Monetary and Financial Conference. At this meeting there were representatives of forty-four United and Associated Nations. In addition the Danish Minister to the United States was present in his personal capacity. Agreement was reached on the establishment of an International Monetary Fund and of an International Bank for Reconstruction and Development. There were also agreements on certain other matters. All the agreements are in draft form to be submitted to the various governments, none of which is bound to accept them.
>
> The International Monetary Fund aims at the restoration of conditions under which transactions arising out of foreign trade could be settled smoothly with the elimination of unnecessary risks and harmful pressures on the economies of participating countries. The Fund is not intended to correct economic maladjustments in the different countries, but to exert an influence on members to undertake corrective action and to afford them time to make such action effective. It proposes to promote exchange stability and to offer facilities for orderly adjustment of exchanges when necessary to the correction of basic maladjustments.

The International Monetary Fund and, in time, the World Bank—both established in 1944—were a long way from the Treaty of Westphalia three centuries before, in 1648. If the earlier agreement began the process of globalizing political structures, the latter in 1944 strengthened what had been in the works ever since.

A capitalist global system is a system of economic exchanges in which nearly any particular commodity can be traded. As the system became more and more complex it required more rational standard units of economic values. In *Seeing Like a State* (1998), James Scott shows that for a while late in the eighteenth century scientific forestry in Germany gave the modern system a measure of timber as a unit of value. Though timber did not become an enduring international standard, one important effect of scientific forestry was to buttress a theory of modern science as subject to a science of management—hence of relative values. At times in various places, spices, precious metals, even slaves, served as standardized units of exchange. Yet, as Karl Marx so brilliantly explained in the first volume of *Capital* in 1867,

*Globalization in the Modern World-System, 1500–1914*   75

a commodity of no inherent value, like money, inevitably imposes itself on the global system of capital exchanges. Not the least of the advantages of money, according to Marx's theory of capital and surplus value, is that money served in the factory system to disguise the extent to which human labor is the only commodity from which surplus value can be extracted. Hence the subtly evil system in which the exploitation of industrial workers derives from the pressures they suffer to work days much longer than the hours required to generate their meager wages. What presented itself as a free-labor market was in fact a liberal form of virtual slave labor.

## KARL MARX: THE BUYING AND SELLING OF HUMAN LABOR POWER

The change of value that occurs in the case of money intended to be converted into capital, cannot take place in the money itself, since in its function of means of purchase and of payment, it does no more than realize the price of the commodity it buys or pays for; and, as hard cash, it is value petrified, never varying. . . . In order to be able to extract value from the consumption of a commodity, our friend, Moneybags, must be so lucky as to find, within the sphere of circulation, in the market, a commodity, whose use-value possesses the peculiar property of being a source of value, whose actual consumption, therefore, is itself an embodiment of labour, and, consequently, a creation of value. The possessor of money does find on the market such a special commodity in capacity for labour or labour-power.

By labour-power or capacity for labour is to be understood the aggregate of those mental and physical capabilities existing in a human being, which he exercises whenever he produces a use-value of any description.

But in order that our owner of money may be able to find labour-power offered for sale as a commodity, various conditions must first be fulfilled. The exchange of commodities of itself implies no other relations of dependence than those which result from its own nature. On this assumption, labour-power can appear upon the market as a commodity, only if, and so far as, its possessor, the individual whose labour-power it is, offers it for sale, or sells it, as a commodity. In order that he may be able to do this, he must have it at his disposal, must be the untrammeled owner of his capacity for labour, i.e., of his person. He and the owner of money meet in the market, and deal with each other as on the basis of equal rights, with this difference alone, that one is buyer, the other seller; both, therefore, equal in the eyes

# 76 ✺ CHAPTER FOUR

> of the law. The continuance of this relation demands that the owner of the labour-power should sell it only for a definite period, for if he were to sell it rump and stump, once for all, he would be selling himself, converting himself from a free man into a slave, from an owner of a commodity into a commodity. He must constantly look upon his labour-power as his own property, his own commodity, and this he can only do by placing it at the disposal of the buyer temporarily, for a definite period of time. By this means alone can he avoid renouncing his rights of ownership over it.
>
> The second essential condition to the owner of money finding labour-power in the market as a commodity is this—that the laborer instead of being in the position to sell commodities in which his labour is incorporated, must be obliged to offer for sale as a commodity that very labour-power, which exists only in his living self. (Marx [1867] 1976, Vol. 1)

Marx, in effect, was the first to provide an explanation for how our capacity to create value by our labor is measured, harshly, in the capitalist system as a mere commodity sold for profit.

In this sense, the measurements of money, time, space, and values are more than simply necessary to capitalism. They are, when examined by (only apparently) objective measures, at the foundation of the capitalist economy. This is because standardized systems of measurement create the appearance of a rational—hence fair and free—system of trade. When, for example, the space of factory relations is organized to speed up the time of work in order to extract maximum money value from the labor process, the human worker is reduced to no value other than the marginal value of money wages against the prolonged working day from which surplus value is gained. In its way, therefore, capitalism can be as brutal as empires, even ones based on enslavement. The capitalist system pretends to use violence only as a last resort, never to conquer others. In fact, to the extent that universal measures are by their nature abstract, the human lives necessary to harvest or otherwise make the products bought and sold are left out of the equation. Much is made today, for example, of the quality of organic food products. Who can argue? Yet behind the dollars spent on apples we never see those who pick the apples on local idealized farms. Some are humane; some are not—and least of all, the produce shipped to our stores from across the world is handled and trucked by men and women working on the financial margins.

## THE NAVIGATING SELF

Measurement alone was not the heart and soul of the early capitalist world-system even though standardized units of time and space led to faster navigation and thus, in effect, shorter times over which goods are shipped. Yet from the earliest days of the global trade system it was often, if not always, technological advances that shortened time and distances from production to marketplace.

In the seventeenth and eighteenth centuries, first Robert Boyle in 1662 discovered the law of pressure by which the smaller the volume of the container of a gas, the more the pressure increases; then a century later, between 1763 and 1775, James Watt applied Boyle's law to the invention of the steam engine, which led to the steam ship and the locomotive. Then another century later, in 1856, Henry Bessemer first announced the process whereby iron can be converted into a much more durable metal. Steel led to vast and efficient rail systems that, in turn, assured the rapid development of heavy industry. The story went on from there to the automobile and truck, then air freight and travel, highway systems and all that today we take for granted. Normally one supposes that technologies are material inventions. For the most part they are. But recall that Magellan's log book was in effect a technology in the sense that it was a system of orderly records. Strictly speaking, a technology entails, as its root term suggests, a technique, which therefore must embrace ideas that alter not just the way people think but how their thoughts affect their lives. Modern rational methods did indeed lead to new technologies that led to speed, shortened distances, and new relations of people to the earth as to one another. But before and behind a willingness to venture forth near and far there must be an idea that justifies the adventure, whatever its purpose.

The idea of the migrating self arose in different forms early in the modern era. The earliest source for the cultural idea of the individual as an independent source of action are, as we have seen, the ideas of the Protestant Reformation, when Martin Luther's *Treatise on Christian Liberty* in 1520 enunciated the doctrine of the individual Christian conscience, which not only challenged the prevailing dogma of the Roman Church, but began the dissolution of medieval and even ancient cultures in which the autonomous individual was, at best, an afterthought—and, importantly, put forth a new idea of political rights. John Calvin, subsequent to Luther, took a similar view of faith as personal, but in time Calvin added the idea that faith must be expressed by acting in the world; or, as Christian theology puts it, to demonstrate faith by, in effect, improving God's creation.

CHAPTER FOUR

> **MAX WEBER ON CALVINISM AND WORLDLY ASCETICISM**
>
> It seems at first a mystery how the undoubted superiority of Calvinism in social organization can be connected with this tendency to tear the individual away from the closed ties with which he is bound to this world. But, however strange it may seem, it follows from the peculiar form which the Christian brotherly love was forced to take under the pressure of the inner isolation of the individual through the Calvinistic faith. In the first place it follows dogmatically. The world exists to serve the glorification of God and for that purpose alone. The elected Christian is in the world only to increase this glory of God by fulfilling His commandments to the best of his ability. But God requires social achievement of the Christian because He wills that social life shall be organized according to His commandments, in accordance with that purpose. (Weber 1992, 64)

This idea allowed, explicitly, for rebellion against civil magistrates that, to the Roman Church, had been called by divine right. In addition, and in the long run more importantly, Calvin in particular introduced the key principle of modern rationality—that the Christian expresses faith not by good works in the Church, but by acting by faith in the world. This, of course, was the interpretation that Max Weber much later, early in the twentieth century, characterized as the Protestant Ethic (or, in popular jargon, The Work Ethic—with a capital *T*).

Three elements made Protestant ideas, in particular those of Calvin, a source of what Weber called the spirit of capitalism—the relative freedom of the individual to think (thus act) for herself, the importance of acting in the world, and the somewhat confounding notion that, for the Christian, the action in God's world was, in effect, a gamble that by good work one will be rewarded. The three elements were, of course, shockingly at odds with Catholic doctrine, and none more telling than the third. The reward hoped for by the Protestants of that day was not assured or even promised. The whole thing was a gamble—thus distinct from the Roman Church's idea of indulgences, whereby obedience through gifts to the church assured some sort of a return.

We should note here that since the Reformation, the Roman Catholic Church has changed in numerous ways, eventually by encouraging adherents to read the Bible and by offering the Mass in languages other than Latin. Still, one of the strangest of sociological facts that Weber observed about the beginnings of capitalism is that early capitalism was most robust in Protestant regions—England, North America, Germany, Scandinavia, for example—and delayed in Catholic areas like Mediterranean France, Italy, Spain. Today those differences are less striking, but they linger on. France, for example, is fully industrialized and thoroughly capitalist economically but has never quite become as economically powerful as Germany or Great Britain.

Was the idea of the free individual, bound to work in the world on the gamble of a payoff, a technology or even a technique for living? It was, it seems, at least the latter and thus is as good being the former. In either case, it was an idea that took hold of the popular imagination, and not just in areas that remained Catholic. Perhaps the more convincing idea of the migratory self was that of a Frenchman, writing in 1637 in the Netherlands where, his Catholic background notwithstanding, he enjoyed Holland's philosophical freedoms and vibrancy. René Descartes's *Discourse on the Method for Rightly Conducting the Reason and Seeking Truth in the Sciences,* more commonly called the *Discourse on Method,* is the most explicit source of the migratory self. Its antiquated, even tiresome, title notwithstanding, the essay is famous for one short line that, even in Latin, is memorable: *Cogito, ergo sum—I think, therefore I am.* Clearly, though not in the least religious, the essay echoes Protestant individualism of the century before in rejecting not only traditional scholasticism but, in effect, all grand metaphysical systems of thought. Yet Descartes began his famous philosophical essay with a longish personal reflection on his own journey with his self-consciousness as the basis not just for thought, but for personal existence.

## RENÉ DESCARTES, *DISCOURSE ON METHOD* (1637)

For myself, I have never fancied my mind to be in any respect more perfect than those of the generality; on the contrary, I have often wished that I were equal to some others in promptitude of thought, or in clearness and distinctness of imagination, or in fullness and readiness of memory. And besides these, I know of no other qualities that contribute to the perfection of the mind; for as to the reason or sense, inasmuch as it is that alone which constitutes us men, and distinguishes us from the brutes, I am disposed to believe that it is to be found complete in each individual; and on this point to adopt the common opinion of philosophers, who say that the difference of greater and less holds only among the accidents, and not among the forms or natures of individuals of the same species.

## 80 ✦ CHAPTER FOUR

Man, so to speak (the modern individual), knows he exists—which is to say he knows who and what he is—*because* he thinks.

Individualism here again is the theme that would recur over the years of modern philosophy. Late in the eighteenth century Immanuel Kant asked *what is enlightenment?*—to which his first and simplest answer was *dare to know.* In France and Germany, as in Holland and the British Isles, modern philosophy and Enlightenment took on many different meanings, but they all sooner or later came down to some version of Descartes's theme that rational method was the work of the thinking subject. Gottfried Leibniz, in Holland, used the term *monad,* as later in England Jeremy Bentham and the Utilitarians invented classical political economic philosophy around the *utility of enlightened self-interest* as the motive force of the kind of economic theory that Marx later devoted himself to attacking.

The Utilitarian philosophy on the eve of modern industrial capitalism was through and through modern, yet it bore the qualities of the best of ancient philosophy—which was, as the word "philosophy" means, a love of wisdom. This may account for the fact that writers like Marx and others since have made mincemeat of the Utilitarian idea that market forces will take care of themselves so long as individuals pursue their enlightened self-interest—a pursuit, as Bentham thought, that seeks pleasure and avoids pain. This idea still holds sway in much of the modern, especially

---

### JEREMY BENTHAM ON THE PRINCIPLE OF UTILITY (1789)

Nature has placed mankind under the governance of two sovereign masters, pain and pleasure. It is for them alone to point out what we ought to do, as well as to determine what we shall do. On the one hand the standard of right and wrong, on the other the chain of causes and effects, are fastened to their throne. They govern us in all we do, in all we say, in all we think: every effort we can make to throw off our subjection, will serve but to demonstrate and confirm it. In words a man may pretend to abjure their empire: but in reality he will remain subject to it all the while. The principle of utility recognizes this subjection, and assumes it for the foundation of that system, the object of which is to rear the fabric of felicity by the hands of reason and of law. Systems which attempt to question it, deal in sounds instead of sense, in caprice instead of reason, in darkness instead of light.

## Globalization in the Modern World-System, 1500–1914  81

Anglo-American, popular mind, not to mention powerful, if conservative, economic policies the world over. Writers like Bentham, being preachers of the public good, attended to the popular mind, as is well illustrated by a fragment from an 1830 letter Bentham wrote giving advice to a young girl:

> Create all the happiness you are able to create: remove all the misery you are able to remove. Every day will allow you to add something to the pleasure of others, or to diminish something of their pains. And for every grain of enjoyment you sow in the bosom of another, you shall find a harvest in your own bosom; while every sorrow which you pluck out from the thoughts and feelings of a fellow creature shall be replaced by beautiful peace and joy in the sanctuary of your soul.

The contrast between Marx and the Utilitarians lies in the fact that for Marx human labor power is a collective reality, subject to the iron laws of capital ownership while for Bentham, in particular, it is the human individual who is subject to the search for pleasure and avoidance of pain, from which all things social arise. Marx bemoaned the alienation of the modern individual under capitalism; the Utilitarians affirmed the centrality of the utilitarian quest of individuals in the social and economic marketplace.

Modern philosophies, as philosophies always do, can stray quickly into the abstract. The untrained eye cannot easily read Descartes or Kant, much less Adam Smith and Bentham, or the earlier Luther and Calvin. Easy or not, what matters, as Weber said of Calvin, is that their key ideas both entered public discourse and grew over the years of their own accord to influence political and economic life. To be sure, there were many serious critics of the varieties of individual rationalism—most notably Marx himself, as well as both early socialism and much later post–World War II French social theory.

But even in places one would not think to look, some reflection of early modern rationalism's individualism can be found. One normally does not think of Napoleon Bonaparte along these lines but, leaving aside his political ideas on civil order, as a brilliant general of the army he understood the victorious forces to be a war machine. "What are the conditions," he asked, "that make an army superior?" His answer: organization, experienced leadership, and *self-confidence*: "that is, all the moral resources supplied by the idea of the self."

## 82 CHAPTER FOUR

> ### CHARLES DARWIN, *THE ORIGIN OF SPECIES* (1859)
>
> Although much remains obscure, and will long remain obscure, I can entertain no doubt, after the most deliberate study and dispassionate judgment of which I am capable, that the view which most naturalists entertain, and which I formerly entertained—namely, that each species has been independently created—is erroneous. I am fully convinced that species are not immutable; but that those belonging to what are called the same genera are lineal descendants of some other and generally extinct species, in the same manner as the acknowledged varieties of any one species are the descendants of that species. Furthermore, I am convinced that Natural Selection has been the main but not exclusive means of modification.

Charles Darwin's *The Origin of Species* in 1859 was more or less pure science. But it so outraged traditional religious people only partly because it attributes the origin of man to an evolutionary process common to all of nature. Just as much, it seems, it offends some because Darwin's idea, far from accounting for the role of a god in these origins, explains them according to rational theory based on his own systematic study of nature.

The theory itself, which over the years has been put to a good many uses (many of them foolish), turns on the idea that the first evolutionary fact is the survival of the fittest. He refers to the emergence of species by natural selection, but behind the theory was the implication that a first survivor must be some individual who passed on the genetic information.

One can hardly read anything worth reading in the nineteenth century without encountering one or another claim for (or against) individualism—a pattern that continues in our time in commentaries on the weakening of modern values: the lonely crowd, status seeking, conformism, bowling alone, and much else.

## TECHNOLOGIES AND CAPITAL ACCUMULATION

From the medieval stirrup and the astrolabe to Gutenberg's movable-type printing process, to the steam engine and steel manufacturing, to the railways and highways, jet engines and today's computers and cell phones, hard material technologies have driven the evolution of global capitalism. But a

## Globalization in the Modern World-System, 1500–1914    83

tool without an idea of what it means is worthless. It may be too strong to suggest that the modern philosophy of rationality was and is a technology, but it was a mental technique that changed not only how moderns thought, but what they did.

Our word *technique* comes from the ancient Greek *techne,* which meant, variously, craft, craftsmanship, and much else of the sort, including, under certain circumstances, art. Thus the modern idea of a migrating and rational self was every bit a well-crafted technique for locating human thought and action in the world as were techniques of longitudinal reckoning and jet transport—and much between and since. Tools, well understood in the modern era, include both material things and ideas that serve as tools for precisely locating and engineering human movement on the globe. Without either (and much else), the very idea of capital accumulation would have never emerged.

Capital accumulation requires ever greater and newer products made, bought, and sold in no less great and new labor, capital, and financial markets. Relatively cheap labor in parts of South and Southeast Asia is labor on the backs of the relatively poor who are pressed to work ever faster in routinized labor, on ever faster machines, to make the shoes and personal computers sold the world over—pressed, that is, until the normal rise in wage demands accompanied by increased taxes by a variety of state and interstate actors exhaust the value of a labor market just as products saturate consumer markets. Today's DVDs are headed to the same dumps or attic corners as yesterday's eight-track tape recordings, just as are all the old black-and-white TVs, ancient computers, and outmoded cell phones. All of this junk, especially the electronic stuff, eventually is shipped to distant dumping sites, often in China or India, where children pick at the dangerous leavings for something of value—children, that is, who pick because their parents lost or failed to get meager jobs at nearby call centers, construction sites, or now-fading production centers.

It was Karl Marx who, with Friedrich Engels, first said in *The Manifesto of the Communist Party* that the first fact of capitalism is that "all that is solid melts into air." Capitalism has been the engine that built and moves the modern world-system. From it much that is good in the lives of many was made both possible and available at affordable prices. But, following in Marx's footsteps, others today—notably Zygmunt Bauman in *Liquid Modernity* (2000)—say that modernity, and hence capitalism, underneath the shining new and hard metals, is a melting liquid. What has been made

# 84 ⊕ CHAPTER FOUR

and for a moment admired and possessed fades away in a flood of destruction. Not all would describe the capitalist world-system so severely, but few who have studied the long sweep in its history could deny the facts of capitalism's wasting of persons, resources, and products. At least none could deny it without a willful intent to ignore the facts.

Immanuel Wallerstein has summarized the factual realities of capitalism this way (2006, 23–24):

> Capitalism is not the mere existence of persons or firms producing for sale on the market with an intention of obtaining profit. Such persons or firms have existed for thousands of years. Nor is it the existence of persons working for wages sufficient as a definition. Wage-labor has also been known for thousands of years. We are a capitalist system only when the system gives priority to the *endless* accumulation of capital. Using such a definition, only the modern world-system has been a capitalist system. Endless accumulation is a quite simple concept: it means that people and firms are accumulating capital in order to accumulate still more capital, a process that is continual and endless. If we say a system "gives priority" to such endless accumulation, it means that there exist structural mechanisms by which those who act with other motivations are penalized in some way, and are eventually eliminated from the social scene, whereas those who act with the appropriate motivations are rewarded and, if successful, enriched.

No one has done more than Wallerstein to advance the concept of the modern world-system as a capitalist system, different in kind from any and all early systems, including the Asian one that began in the Han Dynasty. Before the modern era, there had been, to be sure, certain particulars of the modern system—production for profit, wage labor, and even the firm had their start in feudal institutions. But a capitalist world-system is something structurally different.

*Endless capital accumulation,* if one stops to consider this superficially simple characterization, is more or less normal in our times, but looking back to the beginning of the modern world-system around 1500, one sees that, over time, it represents a stunning, even alarming, revolution in mankind's relation to the globe. Capital accumulation is necessarily a rational ethic but an ethic that, once established, changes everything—the mode of life for those given over to future goals, the economic and political structures that deeply affect social life, even the material resources and built environments mined and constructed to house the people and institutions that do the work of endless profit-making. Here precisely is why globalization must be understood as, first and foremost, an endless process that must, for its own sake, select out those who serve its goal of accumulating capital by endlessly creating markets of all kinds while relentlessly expanding wherever they can be found or made.

## THE GLOBAL ECONOMIC SYSTEM

Globalization, again, entails two meanings—a process that in time covers and affects the world as a whole and a process that, at any given time, is total, which is to say accounting for and altering everything in a given sphere. The former meaning refers to a process, the latter to an enduring structure that orders all within the whole it organizes.

The modern global system was, to state the major instances, Iberian in the sixteenth century, then Dutch in the seventeenth, then French in the Napoleonic era, then British until 1940, then American for the time being. Yet to list any particular nation as representing the system as a whole is misleading. Iberia—first Portugal, then Spain—was in truth the core state even before the modern idea of a state was agreed upon. Its ventures into Indonesia and Brazil, the Americas generally, as well as a variety of outposts in the Pacific, were economic thrusts into areas found to possess valuable products like spices, teas, and coffee beans, among others that could be shipped back home for profitable marketing. These were peripheral regions sometimes without any sort of state structure—or, where states existed, they did so more in name than in real authority. The culturally and economically stable Aztecs under Montezuma in Mexico, for example, were crushed in 1519 by Hernán Cortés and the Spanish *conquistadores*.

The structure and process of the early system is well enough illustrated by the Atlantic slave-trade triangle that endured from late in the sixteenth century until well into the nineteenth. Its structure is plain enough. Once Europeans settled in their new world and failed to press local native peoples into slavery, they captured or bought slaves from West Africa to labor in the harvesting of spices, tobacco, and sugar—which were then shipped in the second major leg of the triangle for sale in Europe at sufficient profit to purchase more slaves for labor in the Americas, and on and on endlessly. Clearly, in the first centuries of global colonization after 1500 the global system was uneven. To the extent that the Americas were a primary target of

## 86 CHAPTER FOUR

world trade with Europe it was because of proximity as much as anything. In fact, the Americas were ill-developed for the production of commodities that over time would have to be mined or grown.

By far the most stabilizing and wildly profitable commodity of the Atlantic trade triangle was cotton, dating from about 1620 when simultaneously slave labor was imported from Africa. The American South became the center of cotton production in the century following that and, even after the United States won independence, the South remained a global peripheral area—a region in which life and work were structured not only around a slave economy but, even after the formal end of slavery in 1863, a near-feudal plantation system. Raw cotton was shipped initially to the north of England and by the 1800s to the burgeoning milling towns in New England, where it was milled and prepared for market.

Thus a typical trade pattern was ships sailing from Bristol, England, to West Africa to trade on the cheap for slaves captured by indigenous entrepreneurs. Slaves were shipped along the notorious Middle Passage to Charleston, South Carolina, and other American ports then sold into the plantation system. The raw product of the field was then sold to mills in Lawrence, Massachusetts, for weaving into bolts—after which some, of course, were marketed in the Americas but most were shipped, typically to Liverpool and other ports in England, to be sold in bulk throughout Europe, where cotton clothing had become the rage. Capital profits were then invested back into the cycle for more and more capital gain. Naturally, the early trade system was more complex than this, but the Atlantic slave-trade triangle serves to illustrate the classic structural elements of the capitalist world-system and, in this case, to demonstrate how the modern North Atlantic nations were united first in the interest of capital accumulation.

The outlines of the capitalist world-system were, by this important historical system, painfully straightforward. Labor and raw material in the *periphery* (Africa and the American South) were sent for production in New England, which was in effect a *semiperipheral* political entity from which, at least in the case of cotton trade, the raw or primitively milled commodity was sent to an emerging *core* nation, England. Of course, by the twentieth century the American South became a semiperipheral region, and the United States a full-blown semiperipheral state that became a principal geopolitical ally of England until early in the 1940s, when the United States and the UK traded positions, with the former as the new global core and the latter as its semiperipheral partner. A peripheral region, a series of semiperipheral national economies, and a stronger core state—these are the key and enduring concepts of world-systems analysis.

As most general concepts are, these key concepts—periphery, semiperiphery, and core—are subject to change and thus are inexact in their applications. Still, over the centuries, as the world-system evolved some elements remained relatively constant. Much of Africa today remains an impoverished peripheral region, still rich in resources extracted by the core states. Also, the core states were themselves always in flux as their economies and their states rose and fell. But it is relatively easy to identify the major successive cores—Portugal and Spain, the Netherlands, France and Britain (with Britain having the upper hand), and the United States. Today the key semiperipheral states have changed, with Western Europe, South Korea, and Japan (all with major US military bases after WWII) functioning in relation to the United States.

The modern world-system analytic scheme has been subjected to a good bit of criticism and no small degree of discrediting by a studied refusal on the part of established foreign-policy and political-economy policy makers even to give it serious attention. Academics, of course, criticize for their own considered reasons. Policy makers and think tanks, such as the Council on Foreign Relations, also have their reasons for largely ignoring the degree to which world-systems analysis is so sharply at informed odds with the longtime and still-liberal notion of the global system: modernization theory.

Modernization theory, which was codified after World War II, initially in the United States, holds that to the extent that the world is globalized it is because economic development moves linearly along a historical path from the poorest regions called *underdeveloped* (again, Africa is among the instances) toward, under certain conditions, *developing* (Nigeria with its oil wealth is today apparently moving into this category), then *developed* (Western Europe and the United States), and *post-developed* (Scandinavia).

The implicit background doctrine of modernization theory is that underdeveloped areas are poor because, in effect, they are culturally and economically not ready for modernization. They remain traditional because they lack a well-educated class of leaders that could provide the entrepreneurial energy applied to local wealth (especially natural resources) in disciplined ways—which, in turn, would allow the regions to form strong states able

## CHAPTER FOUR

> ### W. W. ROSTOW, QUESTIONS OF THE FIVE STAGES OF ECONOMIC GROWTH
>
> How, for example, should the *traditional society* react to the intrusion of a more advanced power: with cohesion, promptness, and vigor, like the Japanese; by making a virtue if fecklessness, like the oppressed Irish of the eighteenth century; by slowly and reluctantly altering the traditional society, like the Chinese?
>
> When *independent modern nationhood* is achieved, how should the national energies be disposed: in external aggression, to right old wrongs or to exploit newly created or perceived possibilities for enlarged national power; in completing and refining the political victory of the new national government over old regional interests; or in modernizing the economy?
>
> Once growth is under way, with the *take-off*, to what extent should the requirements of diffusing modern technology and maximizing the rate of growth be moderated by the desire to increase consumption per capita and to increase welfare?
>
> When technological *maturity* is reached, and the nation has at its command a modernized and differentiated industrial machine, to what ends should it be put, and in what proportions: to increase social security, through the welfare state; to expand mass-consumption into the range of durable consumers' goods and services; to increase the nation's stature and power on the world scene; or to increase leisure?
>
> And then the question *beyond*, where history offers us only fragments: what to do when the increase in real income itself loses its charm? Babies, boredom, three-day week-ends, the moon, or the creation of new inner, human frontiers in substitution for the imperatives of scarcity? (Rostow 1960, 15–16; emphases added)

to drive development. Some today (many Chinese leaders included) would classify China as a rapidly developing nation. Certainly China is well beyond the initial stages of "take-off" and in some respects is close to the stage of economic maturity. Others consider India in this light.

At the same time, Rostow's scheme implicitly, if not overtly, explains the impoverishment of many parts of the world as a consequence of underdeveloped regions' and nations' failure to modernize. Rwanda, for example, is sometimes glibly called a failed Norway. Who claims the credit when a

*Globalization in the Modern World-System, 1500–1914* 89

region or a nation enters into the developing category? Unabashedly the economically wealthy states do. It is they that, since the Bretton Woods agreement in 1944, support World Bank and International Monetary Fund programs and loans intended to stimulate underdeveloped economies.

World-systems analysis explains the flaws of First World development programs by the cutting phrase "the development of underdevelopment." Its view of simple modernization programs is that peripheral and underdeveloped regions do not develop, to be sure. But they do not because the more powerful core and semiperipheral states actively undermine those regions. Whether they do this intentionally or by willful indifference, their interests in the resource wealth of the poorer regions would at least suggest one reason why so many states in the peripheral regions are politically unstable and economically limited. The rich want to extract their wealth at the cheapest price. Even now that all but a very few once-colonized states are liberated, it seems clear that even the labor power of the poor is for sale for harvesting and mining natural resources from the poorest regions. When the less obviously brutal forms of postcolonial economic colonization fail to work, it is not uncommon that the powerful states will use economic pressure and surreptitious undercover means to assassinate unfriendly—often rebel—leaders. When that doesn't work, they resort to direct military action under the thinnest of pretenses, such as defending freedom in Vietnam and later Iraq.

Naturally, different thinkers for different reasons make their own decisions about the underlying nature of modernization as a global process. In official international discourse, modernization remains the leading theory. The problem is that in spite of billions of dollars of foreign aid by state and nongovernment agencies the number of global poor is at best constant if not worse today. Plus which, there is strong evidence for the belief that the economically powerful corporations and nations, not to mention individuals, have little true interest in liberating the poor. One need not insist that, today, the United States is thoroughly or even majorly a vicious exploiter of the poor to conclude that the wealthy world economies enjoy much of their wealth at the expense of the global poor. Otherwise, the global map of poverty—still mostly that of a rich North and a relatively poor South— would not be so stark.

In a word, a world-system, being capitalist, is of course rational in an entrepreneurial sort of way. The endless accumulation of capital is its reason for being and such a purpose, by definition, always in the end bets not on

# 90 CHAPTER FOUR

human generosity but on investments that keep the system going—even to the extent of excluding those unable to serve its interests. Between modernization theory and world-systems analysis there remains, intellectually, much room for debate. Then too, there is the question of what happens if the modern world-system enters a period of structural crisis.

## "THE STRUCTURAL CRISIS: MIDDLE-RUN IMPONDERABLES"

Immanuel Wallerstein posts commentaries on global events every two weeks or so. One way or another, each is consistent with his general analytic idea that the world is more or less systematically organized around dominant core states and semiperipheral states of varying kinds and number that, for the most part, are willing economic allies of the core state. Together the dominant states effectively exploit people living in the world's poorest or peripheral regions. In the last few decades Wallerstein has become more and more convinced that the modern world-system, established in the long sixteenth century, fell into a crisis of uncertainty late in the twentieth century. The following selection from one of Wallerstein's (2013b) comments describes that crisis from the point of view of specific global imponderables that aggravate the system's uncertainties:

I have previously laid out why I think the capitalist world-system is in a structural crisis, and why this leads to a worldwide political struggle over which of two alternative outcomes will prevail: one that results in a non-capitalist system that retains all the worst features of capitalism (hierarchy, exploitation, and polarization); or one that lays the basis for a system that is based on relative democratization and relative egalitarianism, a kind of system that has never yet existed.

There are however three imponderables in the process of systemic transition. These are three phenomena whose roots are in the historical developments of the modern world-system, and which could "explode" in some sense in the next twenty to forty years in an extremely destructive manner, with very uncertain consequences for the worldwide political struggle.

These three imponderables are climate change, pandemics, and nuclear warfare. They are not imponderable in the dangers they pose for all of humanity. They are imponderables in terms of the timing of any disasters. Our knowledge about each of these is extensive but there are enough uncertainties and differences of views among those who have studied seriously these issues that I do not believe we can be sure what exactly will happen. Let us discuss each in turn.

Climate change seems an unquestionable reality, except for those who reject this reality for political or ideological reasons. Furthermore, everything that has been causing climate change is actually accelerating rather than slowing down. The political differences between wealthier and less wealthy states as to what should be done about climate change make an accord that would mitigate the risks appear unattainable.

However, the earth's ecological complexity is so great, and these changes so extensive, that we do not know what kinds of readjustments will occur. It seems clear that water levels will rise, are already rising, and this threatens the drowning of vast land areas. It also seems clear that the average temperatures in various parts of the world will change, are already changing. But this can also result in shifting the location of agricultural production and energy sources to different zones in ways that might in some sense "compensate" for the acute damage to other zones.

The same thing seems to be true of pandemics. The enormous "advances" of world medicine in the last hundred or so years that have seemed to bring so many diseases under control have simultaneously created a situation in which humanity's ancient enemy, the germ, has found new ways to be resistant and to create new kinds of maladies that our medical forces find extremely difficult to combat.

On the other hand, we seem to be beginning to learn that germs can sometimes be humanity's best friend. Once again, our knowledge seemed great but, when all is said and done, turns out to be pitifully small. In this race against time, how fast will we learn? And how much must we unlearn, in order to survive?

Finally, there is nuclear war. I have argued that there will be significant nuclear proliferation in the decade or so to come. I do not see this as a danger in terms of interstate warfare. Indeed it is almost the contrary. Nuclear weapons are essentially defensive weapons and therefore reduce, not increase, the likelihood of interstate wars. . . .

It is perfectly possible that the world weathers the global transition to a new world-system or systems without any of these catastrophes occurring. But it is also possible that it doesn't. And, if it does weather the transition, it is also possible that the new world-system will take the kinds of measures that will reduce (even eliminate) the likelihood of any of them coming to fruition. . . . Obviously, we cannot simply sit back and see what happens.

## 92 CHAPTER FOUR

> We need to pursue whatever measures we can in the immediate present to minimize the possibility of the "explosion" of any of these three imponderables. . . .

When it comes down to the realities of globalization, it seems more likely that capital growth and accumulation account better for the terrible dark side of globalization. For all its glittering wealth and technical genius, the world as a whole is not today more fair than before. The poor are still many. They face the world as best they can, against terrible odds. Somalia may one day overcome its tragic conflicts and pervasive poverty, but places like it stand hard against the promises that the globalizing world is more modern and more humane.

CHAPTER FIVE

# CHANGING GLOBAL STRUCTURES IN THE SHORT TWENTIETH CENTURY, 1914–1991

Modern times have always pushed forward toward the global. As the oft-abused term "modernization" suggests, the modern is necessarily oriented to progress beyond a past and through the present. Even if modernization theory implies that those who lag behind are somehow lesser than those fully developed, the concept still makes a claim about the restlessness of the modern.

It must be asked, just the same: *Does the modern ever reach a limit, a point in its own history, where the process stops or changes so fundamentally that it becomes necessary to speak of a subsequent something?* Of course, when one claims, as many do (myself included), that globalization was always part and parcel of the modern global system, the question changes: *Is there some point when globalization takes over and, in effect, modernization ends?* This question became commonplace in the 1990s in the global academy's less hip places, like the United States. Chiefly but not exclusively among the aggravating concepts was the much-despised postmodernism. To those not disposed toward then new modes of thinking, postmodernism was, oddly, considered reactionary because some thought (incorrectly) that it stood for the rejection of all that was good in the modern world. Quite apart from the evidence that those who made remarks of this kind knew little or nothing

## 94 ⊕ CHAPTER FIVE

about the postmodernists they so loathed, the idea was not very realistic about how history works.

Yet, quite apart from intellectual debates about modernization or postmodernist theories, world-systems analysis had already staked a claim, still good today. Though it has its critics, world-systems analysis at least avoids more commonplace ideas by resting its case on historically demonstrated ideas of the origins and development of the modern world as primarily but not exclusively based on an economic system of world trade. This approach hardly requires either the infantilizing of the premodern or the destruction of the modern. The beginning of the modern system in the sixteenth century did not entail the end of earlier systems, least of all the feudal and slave economies. There is no better illustration of this than the fact that the American South was originally based in the 1600s on a feudal-slave economy that was formally abolished in 1863 by Abraham Lincoln's Emancipation Proclamation, but it endured in practice long after. When the post–Civil War program of economic and social reconstruction collapsed in 1877 the American South reverted to a de facto plantation system that kept some four million freed men and women under the same old racial and economic oppressions (Du Bois 1935). In effect a feudal economic system in the American South did not begin seriously to modernize until after the 1965 Voting Rights Act. Then too, today untold millions of women are bought and sold into the underground economy of sexual slavery. An older system, however nasty and illegal, can endure seemingly without end when a new dispensation takes over.

Likewise, globalization before the concept emerged was a crucial aspect of early modernity, and thus not in and of itself necessarily at odds with the modern. At the same time, it is possible that the modern world-system, by whatever name, can itself undergo deep structural changes that turn it into a form of capitalism so different from the early factory system in the nineteenth century that not only are capitalist farms and factories obsolete, but capitalism becomes a horse of another color. Over the centuries the modern economic system has proven able to change while coexisting with prior and less modern economic structures.

Herein lies the central question of global realities in our time early in the twenty-first century: *Is globalization a proper name for the apparent changes in the world as we and our ancestors knew it?* As with all questions of very large and global changes, it is tricky business to argue *when* such a change has or might have occurred. Modernization, as we have seen, began anywhere

*Changing Global Structures in the Short Twentieth Century, 1914–1991* 95

from the fourteenth to the nineteenth century—depending on the point of view taken. At the least it is nearly impossible to argue persuasively about the facts of present history. Globalization, whenever it began and however much it preceded the present time, has today become a subject of interest and concern to people well beyond academic historians and theorists. This fact, in and of itself, cannot be taken as an assurance that it is new. But it can and should alert us to think anew about it. But how does one think about globalization, especially as it came into popular consciousness late in the twentieth century?

## GLOBAL SPACES

Globalization, like other big social things, including the modern world, is both a process and a structure. If the modern system is a process of endless accumulation of capital based on an acutely rational practical ethic and a relentless economic system, then what is the structure formed by that process?

It is one thing to call that structure an economic world-system. But, as history shows, that very system over at least a half millennium has been subject to a restless process of change. Core states change, peripheral regions are differently subjugated, labor and resource markets are constantly moving about the world, and consumption patterns change as new forms of buying and selling arise. Even in the wealthier parts of the world economy a degree of affluence has made workers and other middling laborers able to buy homes, take holidays, own cars, send kids to university. And, of course, as everyone who works to pay for commodities like these knows, early in the twenty-first century the once-certain benefits of modern life are at risk of disappearing as the few who are rich get richer and the rest get poorer. These and more are aspects of the structures of the modern system. There can be little doubt that many of the causes of changes like those in the earlier and later modern world are structural.

---

### WHAT IS A STRUCTURE?

I once, perhaps unwisely, accepted an invitation to speak to a group of graduate students in architecture. One fact about their lives that I had known but forgotten is that they work very hard, often through the night, on design projects necessary for their training. As a result, they tend to be engaged in an intense process in a setting where, side by side,

## 96 ⊕ CHAPTER FIVE

the work of one can be judged by any of the others. They also tend to be tired, which makes it a particularly bad idea to try, as I did, to speak to them late in the afternoon. Just the same, I held forth.

After a while, when it was obvious that the whole thing was going poorly, I changed what I was saying by introducing the concept of social structures. Somehow I thought this would get their attention. Actually it did, but not as I supposed. I tried to draw the comparison between the physical structures they were designing and social structures that sociologists attempt to describe. They were completely unconvinced. The first issue, I should have anticipated, was that the design of any building always involves a physical site, whether a residential lot, a parcel in a flood plain, an already-built-upon city block, an open (or openable) space for a football stadium, or whatever. Sites always limit what can be done. A skyscraper cannot be built on sand. A home cannot be constructed without consideration of springtime floods. A stadium cannot be constructed too far from the population center that will supply fans.

By contrast, a social structure can be anywhere, at least in principle. Nomadic populations can organize a life on vast expanses of desert. Urban populations find a way to organize themselves when tightly crowded together far from natural food and water supplies. Whole nations, like Canada, can live mostly on a narrow strip of territory at their southernmost borders while harvesting oil and timber wealth from their enormous Arctic north. Australians crowd, similarly, in their generally pleasant coastal cities while eating beef and drawing mineral wealth from their otherwise-barren outback interior. Still, all have social structures that stand up without a fixed relation to their physical territories. Plus which, social structures of various kinds are, for all intents and purposes, invisible to the naked eye. In the days of its global empire where, exactly, did British social structure begin or end? Is Russian social structure European or Asian? Given that Canada hugs the northern border of the United States, does not American social structure leak into Canada? And if all this, what sense is to be made of the concept of a global structure? The modern world-system is capitalist, to be sure; but what kind of capitalist structure has it become?

The modern system late in the twentieth century was vastly different from the early structures of the colonizing world-system of the sixteenth century—and no less so now early in the twenty-first century, when for so

*Changing Global Structures in the Short Twentieth Century, 1914–1991*

many what was gained seems to be fading away. We now must, some think, speak of a global social structure. This is not unreasonable. But where and what is it? All structures called social, whether global or tiny, present this problem. Yet who would dare to say that, for better or worse, the world is not structured, lacking any definite and enduring order? Global structures may not be so straightforward as to have the earth as their site, but they are there playing out their engendering effects.

What, then, are global structures in our day? Whatever the world is now, it is not, surely, simply a result of events during the last quarter century. As history goes, a period of twenty-five years would be our "present," even for those born sometime late in that span.

We cannot, therefore, arbitrarily name any one period as in and of itself the beginning of this or any other present time. A historical present comes and goes. People live in a present, not in a given moment in their lives. We move, our loved ones die, we start jobs or lose them, we have kids or don't, and so on.

> ### WHAT IS A PRESENT TIME?
>
> My daughter was born in 1998. Her sensibilities and tastes are very twenty-first century. But as present as she is, her mother and I, so much older than she, cannot help but become, as best we can, more twenty-first than twentieth century. This is in part because of our daughter, but generally because that is the way this world works.
>
> We all have some version of the history into which our family ties are set. My other mother, who brought me up, was born about the time of my parents, a bit earlier (no one knows for sure). She was black, born in the American South. Florence migrated north around the time I was born to my white parents. She came north, as did so many in her family, to find a better life outside the racially segregated Deep South. Florence never knew, and did not care, which of her ancestors had been slaves. Some surely were. She was not formally educated, so she knew but a few of the fine facts of the history of the American Civil War. But she most surely knew who Abraham Lincoln was and what he meant to African Americans. Was emancipation in 1863 the beginning of Florence's present? Perhaps in some sense it was, even though she lived very much in her own present, during which she kept me as a kid on a sort of straight and narrow path.

## 98 ⊕ CHAPTER FIVE

No present history is definite. It changes not just with time, but is different for different people with different personal histories.

Still, given all the variations and confusions between personal and global histories, it is possible to say when the global structures of the modern world began to change—or at least to change in ways that would eventually lead to a possible deep structural change in the world as it is lived. It is possible, of course, because in modern times, a world of continuous change, it is impossible not to imagine where the world is going. As in personal lives, we are assured of a time when we began to become who we are, and when thinking about the nature of global structures there must be some sort of reckoning with its beginning—a "zero degree" of time from which all must measure the passing years.

To think about global structures it is necessary, therefore, to have a theory of structural histories. Structures like a world-system endure very much longer than any personal life. This insight is one of the most important contributions of Fernand Braudel, who until his death in 1985 was France's most distinguished historian. Braudel remains today the historian who, more than any other, forced social historians to think of structural time. He was, thus, an important source for world-systems analysis. Chief among Braudel's contributions was his criticism of what he called *event history*—more or less that sort of history that hurts the hair of young school students: the history of events with dates, usually taught with an emphasis on famous individuals, as in "the American Civil War from 1861 to 1865 began and was ended by Abraham Lincoln." As great as Lincoln was, this one event was part of a much longer enduring series of events from the earliest plantations and the slave system in the 1660s through the political battles over states' rights early in the 1800s, through the Civil War itself and until the civil-rights movement in the 1950s and 1960s.

For Braudel, historical time was not simply a series of events typified by great individuals, wars, and such momentous occurrences. There are three categories of historical time that, as he put it, "dissect history into various planes, or, to put it another way . . . divide time into geographical time, social time, and individual time" (Braudel 1972 [1949], 21). If, thus, event time is essentially individual time, then social time is long-enduring structural time, and geographical time is the still-longer-enduring time of the physical world. A world-system therefore is social time set against geographical time. Braudel began his most important book, *The Mediterranean and the Mediterranean World in the Age of Philip II* (1972 [1949]), with a chapter

## Changing Global Structures in the Short Twentieth Century, 1914–1991  99

titled "The Mountains Come First," followed by essays on the seas and coast lines, the Atlantic Ocean and the Mediterranean climate; then, nearly 300 pages into the book, he introduces human communication and cities. As the title makes clear, the book is about the geographical time of the area before it is the account of the Mediterranean world in which Philip II figures less as an individual but as the name of an age—of, that is, the sixteenth century, when Spain was still the dominant global power.

Hence Braudel's particular influence on world-systems analysis is that social time is structural in the sense that, as he puts it elsewhere, social time is "something organized, something coherent, in relations rather fixed between social realities and groups ... a time only slightly altered by time but one long enduring" (Braudel 1969, 50). Thus it is evident that, apart from many other influences on how history must be understood, Braudel's social time set against geographical time is essential to understanding just how, over time, the structure of globalization has remained stable and continuous in spite of its most salient junctures.

## THE SHORT TWENTIETH CENTURY

Returning to the twentieth century, the key question is, *Does it not appear that somewhere in the twentieth century, global capitalism began to restructure itself such that a departure, if not a decline, in preexisting capital structures became evident?* The twentieth century was a "short" century because its most salient structural transformations occurred on either end of a condensed period—from 1914, when WWI began, to 1991, when the Cold War ended. Some (Arrighi 1994) have identified the twentieth century as long—from 1848, when the revolutionary era was more or less settled in favor of a liberal economic regime, until at least the end of the Cold War. The argument for its having been short makes more sense because with the world war of 1914 it became clear that economic structures as such were definitively altered. Eric Hobsbawm, in *The Age of Extremes: A History of the World, 1914–1991* (1994), was the most persuasive of those to make this argument. Like many other historians who hold a strong structural view of history, he was avowedly Marxist, a conviction to which Hobsbawm, unlike many others influenced by Marx, made an explicit lifelong political commitment. Politics aside, however, it was Marx, more than any other modern thinker in the nineteenth century, who insisted that capitalism was not just a structure with global reach—but also a structure that was, at

## 100 &#x1F310; CHAPTER FIVE

one and the same time, sharply discontinuous with all preceding economic systems while remaining as harshly exploitative as any other, including the feudal and slave systems.

Many conservative Americans are still relatively naive in thinking of Marx and socialism as the evil beast of capitalism. Yet in a broader sociological sense, one can say that, as critical as Marx was of capitalism, it is hard today to appreciate capitalism's true nature without historical insights provided by Marxism—all the more so today with the weakening of many of the social democratic economies in Europe and the transformation of China's economy into a bastardized capitalism thriving under a one-party regime. Capitalism, since 1991, has become the only economic game in town, globally speaking, notwithstanding its own varieties of social democratic, neoliberal, third way, and other brands of market philosophies. Those with a historic debt to capitalism (most of the modern industrial nations and regions) are inclined to interpret the decisive dates 1914–1991 as a period that began as trouble but ended as the final triumph of capitalism.

But had the collapse of strict socialist economies in 1991 been, in fact, an unbridled triumph of capitalism, one would expect all that came in the more than a quarter century since to have represented the decisive spread of relative global wealth and the drawing near of the modern ideal of the good society. Globally, as we have seen, poverty, war, and violence, even environmental decay, along with every other evil humans have shown themselves capable of, should have declined. Hence, among much else, whatever globalization is, it is not some sort of giant step toward the perfecting of modernization on a global scale.

Hobsbawm called the twentieth century, from 1914 to 1991, a short century in part because it was also an age of extremes. The wars and economic bust of the period from 1914 to 1945 were followed by one of modern capitalism's more striking economic booms. Affluence promoted by wartime industrial growth not only cured the ills of the Depression of 1929, but left the United States the global economic titan. Soon after, the Americans rebuilt economic markets in Europe and Asia that, with their allies, they had destroyed. Though the rebuilding was presented as sheer altruism, it was engaged more out of American economic interests in creating global markets for its goods and services. Japan, Italy, and Germany—as well as the Allied economies in Western Europe, also devastated by war—rapidly regained their industrial strength. The Soviet Union never rivaled Western capitalism as a producer of the very consumer goods the rest were enjoying.

*Changing Global Structures in the Short Twentieth Century, 1914–1991* 101

The Soviet Union's key role in the defeat of the Nazis had assured it a major stake in Eastern Europe and Central Asia, from which it asserted global political power backed by its military threat to the so-called free world. The productivity of the West's global economies also exposed Mao Zedong's failure in China to make his great economic leap forward after 1958. China's economic growth would come well after Mao's death, when the Communist Party gradually opened China after 1972 to Western ideas and, eventually, to global capital investments encouraged by Deng Xiaoping in the 1980s and early 1990s, when China's economy grew by nearly 10 percent per year. Hence, the extremes. This short century began in deep structural economic ruin that led, after World War II, to an economic recovery greater, on a global scale, than any before.

It is all too easy to see the twentieth century as ultimately a triumph for capitalism and, by implication, for the world. Yet affluence for some does not global progress make. Today's India, for example, has enjoyed economic progress that has brought millions into a life of financial well-being celebrated in Bollywood films and the famously glamorous sections of cities like Mumbai. Yet according to the World Bank, two-thirds of India's people live on less than US$2 a day; at least a third suffer poverty, according to international standards of US$1 a day. India, thus, is a reasonable, if extreme, illustration of the fate of the world at large. Amid much good, there remains a stubborn world of human exclusion.

Is capitalism, pure and simple, the cause of all this misery? Aside from whether capitalism caused today's global poverty (a difficult but often-argued proposition), it can be said that the global triumph of capitalism, especially after 1991, has *not* made the world better for the most poor. The global core may no longer be a single national economy, but the global periphery remains much as it long has been, even as capital wealth and modern cities have grown up in peripheral regions. Lagos is not even as developed as Mumbai, but it is rapidly developing and in many ways modern if not quite postmodern. Mexico City is one of the great world cities from the point of view of art and culture, and since 1991 of financial wealth, but its population of nearly nine million is but the hub of a metropolitan agglomeration of twenty million, many of whom are among the nearly 30 percent of Mexico's marginally poor. Economically, Nigeria has one of the world's highest growth rates, largely because it is the world's fifth-greatest exporter of petroleum. At the same time, Nigeria's rate of poverty also ranks among the world's worst. Its gross domestic product ranks 140th out of 184

102   CHAPTER FIVE

nations—63 percent or more of Nigeria's people, many crowding around Lagos, are living on US$1 per day.

Since the boom decades of the post–World War II era, capitalism has produced much global wealth and, it must be said, very much technological and economic good for many. But capitalism's structural foundation in capital accumulation means that, even as it produces wealth, economic growth necessarily leaves those unable to contribute to capitalism's economic demands out of the equation. The very wealthy gain at the cost of a growing number of poor. It is not for me, here, to try to judge whether a newer, more generous kind of capitalism could do better for all people in the world. But, if it can, it surely has not come close to that possibility since the short twentieth century, when global capitalism changed just how it generates capital wealth while managing to restrict its direct benefits to a smaller and smaller core of the extremely wealthy.

Still, why was the start of WWI in 1914 the beginning of this short century? What did that war, however worldly, have to do with capitalism and the world-system?

## GLOBAL RESTRUCTURING AFTER 1914

The Great War of 1914 was, first of all, a world war less because all parts of the world were involved in the hostilities than because that war and all that followed from it signaled, and in many respects directly caused, the four major global restructurings of the century: (1) That war gave rise to a global warfare that in effect erased the vestiges of imperial empires that remained in a shrunken form through the nineteenth century. (2) Its conclusion in the peace treaty of 1919 far from assuring peace, provoked a continuing series of struggles for global control, of which the Cold War after 1945 was the most complex. (3) After 1914, the prewar global powers, especially in Europe, were caught in what turned out to be a long war from 1914 through the end of World War II in 1945, which made it possible for their colonies to engage in their own wars of decolonization, beginning with India in 1947. (4) In the breach left by the gradual decline of the European and, in Asia, Japanese colonizing powers, new global forces, including very different forms of capitalism, arose to change the form of the modern nation-states.

If there could be a single name, however metaphoric, for these changes as a whole, it might be one invented in 1941 by an American magazine editor Henry Luce, who called the twentieth the American Century.

*Changing Global Structures in the Short Twentieth Century, 1914–1991*   103

> ## HENRY LUCE: THE TWENTIETH CENTURY IS THE AMERICAN CENTURY (1941)
>
> Consider the 20th Century. It is ours not only in the sense that we happen to live in it but ours also because it is America's first century as a dominant power in the world. So far, this century of ours has been a profound and tragic disappointment. No other century has been so big with promise for human progress and happiness. And in no one century have so many men and women and children suffered such pain and anguish and bitter death. It is a baffling and difficult and paradoxical century. No doubt all centuries were paradoxical to those who had to cope with them. But, like everything else, our paradoxes today are bigger and better than ever. Yes, better as well as bigger—inherently better. We have poverty and starvation—but only in the midst of plenty. We have the biggest wars in the midst of the most widespread, the deepest and the most articulate hatred of war in all history. We have tyrannies and dictatorships—but only when democratic idealism, once regarded as the dubious eccentricity of a colonial nation, is the faith of a huge majority of the people of the world.
>
> And ours is also a revolutionary century. The paradoxes make it inevitably revolutionary. Revolutionary, of course, in science and in industry. And also revolutionary, as a corollary in politics and the structure of society. But to say that a revolution is in progress is not to say that the men with either the craziest ideas or the angriest ideas or the most plausible ideas are going to come out on top.

The year 1941 would seem an improbable time for anyone to claim that the century ought be called the American. It was the beginning of full hostilities of the Second World War, for which the United States was ill prepared. But Luce was calling for America not just to engage fully in the war but to do so in order to claim its providential calling to be the new global leader, one unlike any before. And that was, at least for a time, just what happened. Then, the Cold War quickly stalled any idea of America as the sole world power.

Notwithstanding the fantasy in Luce's proclamation, how could such an idea, much less a version of the reality, have owed to 1914? In two ways: first, WWI deeply confused Europe's sense of itself as the leader of the global authority, and second, economic innovations in the United States would fundamentally change industrial production and global capitalism.

CHAPTER FIVE

> **THE CHRISTMAS TRUCE OF 1914**
>
> World War I in Europe is etched in memory by a true-to-life scene that recurs in various popular movies. The best-known historian of the First World War in Europe, Paul Fussell, tells of a dramatic Christmas Eve truce in 1914, when, it seems, the Germans, in their trenches, sang "Stille Nacht," to which the British responded in English with "Silent Night." The trenches in that war were just that close and the cultures so similar that the one enemy could hear and understand the other. The men stepped out of their respective trenches, shared Christian greetings. Then in the morning they recommenced killing each other. The story was, in effect, recently retold in a fictional movie, *War Horse,* the story of a war horse so magnificent that when it was caught in barbed wire at the front, German and English soldiers joined in freeing it.

The Christmas Truce, in retrospect, is so touching because the war itself was so brutal. In *The Great War and Modern Memory,* Paul Fussell summarized the effect of that war as the deathblow to the long-held nineteenth-century myth that the human condition is always, necessarily, getting better. "Every war," said Fussell, "is ironic because every war is worse than expected. . . . But the Great War was more ironic than any before or since. It was a hideous embarrassment to the Meliorist myth which had dominated the public consciousness for a century" (1975, 8). World War I in Europe was war as never before. In fact, the American Civil War in the 1860s was the last major war in which lines of troops systematically aligned themselves on opposing sides of a battlefield to move rationally against each other's flanks if not to attack the opponent straight on. This was Napoleon Bonaparte's logic of military conflict. His defeat at Waterloo in 1815 was not due to a failure of orderly military warfare, but to the terrible storms that gave the duke of Wellington the advantage his forces needed to crush Napoleon and end his imperium.

By 1914, railroad systems had so sped up the ability of combatants to move and shift their forces that war was fought in trenches stretching great distances across the contested territory. The German advance was along a front from Lorraine to Belgium. The British forces were able to hold the line, and thus to prevent an expansion of the western front. Some nine million were killed in the war, one of the bloodiest in history, but the horror for Europeans was that the war occurred in the first place. The trenches

*Changing Global Structures in the Short Twentieth Century, 1914–1991*    105

forced combatants into such close range that they could hear the cries of pain on both sides. The horror was iconic. At the same time, this was the war in which air and submarine forces introduced killing at a distance. The proximity to slaughter in the trenches was doubly felt in the distances by which air and naval forces killed. Neither was known before on such a scale.

The Americans entered the Great War after 1917. Their soldiers died and suffered, but the war as a whole did not touch them in the same way. The fact that their relatively short engagement contributed to the defeat of the Germans only enhanced the already-robust American sense of itself as a special, if still rising, global power.

The year 1914 was very different in the United States than in Europe. As World War I deflated Europe's self-confidence as well as its ability to remain the dominant force in the world, 1914 marked the beginning of the radically new departure in American industrial capitalism. If the United States suffered an end to its nineteenth-century idealism, that end did not come until the crash of 1929, from which it recovered in just more than a decade and a half, in 1945.

Meanwhile, in 1913 as war was coming to Europe, the American industrialist Henry Ford introduced the assembly line to the manufacture of automobiles. Though the system was not entirely new to the Ford Motor Company, its application to the production of the Model T is considered a perfection of the method of line assembly of parts. The method meant that no worker could be said to have "made" a given car. Assembly was achieved along a mechanized line on which workers each assembled no more than a part of the whole. Today this hardly need be explained. If we think of industrial manufacturing at all, the assembly line is the image that comes to mind. Charlie Chaplin's 1936 film *Modern Times* is memorable for its scenes of Chaplin's assembly worker so caught in the manufacturing line that he becomes trapped in the gears driving production. This is but the most famous of popular culture's often-scathing images of the assembly line: the worker as a cog in the machine. With Ford Motor Company's Model T line, the assembly line was originally heralded as a brilliant new industrial process, a notion that Ford encouraged by paying a wage far greater than the industrial norm (a wage he took back by temporary layoffs of workers, by which he saved paying the wage for a full year). In effect, the assembly-line process not only produced standardized products, but standardized workers.

Ford's fame as an industrial innovator is associated with a book published in 1911, F. W. Taylor's *The Principles of Scientific Management*.

## 106 CHAPTER FIVE

> ### F. W. TAYLOR'S *THE PRINCIPLES OF SCIENTIFIC MANAGEMENT* (1911)
>
> Under the old type of management success depends almost entirely upon getting the "initiative" of the workmen, and it is indeed a rare case in which this initiative is really attained. Under scientific management the "initiative" of the workmen (that is, their hard work, their good-will, and their ingenuity) is obtained with absolute uniformity and to a greater extent than is possible under the old system; and in addition to this improvement on the part of the men, the managers assume new burdens, new duties, and responsibilities never dreamed of in the past. The managers assume, for instance, the burden of gathering together all of the traditional knowledge which in the past has been possessed by the workmen and then of classifying, tabulating, and reducing this knowledge to rules, laws, and formulae which are immensely helpful to the workmen in doing their daily work. In addition to developing a science in this way, the management take on three other types of duties which involve new and heavy burdens for themselves. . . . It is this combination of the initiative of the workmen, coupled with the new types of work done by the management, that makes scientific management so much more efficient than the old plan. . . . These new duties are grouped under four heads:
>
> > First. They develop a science for each element of a man's work, which replaces the old rule-of-thumb method.
> >
> > Second. They scientifically select and then train, teach, and develop the workman, whereas in the past he chose his own work and trained himself as best he could.
> >
> > Third. They heartily cooperate with the men so as to insure all of the work being done in accordance with the principles of the science which has been developed.
> >
> > Fourth. There is an almost equal division of the work and the responsibility between the management and the workmen. The management take over all work for which they are better fitted than the workmen, while in the past almost all of the work and the greater part of the responsibility were thrown upon the men.

Whether Ford himself was a scientific manager, as opposed to a brilliant if ruthless capitalist, is open to debate. What is not is that Ford's assembly line gave rise to an enduring name for a departure in manufacturing process, Fordism. Scientific industrial management, in practice, was well illustrated by Ford's Model T manufacture after 1913. The Model T was wildly popular among the masses because it was priced so that workers and middle-class people could own one. By 1914 Ford Motor Company produced more automobiles than all the world's manufacturers. The hidden cost, of course, was the rigidifying of work life and life itself. Industrialists, including Ford himself, sought to control, with some success, not only where the workers lived (often in factory-built and -owned housing villages), but how they lived. Not any worker would do. Only the compliant and patient were wanted. As the century moved on, not only did the Ford assembly process spread, but so did the theory of scientific management.

By the 1930s and decidedly by the war years after 1941, industry was managed not just by scientific managers. Increasingly the family owners of industrial factories gave way to a new class of managers who did the bidding of public stockholders governed, theoretically at least, by an elected board of directors.

The 1929 stock-market crash was, at its most basic, a collapse in stock prices. Manufacturing was by then a different process from, in particular, Marx's idea in the 1860s of a bourgeois class of owners of the means of production. Stockholders then were, of course, the American equivalent of a bourgeois class but only in the sense of being those with sufficient wealth to purchase stock shares and thus a stake in a range of industrial manufacturing companies. Though the process of scientific management took a long time to develop fully, it soon was, as it is today, the norm in privately owned companies as well as public ones. Today the Ford Motor Company is one of the world's largest multinational corporations. It is publicly traded but controlled by the Ford family. Still, it has been the better part of a century since any one member of the Ford family was the sole manager of the company as a whole. Fords are still at work in the company that bears their name, but no one individual can manage so enormous a global corporation. Not only has the management of industry changed, but the size of corporations has grown such that one individual can do little more than be the final arbiter of the most general companywide policies. Ford and Toyota, therefore, are managed much as is General Motors. The family name is more a brand than the basic truth of corporate process.

To be sure, scientifically managed industries have long been a global process. The Ford assembly line of 1913 is very much in the past, though a version of it remains in newer industries where, in China for example,

108 &#x2295; **CHAPTER FIVE**

a great many of the world's personal computers are assembled on an on-demand basis. Order a laptop by any brand-name company, and very often the order is sent electronically to China, where the machine (which is no longer a machine in the older sense) is assembled and shipped to you for delivery the next day. When it comes to cell phones, personal computers, televisions, and most electronic products there is no such thing as a boutique manufacturer (as there may still be in specialty high-end furniture) or even a single factory town. This reality is one of the reasons that Detroit—in Ford's day the world's automobile-manufacturing capital—went broke a century later. Detroit is slowly rebuilding as a lesser center of capital commodities, but many of those products are not material things. Twitter, for example, has opened a corporate center in downtown Detroit. Whatever Twitter sells, it is nothing like a car. In fact, in Ford's day Twitter or Facebook would not have been thinkable.

Fordism became the name for a much different process of both manufacturing and industrial management—and, eventually, of the type of products produced. In the 1920s advances in management and manufacturing were salient, if not always humane, advances in global capitalism. Then the crash of 1929 struck the world's economic system. Its commodity wealth was helpless against the collapse of confidence in financial institutions. First stock values and markets declined precipitously, then dramatically the banks and related financial institutions failed in the face of a widespread demand for cash—all to disastrous effects. Still, Fordism continued, during and after the Depression. It was *one* of the reasons the United States—slow to engage in World War II and far behind Germany and Japan in its ability to produce military arms and equipment—so quickly caught up after the attack on Pearl Harbor on December 7, 1941. In four relatively short years, as these things go, the United States became the world's most formidable military force because it was far and away the world's most efficient and productive industrial economy.

Meanwhile in Europe, hardly a slacker in industry, every possible wrong move was made at the end of the Great War in 1919. Most notoriously, the Versailles Treaty was so financially punitive toward Germany as to make it nearly impossible for even a version of its prewar parliamentary form of government to regain its footing. In *The Downfall of Money: Germany's Hyperinflation and the Destruction of the Middle Class* (2013), a current-day historian of modern Germany, Frederick Taylor (not, by the way, the F. W. Taylor of scientific management), put the failure of 1919 bluntly:

the Versailles peace treaty meant "loser pays all." During the war, Britain, understandably, all but destroyed Germany's ability to trade in the North Atlantic. In Taylor's words the harsh terms of the peace treaty aggravated the weakness of Germany's postwar economy:

> Germany's inability to trade meaningfully also reflected her inability to participate in what was left of the global financial system. Britain and France could continue, to some extent, to import and export, and to raise money for the war through borrowing on the international markets. In the four years between 1914 and 1918, Britain earned £2.4 billion from shipping and other "invisible" sources, sold £3.6 million of its foreign investments, and borrowed almost £1.3 billion abroad. Before August 1914, Germany had held overseas investments of between £980 and £1,370 million in countries with which she later found herself at war. At least 60 per cent of these were subjected to outright confiscation. Moreover, unlike Germany, Britain and France remained in possession of large overseas empires. (Taylor 2013, 29)

Germany's financial ruin meant that it had financed its war effort almost entirely on domestic internal borrowing, which landed a crushing postwar blow to its economic stability. The German mark fell in exchange value from roughly four to one against the American dollar to an unimaginable four trillion German reichsmarks to one US dollar in 1923. Germany's money was worthless; its economy and all that an economy must provide, notably food and shelter, were so weak that Hitler's rise to power was if not assured, almost predictable in retrospect. Hitler had joined what would become the National Socialist Workers' Party in 1919.

> ### ADOLF HITLER, *MEIN KAMPF* (1925)
>
> The function of propaganda does not lie in the scientific training of the individual, but in calling the masses' attention to certain facts, processes, necessities, etc., whose significance is thus for the first time placed within their field of vision. . . .
>
> All propaganda must be popular and its intellectual level must be adjusted to the most limited intelligence among those it is addressed to. Consequently, the greater the mass it is intended to reach, the lower its purely intellectual level will have to be. But if, as in propaganda for sticking out a war, the aim is to influence a whole people, we must avoid excessive

# 110 CHAPTER FIVE

> intellectual demands on our public, and too much caution cannot be extended in this direction.
>
> The more modest its intellectual ballast, the more exclusively it takes into consideration the emotions of the masses, the more effective it will be. And this is the best proof of the soundness or unsoundness of a propaganda campaign, and not success pleasing a few scholars or young aesthetes.
>
> The art of propaganda lies in understanding the emotional ideas of the great masses and finding, through a psychologically correct form, the way to the attention and thence to the heart of the broad masses. The fact that our bright boys do not understand this merely shows how mentally lazy and conceited they are.

*Mein Kampf* was published in 1925, soon after Hitler had made his first political moves toward 1933, when he was appointed chancellor by President Paul von Hindenburg. Thereafter, the tragic story of Germany's deterioration and turn to fascism is generally well known. What remained of the prewar Weimar Republic was finished. The Nazi war machine was, in effect, scientifically managed to the most appalling end, and in many ways typified the logical historical outcome of assembly-line standardization of production, most gruesomely the standardization of human work in a new industrial system.

## 1945 AND THE COLD WAR

After 1945, America reigned supreme economically—until, of course, the major European nations rebuilt. Until reconstruction in the 1950s Europe's industrial powers were so depleted by war as to remain relatively primitive from a capitalist point of view. Then too, those parts of Germany, Eastern Europe, and Central Asia that were subjugated to the status of client economies in the Soviet system were at best an external zone of the capitalist world.

The Cold War was most dramatically symbolized by the East's construction of the Berlin Wall in 1961, which cut off West Berlin from the rest of Germany. John F. Kennedy's 1963 *Ich bin ein Berliner* speech in Berlin was a dramatic moment in the Cold War. But the Cold War's most memorable public beginning was hard on the heels of the end of World War II in 1945, in another famous speech that introduced the phrase "Iron Curtain" to public discourse.

Changing Global Structures in the Short Twentieth Century, 1914–1991  111

> ## WINSTON CHURCHILL, COLD WAR, AND THE IRON CURTAIN (1946)
>
> A shadow has fallen upon the scenes so lately lighted by the Allied victory. Nobody knows what Soviet Russia and its Communist international organization intends to do in the immediate future, or what are the limits, if any, to their expansive and proselytizing tendencies. I have a strong admiration and regard for the valiant Russian people and for my wartime comrade, Marshal Stalin. There is deep sympathy and goodwill in Britain—and I doubt not here also—towards the peoples of all the Russias and a resolve to persevere through many differences and rebuffs in establishing lasting friendships. We understand the Russian need to be secure on her western frontiers by the removal of all possibility of German aggression. We welcome Russia to her rightful place among the leading nations of the world. We welcome her flag upon the seas. Above all, we welcome constant, frequent and growing contacts between the Russian people and our own people on both sides of the Atlantic. It is my duty, however, for I am sure you would wish me to state the facts as I see them to you, to place before you certain facts about the present position in Europe.
>
> From Stettin in the Baltic to Trieste in the Adriatic, an iron curtain has descended across the Continent. Behind that line lie all the capitals of the ancient states of Central and Eastern Europe. Warsaw, Berlin, Prague, Vienna, Budapest, Belgrade, Bucharest and Sofia, all these famous cities and the populations around them lie in what I must call the Soviet sphere, and all are subject in one form or another, not only to Soviet influence but to a very high and, in many cases, increasing measure of control from Moscow.

On March 5, 1946, in Fulton, Missouri, Winston Churchill, using the language as only he could, said, "From Stettin in the Baltic to Trieste in the Adriatic an iron curtain has descended across the continent." Stalin reacted by sneeringly calling America and her "friends ... war mongers." After the wall in 1961 the United States airlifted economic supplies into West Berlin. West Germany, including the isolated West Berlin, remained a vital intellectual, scientific, and economic nation and city, an especially intimate reminder to the Union of Soviet Socialist Republics of the lesser capabilities of its economic system. At the same time, the vitality of so-called free-world capitalism aggravated ever more the military and political

## 112 CHAPTER FIVE

competition between East and West. China through most of the Cold War was not the economic threat to the West that it is today.

The political architecture for the Cold War was drawn at the Yalta Conference in 1945, where real differences between Stalin and Churchill and a terminally ill Roosevelt redrew the map of Europe. Stalin's insistence on a partition of Europe was claimed on the basis of its war effort but in reality it was an outgrowth of a deep Russian Socialist hostility to global capitalism. However ideological Soviet Socialism was, its roots were dug in Russia's revolutionary struggles since 1917 to replace the lingering effects of a feudal czarist rule with a radical people's republic based on rapid industrialization. Mao's catastrophic Great Leap Forward from 1958 to 1961 was a comparable goal arising from the Chinese communists' own long revolution struggle with the nationalists from 1911 to 1949. The Soviet Union, like the People's Republic of China, had its beginnings in premodern agrarian economies. By the late 1950s the Soviets, like China's Communist Party, had failed at industrializing. The industrial capacity of the United States and Western Europe, not to mention of Japan, had been well if elementarily formed since the early years of the short twentieth century. Fordism does not entirely explain the differences, but Ford's assembly innovations after 1913 were a reliable point of origin for them.

Fordism was and remains a single-minded method based on strict control of the manufacturing process for standardized products by standardized workers. It served capitalism's goal of endless capital accumulation at a crucial point of departure in the industrialization of production. Whatever Fordism's initial value to production efficiencies and the mass production of commodities, it is not an economic method suitable for global economies. During, between, and after the two great world wars global investments and borrowing abroad had become a vital prospect for national economies and for the earliest instances of multinational corporations. If, as some claim, the Portuguese global system in the sixteenth century and the Dutch East India company in the seventeenth were the first multinational corporations in the modern era, the true modern form of firms able to capitalize in global trade early in the 1800s depended on heavy industrial production. Obviously the modern economic system depended on a global marketplace for the mining of metals and the growing of cotton. Natural resources of the sea and land were, ever more than before, key to the production of capital commodities. In 1855 Henry Bessemer invented the method for efficient steel production. In the 1860s Bessemer's method revolutionized steel production that, in turn, made possible the railway systems that united both the North American and European continents.

Standardized hard industrial manufacturing thus propelled global capitalism and trade toward an ever-more-mature stage of productivity. The innovations in automobile manufacture by Ford in the United States in 1913 and, years later in 1937, by Volkswagen in Germany, were pioneering instances of efficient production applied to relatively affordable consumer products. Though the price of automobiles today has skyrocketed, in those early beginnings cars were a miracle of popular commodities. There is a reason that Volkswagen was the people's car, as was the Model T. But even then, and certainly now, the purchase of higher-ticket commodities like cars, however reasonable the price, demanded credit, which in turn required a trustworthy international financial market. I once ordered and paid for a Saab, once truly a Swedish car, in the United States and by agreement picked up the car itself in Copenhagen some months later. This is still possible but far from the normal method for purchasing a valuable or desirable commodity like a personal computer or cell phone. Still, then as now the system relied on an international agreement as to the value of currency used for trade. This was the first stage in global market exchanges for which, in principle, any valuable commodity—whether timber from Germany or gold mined in South Africa or theoretically any other commodity—could serve as the standard.

Precious metals as an international standard for trade are mostly arbitrary. Gold, for one example, has some applications in industry and dentistry but in and of itself it was and, to a degree, still is a standard for exchange values simply because gold has long been a sought-after metal. Gold itself has no particular utility other than in the decoration of churches, government buildings, and wealthy high-society ladies. As things turned out, the gold standard was inconvenient. Then as today, nations could claim to possess a certain amount of gold in a secure location like Fort Knox, but the actual quantity held was held in trust. To a considerable extent precious metals have been replaced by abstract currencies. As an example, the British pound sterling, while at first produced of sterling silver, is today a paper note representing an attributed quantity of the precious metal. Even if global trade requires confidence in one's trading partners, business is business such that there comes a time when a currency must pay out and up. When wars and stock-market crashes arise, artificial (one could say *alleged*) monetary values can disappear in an instant, as they did for the German reichsmark during

## 114 ⊕ CHAPTER FIVE

and after WWI. It is at least possible that the current global state of multiple centers of economic power may eliminate money currencies altogether. In fact, there is a movement under way to establish a new digitalized currency independent of governments and banks—one that works by the trading of values unrelated to paper monies or cash reserves. The Bitcoin project offers itself as a currency reliant on peer-to-peer technology that is designed for open source and public use. This may sound a bit sketchy, but reports are that, in contrast to checks and cash, Bitcoin cannot be counterfeited or stolen because it passes through an ultra secure Web-based system for which there is no single authoritative code. The remarkable thing is that people in some sectors are buying and selling Bitcoin, which from time to time has more book value than gold. Bitcoin, wherever it is, has a value of some kind and therefore must be susceptible to the ebb and flow of world events. Money and its substitutes ride along on the crest of waves that rise up from a bottomless deep.

Political careers and national destinies can be ruined or advanced as the standard value of currencies, whether based on a precious commodity or something else, falls or rises. On this score Marx was, again, correct. There can be no truly stable path to surplus capital values without money. His famous formula is M-C-M+—surplus value suggests the inevitability of money (M) as the standard means for producing a commodity (C), the exchange value of which earns a capital profit (M+). Very simple, save for Marx's story of what the key commodity (C) in the industrial process must be. Again, the famous passage on money, profit, and labor power in *Capital I* (1976 [1867]).

> Moneybags must be so lucky as to find, within the sphere of circulation, in the market, a commodity, whose use-value possesses the peculiar property of being a source of value, whose actual consumption, therefore, is itself an embodiment of labour and consequently, a creation of value.

What begins as seemingly straightforward analysis ends up being a devastating critique of capital process. Surplus value, or profit measured in money values, depends on the ability to the capitalist to press a mass of human labor to the factory floor where labor power is consumed—and consumed from a wage able to earn the capitalist a surplus beyond labor and other costs of manufacture. In this, Marx foretold, if not in so many words, both the evil of Fordism's standardization of human labor and the ultimate emergence of

Changing Global Structures in the Short Twentieth Century, 1914–1991  115

> **PIG'S FEET AND PROFIT**
>
> I grew up in a rural state in the American Midwest where, on midday radio, the big news was from the Chicago commodities market announcing the current market value of wheat, corn, and, mysteriously to me, pig's feet. It was only years later that I learned some of the uses to which pig's feet might be put, and still later when I learned that this commodity can be traded on global financial markets not because investors had an interest in the commodity itself (and less still in the farmers who grew the pigs and the butchers who slaughtered them), but because they were speculating on a possible future value.

financial capitalism, wherein money values are traded in a system in which any given commodity is no more than a means of financial exchange.

Commodity exchanges trade in speculations as to what the price of a bushel of wheat might be at some point in the future, just as today there are markets that trade on the expected (not promised) future value of a barrel of crude oil. Investors who trade in commodities never need to see, nor do they care to see, the oil they are investing in. They bet their money on the prospect that someone will buy back their invested claims for a bushel of Iowa corn (or whatever) in a given future season. Thus one supposes that there are tankers carrying crude oil over the seas without, necessarily, calling on a given port, just as across the American Great Plains one can pass silos of wheat and corn never to be shipped if the market price of the grain will not cover the costs of production.

The trading of pig's feet and barrels of crude oil in this way is a real but extreme extension of Marx's Mr. Moneybags, who, in effect, traded in human labor. In both cases the commodities are always quantified, in the sense of being both reduced to a value and multiplied in number. One might go to a butcher to buy a few pig's feet for a certain recipe, but the commodity itself is a question of the number of units amassed in a given season. Thus, just as a glut of corn on the grain market means that much of it will rot in a silo, a glut of workers means that wages can be reduced to a vanishing point of bare subsistence since there will always be workers for unskilled positions should the currently employed complain about the wages. In this sense the financial aspect of capital accumulation is always a factor, and one that alienates

## 116 CHAPTER FIVE

individual workers from the value of their labor while fetishizing the accumulation of surplus money values. Money is nothing of inherent value, but in and for its sake human values are reduced to nothing human—to things, not beings.

## FISCAL ACCUMULATION AND A NEW CAPITALISM

As capitalism developed since the days of Marx's *Capital* in the 1860s, it changed more or less along the lines predicted by his theory. Hate politics done in Marx's name if you will, but respect the ideas. As it turned out, while Ford and Fordism drastically changed the productive process by multiplying the number of workers who would be integrated into the machinelike assembly line, it would not be anything like the final word on capital accumulation. Capitalism after Fordism required a more flexible method, and one that could (as it would) evolve into a fiscal capitalism. One of the respected authorities on this aspect of capitalism is David Harvey, who describes the new capitalism this way (1989, 147):

> *Flexible accumulation,* as I shall tentatively call it, is marked by a direct confrontation with the rigidities of Fordism. It rests on flexibility with respect to labour processes, labour markets, products, and patterns of consumption. It is characterized by the emergence of entirely new sectors of production, new ways of providing financial services, new markets, and, above all, greatly intensified rates of commercial, technological and organizational innovation. It has entrained rapid shifts in the patterning of uneven development, both between sectors and between geographical regions, giving rise, for example, to a vast surge in "service-sector" employment as well as to new industrial ensembles in hitherto underdeveloped regions.

One might take Harvey's words as a bit too abstract, but closer inspection of the key words suggests just what he is driving at: *flexibility* in labor markets, new *patterns of consumption,* intensification of *technological innovation,* rapid and *uneven shifts in economic development* between differing geographical regions, *service-sector* employment, and *new industrial ensembles* in once-underdeveloped regions.

Many of these new global realities are evident in ordinary life. College students may help pay the costs of tuition by working in the food-service

*Changing Global Structures in the Short Twentieth Century, 1914–1991*    117

industry selling burgers, often in remote impoverished neighborhoods. Their studies are not freely chosen, if only because unless they come from wealthy families (which few do) they must estimate where the jobs are and how to get a degree that leads to one. Still, many are aware when there is a new iPhone on the market for which they may long even though this model adds very little to previous generations of fancy phones, especially when their phones are used as phones or simple texting devices. Still they spend what little extra they have on the newer version of the same, which they use to text in class, which, in turn, helps them overcome the weariness that is part of life, along with grades insufficient to qualify them for the job they thought they wanted but that no longer exists or has already been taken by a Princeton grad. They turn, after school, if not to McDonald's, to some other service-sector work. The better ones are school teaching or social services—careers that pay little but do some good so long as the workers earn just enough to cover the steep debt of college loans. Some end up living at home until they save enough to travel the world for a while, then to return to school for another try at the allegedly better job market, if the jobs have not already been outsourced to Southeast Asia. This sad narrative is not true of all students, of course, but neither is it uncommon. It well illustrates how flexible accumulation comes down on many good young people, not to mention their parents who immigrated so their kids would have a better life.

The larger picture of flexible capital accumulation can be illustrated by China. Until the 1990s, China was at best a developing economy, with many of its rural regions on the stark periphery. Since then, people from the countryside have migrated by the millions to new industrial centers designed for assembly work on products for the global economy. These migrations, though internal to the country, have been called the largest migration in human history, usually to new industrial cities. One of the most successful (from a capitalist's point of view) is Shenzhen in southern China, which is designated a Special Economic Zone. Well more than ten million people are crowded into Shenzhen. The vast majority of them are migrants from the countryside. Until recently, they worked under desperate conditions to save enough to send remittances to support their families back home. In time a good number returned to new cities in once-rural areas as China began to provide better housing, education, and health facilities to all its people.

CHAPTER FIVE

> **FAST CAPITALISM IN CHINA**
>
> In Chinese major cities, like Beijing, even the first-time tourist can see, if not name, the effects of flexible accumulation. If Beijing has a main drag it would be the east-west boulevard, Chang'an Avenue (Eternal Peace Street), which moves traffic to and from Tian'anmen Square. Tian'anmen is an enormous square bordered to the north by the ancient imperial palace of the Ming and Qing Dynasties, the Forbidden City, which is decorated today by a bigger-than-life image of Mao, whose tomb is on the eastern border of the square, across from the Great Hall of the People. Tian'anmen is aswarm with tourists and military police who have been particularly visible since the failed protests on the square in 1989. Tian'anmen and Chang'an Avenue are in effect at once a brilliant urban center and a historical hodgepodge of old and new monuments, as well as new wealth supporting millions of visitors from around China and the world. Travel east on Chang'an Avenue, and you will find a super-modern Hyatt Hotel close to a shopping plaza that could be in central Paris or Manhattan and, a little farther on, a sparkling glass-enclosed Audi dealership. All this is interspersed with Kentucky Fried Chicken restaurants and shops selling souvenirs to tourists. In one hotel where I once stayed (not the Hyatt), the view to the back was of a construction site that never closed, night or day. Workers were, I was told, temporary migrant laborers who worked long shifts only to rest a few hours and eat in shabby worker lodgings.

China is booming as one of the world's most important economies. But its greatest global power lies in the fact that it has saved and bought up American dollars, the global standard for financial exchange. China is not yet the world's banker. But it holds the world's dollars, which gives it geopolitical economic power to further its interests around the world. China thus is a de facto financial global power because of this tradeoff with the Americans and the Europeans.

Behind the appealing speed of the new, whether in Beijing (long a global city) or Shenzhen (in a formerly underdeveloped region of Guangdong Province), none of the new would have been possible under the factory system of Marx's day or even the assembly line of Henry Ford's. Assembly-line work is still done, in some sectors, but it is most visible in the food and

*Changing Global Structures in the Short Twentieth Century, 1914–1991*

hotel service industries. What is truly new about the current methods of accumulation is the degree to which capital itself is the commodity of value. Hidden between the lines of David Harvey's theory of flexible accumulation is the most dangerous of the new capitalism's production sectors and markets: new ways of providing financial services.

Before the crash of 2008, credit was loose. Few were those who could not borrow well beyond their means. Then the system fell apart. Many big banks, insurance companies, and mortgage groups collapsed. Big banks turned out to be bad news in so many ways, chiefly for making bad loans they could not and seemingly never intended to stand behind should the worst happen (as it did). Years after the terrible crash in global finances in 2008, the American and global economies recovered to a degree. In the United States there are thousands still losing their homes by default, and

> ### BIG BANK/SMALL BORROWERS
>
> In the heyday of the economic boom before the crash of 2008, my wife and I decided to refinance the mortgage on our home. Interest rates had declined and everywhere there was a market for borrowers willing to take what amounted to unlimited money. A few years before, when we were looking for the home we bought, our agent, on her cell phone, checked out our credit rating, then asked us, "How much money do you want? You can have a million dollars or more." We were agog and smart enough not to take the leap. We took a modest loan to buy a good house we love at a reasonable rate. Our refinancing story was a different version of much the same. We began by calling the mortgage person at the big bank that held our then current loan. It turned out that our "banker" was a guy in a call center in Texas. He was nice enough and gave us the numbers and assurance that the deal could be closed in a week or so. Before signing we got nervous. Who was this guy we met only on the phone? Why should we trust a multinational big bank? We checked with a local credit union and got a somewhat better deal, but the assurance that our lender would be someone we would know personally. When I told the big banker we had decided to do this, the kid said, "Don't worry, we'll own your home sooner or later." We went with the local lender who, it turns out, sold our mortgage to a company in Michigan. That was annoying, but at least we knew where the lender was.

## 120 &#127760; CHAPTER FIVE

millions still without decent jobs. This while the stock market reaches record highs. Who gets that wealth? The topmost 5 percent gets the lion's share, but within that small group the richest 1 percent are the alpha lions in the pride. This is what flexible, increasingly fiscal accumulation is like today.

The foundations of this ultraflexible new capitalism were laid in the short twentieth century. Through that century's early years from 1914 to 1945, capitalists were hit hard by war and depression, but capitalism survived. It did in some good part because American industrial ingenuity was based then, as now, on the principle of scientific management. America's war effort, as it was called, was so brilliantly, if tragically, successful because scientific management was well applied to espionage and military strategy as to industrial efficiency in the production of the material necessities of war—after which American global wealth fed the rebuilding of many of its former enemies. This to feed the simple logic of endless capital accumulation. In capital markets there may be bad actors like our big bank, but in the long run there can be no enemies. Capital accumulation is rational in this way. It does what is necessary to its end.

When the Cold War ended in 1991, what was left was not a triumphant American Century but a new global economy. We live in the years since then—in the whirlwind of new lavish products, most of which we don't really need—in an ever-changing world of economic prospects for work and income wrapped up and choked by the technological illusions of access to a World Wide Web of endless possibilities. Some travel more. My brother, who is retired, is always enjoying some new part of the world. He earned the ability to do this through years of hard work. I still travel to various places when someone pays me to come to talk or the like. I have been to Beijing, but so far as I know it may be quite changed since a few years ago. Though when last I checked the Grand Hyatt where I didn't stay is still there. But who knows for how long in this world?

In so short a century what has changed most is how money is made and how it moves with lightning speed around the world. The modern system is still capitalist, but capitalism of another kind. So too is the world-system restructured in large part because of the structural time of this short century. America was for a short while the core nation in the system. In 1944, when its dollar became the monetary standard for world trade, the Second World War was near its end and the American Century seemed near at hand. But then the Cold War meant that the United States could not disarm. Since 1945 it has remained more than ever the world's policeman. No other

*Changing Global Structures in the Short Twentieth Century, 1914–1991*   121

nation spends nearly as much on military expenditures. In fact, the next ten militaries combined do not come close to America's military might. In the meantime, Europe and East Asia and many parts of South Asia have experienced their own economic booms.

For a long while, the European Union was supposed to be a new miraculous form of post-state alliance—a democratic system that transcended national interests while enjoying brilliant economic success. But this too has faded. Germany is the dominant European economy. It has grown weary of paying the way for the economically weaker countries like Greece and Spain. The perfect democratic union could well collapse if, as some fear, its currency, the Euro, fails. For the time being, however, the European Union, even with its several weaker economies, stands with the United States and China as the world's most powerful . But each plays its own role and no one of them is anywhere close to occupying the exclusive global place of the earlier core states, from Portugal and Spain to Great Britain. The world-system is wealthy beyond belief but also changed, even troubled, beyond anything the most skeptical or cynical could have imagined in the decades before 1914. The world economy is, at best, multipolar—several powers, with newer ones like Brazil and India rising apace. There no longer is a dominating power and this is probably a very good thing for the world.

Globalization, thus, is nothing if not a new uncertain version of the long-standing capitalist world-system. It is not known, today, if the older capitalist system is dead and gone. Some say it is. Others say it is just transformed. None knows which. It is too early to tell. In the meantime, our kids and their kids will likely have to live through a period when no one knows for certain what comes next.

CHAPTER SIX

# THE GLOBALIZATION DEBATES
## *AFTER THE SHORT TWENTIETH CENTURY AND INTO THE TWENTY-FIRST*

One of the reasons the understanding of globalization is so tenuous is that, since early in the 1990s it has provoked so many competing theories. Still, it would be a mistake to conclude from this that globalization is mostly an idea or a theory. It is an idea, of course—or, better, a number of ideas all at once. Yet underlying the many theories is the empirical reality that, whatever else it is, globalization is also a very material structure and, thus, part and parcel of the shifting sands of a world-system.

Since the Cold War ended, China, to be sure, has become a major force in the global political economy. What now are we to say of Russia, which, more than ever, is driven by capitalist fiscal interests superimposed on the ruins of a now-rusted-out Soviet infrastructure? Russia's post-Soviet state must govern a nation of vast natural riches with a still-unsettled political system. By this standard, Russia is a rising force among the so-called BRIC nations— Brazil, Russia, India, and China. But if China is much more now than a rising economic power, where does Russia fit? The same could be asked of India and Brazil. They too, far from being merely prominent in today's semiperiphery, seem already on the way to joining the elite players among the global economic powers. The BRIC economies are not, to be sure, close to being core states in the older nomenclature. But neither are the United States, China, and the European Union anything more than a multipolar shared core. There are, it is plain, difficulties not only with the rigidities of the modernization scheme but also with the analytic system of the modern world-system. Russia does not seem to be a global player like the others, if only because its politics are so riven by a lingering authoritarian habit. It is far from clear what political forces might budge Russia toward a less repressive leadership able to engage better in rational relations with the rest of the global economy. There is no easy way to figure the global economic system as it seems to be still early in the twenty-first century.

Part of the answer to all this may well be that, in the absence of a hegemonic economic power (and however enduringly poor the periphery remains), the semiperiphery of intermediate economies might continue to assume a stronger, if less orderly, role in the new global system. Then too, there are what, in a new nomenclature, might be called outlier semiperipheral nations, Australia and Canada. Neither is close to being a major economic power, but in many ways both are at least as advanced as, say, the Scandinavian countries. Both have universal health care, strong banking systems that withstood the crash of 2008, generous minimum wages, excellent schools, and world-class universities. Either or both could have been, geography aside, likely members of the European Union rather than members of the British Commonwealth. In certain respects, not including very high criminal rates and a stalled economy, South Africa has many of the same qualities.

Nations like these—along with Brazil, South Korea, Singapore, and Hong Kong—whatever their limitations, present strong reasons not to consider the post–Cold War global political economy a mess. There are many things wrong with the world today, not the least of which is its failure to make any serious progress in eliminating poverty. But neither is the global whole anything like a catastrophe. At the least the twenty-first-century global system is not another lock-step in the prior history of the modern system—a system that since 1500 has changed many times over, even as it settled on a coherent, enduring structure. Modernization theorists, by contrast, think that structure was one of gradual economic development the world over. World-systems analysts think of it as a system with a hegemonic core surrounded by fellow travelers who benefit from its considerable wealth and share in the feeding frenzy off the corpse of an impoverished periphery. Whatever this system, if it is a system, turns out to be as the short twentieth century fades away, it is no longer the same as the older, long-enduring world-system, even if it exhibits structural features of a similar kind.

124 CHAPTER SIX

As a consequence, early in the twenty-first century we are left with something similar to, but different from, what was long considered the historical norm of the modern world. This state of affairs leaves those who consider it their vocation to make sense of the world in a sort of quandary. We can only resort to theory, which is not the worst that can be had.

## THEORY AND GLOBAL CULTURES

All enduring, well-structured systems, especially global ones, have cultures unique to their perceived natures. Cultures, well formed, turn out to be theories that contain some shred of an explanation for how and why a people exists and what they should do about it. Ancient Israel, even after the Babylonian captivity, took the prophet Isaiah at his word that the Hebrew people were a "Light to the Nations" of the world who enjoyed a special covenant with Yahweh. Buddhists, for another example, believe, when they are serious about the Buddha's teachings, that this life is impermanent and that one ought to practice meditation of this essential fact. Charlemagne in 800 CE believed that the Church was ordained by God to establish a Carolingian Empire, which led to a Holy Roman Empire, religious successor to the fallen Romans and one with authority to affirm the divine right of kings. Thus, as well, Americans classically believed, as some still do, that they enjoy a special providence to lead and guard the world. And so on.

Many, if not most, of these deep cultural theories are in their ways preposterous. But when all is said and done they are theories. In time all theories, especially sustained by a larger cultural attitude, are susceptible to being proven, by history, that they are ridiculous, or simply not the way things actually are.

One of the little-recognized but troubling issues associated with globalization, even as a vaguely understood theory, is that somewhere in its bowels is a gnawing suspicion about lesser social orders. If the world is global or globalizing then what becomes of "our" people? This kind of group anxiety has been around for a long while, of course. But today it very often takes the form of local angers about immigrants, multiculturalism, black presidents, women in politics, gays in Russia and Uganda, etc. What presents as xenophobia is a very common collective prejudice. But the prejudice is all the more acute when both theories and realities suggest an old order is losing its luster. This may be one of the reasons that the available theories of globalization are mostly the abstract property of academics and high-minded journalists, writers, and some politicians. The word "globalization," when it occurs, occurs rarely unless pronounced by a certified member of the intellectual elite. In this respect, it is similar to "postmodernism," once quite the rage among academics, today seldom to be heard in public. Then too, there is the oddly popular use of "deconstructed," which is heard daily on cooking shows, sportscasts, and talk radio (and used as if the word owed to Shakespeare instead of Derrida). For that matter, the word "modern" is commonplace enough to lend "modernization" theory a degree of face-value plausibility. All this may seem to suggest that theories are somehow elite nonsense. Sometimes they are; other times not. No one of sane mind supposes that Einstein was a charlatan, even though he was a theorist of the first scientific order. Whenever a theory or a theoretical topic gains any degree of currency, if only among an elite, it is a sure sign that something is going on—whether good or bad, sensible or nonsensical—that sparks the interest of people, plain or fancy. There may or may not be flying saucers or aliens who visit this earth, but something occurs in the night sky to give some people a reason to think there are. Likewise, until recently, no one knew that deep in the physical matter of all things there was such a thing as the Higgs boson, or so-called God particle, which is said to explain the missing link in the theory of all things in the universe. Theories of such things come along for a reason. No proof of flying saucers but now proof of this particle. At the first, was either one more improbable than the other?

So it is with globalization, which, as a matter of fact, is at best a trend of some kind or, if you take seriously certain lines of analysis, a historical fact that began in some long-ago. But in our times, in these uncertain early decades of the twenty-first century, globalization or anything of the like refers to *something* that makes people suppose the world is somehow changing. A word is a word, but when a word becomes a name for something thought to be real it represents a state of affairs that is at least real in its consequences, if not a certifiable fact of historical life. This is where we are with "globalization." Something is changing. Some use the term as a vibrant concept to attempt to name and discuss that thing.

Hence, globalization, such as it is, can only serve as a theory for changes that seem to, and probably do, alter the way the world was thought to be until as late as the end of the short twentieth century in 1991. Where there are theories, there are debates. There are no fewer than three major positions on the nature of globalization, ranging from believers to skeptics of various kinds. Better put, proponents of these three are often called (1) globalists,

126　CHAPTER SIX

(2) antiglobalists, and (3) transformationalists. There is at least one other, postglobalists, which I now think are better identified with the question of the future of globalization. These are not exactly glamorous labels, but they serve well enough.

## GLOBALISTS

Globalists are not necessarily true believers. For their own good reasons they believe that globalization is something real that deserves to be considered.

Naturally, one would have to be seriously cynical to write a book like this one without being a globalist of some kind or another. I admit to it, but with my own way of thinking about globalization—or if not my own way personally, at least a way with its own clear influences, however I may have used or misused them. As a result, in speaking about globalists, I personally hold a somewhat ambivalent position. To the extent that my position is influenced by world-systems analysis in general, and Immanuel Wallerstein in particular, I have used much of its terminology and historical thinking—used them, I should add, in a heterodox way. That being said, the world-systems point of view in general does not clearly fit the globalist position.

To speak of the modern world-system after 1500 as the beginning of globalization as we know it in our day is not the same thing as saying that the modern world has always been in a globalizing process. There is a reason that world-systems analysts generally would not refer to themselves as globalists or anything of the kind. Part of the reason may be that, in their tradition, globalization, by whatever name, is nothing new. Yet it should be said that among those of this line of thought, Wallerstein in particular, there is a recognition that in 1989–1991 something dramatic happened. It would be too easy to say that the world changed with the end of the Cold War. Still, whatever one's theoretical commitments, it should be evident that whatever happened in the short twentieth century began in deep structural changes in capitalism after 1914.

To be fair, there are those, also prominent among world-systems analysts, who think these changes began well before that. Giovanni Arrighi, in *The Long Twentieth Century: Money, Power, and the Origins of Our Times* (1994), makes a strong case that the rise of the United States as a global economic force had begun in the 1870s. By then it was clear that the end of the Civil War coincided with the emergence of American industrial capacity, most famously with the ability of the industrial North to defeat a militarily superior Confederate army under Robert E. Lee. By 1862, the North had already built a considerable railroad system, which late in the 1860s opened the continent and the nation to rail travel and commercial transport. In turn, the railroad and the manufacturing system that created it also made possible important new mass industries, from agriculture and meat packing to commercial trade, and eventually to new and growing markets in the West. St. Louis and especially Chicago became continental hubs of railroad transportation and commerce, destining the Mississippi River and the westward overland trails for obsolescence. Arrighi did not concentrate on this example, but he makes the broader point (which, it is important to add, is not all that different from Wallerstein's idea) that the European revolutions of 1848 were the beginning of the truly modern era. However short-lived, the movements of 1848 were a world revolution because they cleared the political and cultural decks for the dominance of a liberal (in the sense of market-based and rational) ideology. The revolutionary and reactionary tendencies that confused the issue in the years after 1789 in France were in effect defeated so far as their influence on global economic culture was concerned.

Still, with all the economic developments after 1848, 1914 was the decisive starting point for a new, increasingly American, economic modification in the global order of things.

With theories and debates it is always awkward to classify various positions as strictly proper to any one or others. World-systems analysis is clearly globalist in an imperfect sense. Modernization theory might be globalist in the more orthodox sense that it holds the idea that all global economies contain the seed, if not the flower, of modernization, and, thus, that any one local economy is or is not modernized to some degree. World-systems analysis and modernization theory could be said to be the two original versions of globalist thinking. But here we need to recall that at the beginning of the 1990s there were extreme versions of a modernization theory, like Francis Fukuyama's *The End of History and the Last Man* in 1992, which interpreted the end of the Cold War as the conclusive victory for a common brand of liberal modernism. Years later, Fukuyama's book turned out to be an early critique of globalism. Today, a quarter century later, almost no one mentions that book, for which even that short a stretch of history supplied little evidence.

Also in 1992, Samuel Huntington delivered the lecture "Clash of Civilizations," which was an explicit criticism of Fukuyama, once his student.

128 CHAPTER SIX

Huntington saw the world from a kind of radically globalist point of view. He thought that the world was in turmoil due to the threat posed to new emergent cultural, political, and economic forces. At the time, the global Islamic movements and the East Asian economies were, in Huntington's theory, the primary instances, while Africa, South America, and India, with their own traditional forms of religious culture, were close behind. Crudely put, as Huntington's categories encouraged, the clash of civilizations was a structural conflict among Christian, Islamic, Buddhist, and Confucian, as well as, in effect, more primitive kinds of Christian cultures in South America and Africa, themselves intermixed with indigenous religious ideas. Admittedly, this is too strong a way to characterize Huntington's ideas, but he opened himself to the extremes by trying to force an overly general concept of civilizations upon a world that by 1992 was already a mélange of political and economic ideas interspersed with the remnants of traditional cultures.

When Fukuyama's and Huntington's essays in the early 1990s are considered in respect to Stanley Hoffman's 2002 essay, "Clash of Globalizations," one is all too clearly reminded that globalization theories are a sometimes thing, and for the most part several things at once, which is the point of Hoffman's emphasis on the differences and convergences among political, economic, and cultural globalizations.

Globalization in the 1990s came to public attention in large part because cultural notables published essays and books that struck the right note, at least for the then-new theoretical tune. One was Kenichi Ohmae, a successful Japanese management expert, who in 1995 published a book that soon became the rage, especially among global corporate and investment leaders and some political leaders. Ohmae's *The End of the Nation-State: The Rise of Regional Economies* appeared just at the time when the postwar Japanese economic miracle had begun to slip back to something less than miraculous. Just the same, Japan's postwar recovery had been so rapid that, unhindered by military costs (provided by the Americans), its economy had surpassed even the brilliance of its prewar industrial capacity. Japan was for a while considered a global threat to the established capitalist economies. This in large part (if not in accurate part) because Japanese management cultures were thought to be doubly unusual—able at once to demand and get allegiance from its workers while producing greater efficiencies. On top of it all, the Japanese people were strict savers. Japan, thereby, generated huge per capita financial reserves unlike, by contrast, anything known in the

## The Globalization Debates

United States, where income gains were, as they still are, spent immediately on consumer goods creating debilitating levels of personal debt. Still today in Western economies, especially the American, without large social welfare investments and costs, the key to economic growth is considered consumer spending. Naturally, as Japan's economy grew, the well-off Japanese spent lavishly. Somehow, the whole system seemed utterly unique. As it turned out, the Japanese miracle of the 1980s became, as some put it, the lost decades of the 1990s and 2000s.

Still, Ohmae's 1995 book was written with authority, vaguely based on his firsthand experience with the Japanese economy at or near its height. This and the shock value of his claim that regional economies were making the economic world borderless lent *The End of the Nation-State* a haunting sense of plausibility. Many readers took seriously his strong globalist ideas that his version of globalism meant the nation-state was nearing the end of its ability to be a force in global economic policy. There was and is enough truth in the claim as to excite a good many business and academic thinkers, many of whom (especially some academics) had their own reasons for seeing (or wishing for) the end of the state.

> ### STRONG STATE/WEAK STATE
>
> Not all that long ago, I was invited by my friend Yan Ming of the Chinese Academy of Social Sciences to offer a number of lectures in Beijing. Every place I went was interesting in its way, but the most interesting to me was a graduate school of administration established by China's ruling Communist Party. Its purpose is to train future city managers of those Chinese cities, like Beijing and Shanghai, governed by the party. All those seeking such a position are required to be party members. Professor Yan was my interpreter on this and other occasions. She had just finished a long research project studying Beijing's most famous urban village—a neighborhood just off the main commercial and tourist center of the city. Villages of the kind she studied, known as *hutongs*, are rapidly being dismantled to make way for modern buildings. Yet it is well known that these are among the few remaining communities of premodern China. In my discussion with the students I brought up the subject of the *hutongs*. I asked them why the party leaders, some of whom were known to oppose the destruction of ancient neighborhoods, didn't put an end to the urban redevelopment that was turning Beijing

## 130 ⊕ CHAPTER SIX

> into a quite commonplace global city. They said quickly, "Because we cannot oppose the interests of the international investors." China is governed by a strong state system. Yet it is unable to resist the power of international capital. This may not be the end of the nation-state, but it very well illustrates how globalization puts the nation-state in a weaker position than once it enjoyed.

The rapid rise of China's economy in the 1990s supported the claim that capitalism had become the most powerful mover and shaker of the new China. The Communist Party remained the controlling force of the Chinese state but its political power lacked, it seemed, the power or the will to prevent capitalism from being a global force without regard for China's political borders.

Then too, the 1990s were the beginning of awareness of the global power of multinational corporations. Multinational entities had long been a force since, if not the Dutch East India Company, the important steel, oil, and manufacturing corporations with roots in the late nineteenth and early twentieth century were clearly able to breach the political intentions of any given nation-state. Today we speak of Toyota, Shell, and Hyatt, among others, as though they were, as some Americans think, de facto American companies with headquarters, dealerships, and production factories in the United States as well as around the world. Even if they have strong ties to any one nation, multinational corporations are clearly borderless.

One of the less successful globalist arguments was an early book by *New York Times* columnist Thomas Friedman, who since has become quite a bit more restrained than he was in *The Lexus and the Olive Tree: Understanding Globalization* (2000) where he offered a rather shallow theory of globalization as "the Golden Straitjacket." He meant to argue that the productive genius (the Lexus) of globalization challenged important human traditions (the olive tree). The new productive wonders, in effect, doomed people to an extreme of standardization—a fact of economic life that can be traced back to Henry Ford's assembly line. To be sure there is some truth in this in that, for example, much of the non-Arabic world gets its news from CNN, which of course broadcasts everywhere at once (usually in English). In the Arab world, Al Jazeera dominates the news. Important to note, in the 2010s CNN and other global news organizations, like BBC, are experiencing competition from Al Jazeera, which has been broadcasting in the United States and around the world. There are, it seems, a good many

*The Globalization Debates*  131

olive trees blooming around the world. Just the same, Friedman's book, its overly simple claims notwithstanding, served the purpose of popularizing the globalist idea.

A much more thoughtful globalist position is found in the writings of Manuel Castells, especially in a trilogy of books called *The Information Age: Economy, Society, and Culture* that covered virtually the full list of subjects made critical by globalization. The first was *The Rise of the Network Society* (1995); the second, *The Power of Identity* (1997); and the third, *End of Millennium* (1998). Each takes on questions that in the 1990s had become current: among them the environmental and other global social movements (in *Power of Identity*), the Fourth World, the dehumanization of Africa, the global criminal economy (in *End of the Millennium*), and information technology and the flow (a word that has since become common) of global processes (*Network Society*). It would be impossible even briefly to summarize the range of his thinking, except to say that the main theme is that the new global world is a network society. In a latter essay, Castells said, in effect, that globalization is "the formation of a network of global networks [that] link selectively across the planet all functional dimensions of societies" (Castells 2006, 7). It hardly need be said that this way of thinking has an affinity for Ohmae's theory that globalization means borderlessness. But for Castells it is neither the state nor the corporation alone but all economic, political, and cultural institutions and activities that are brought into the global network.

> **GLOBAL NETWORKS IN PERSONAL LIFE**
>
> As Sherry Turkle noted in *Alone Together,* one of the strange effects of informational technologies is that, when in possession of Internet tools, people will use them even when they are but a few paces from each other. I don't think my teenage daughter is alone in texting me from her room when she wants help with something. I am not alone in texting a friend who lives just more than a block away (and doesn't care when I arrive) to confirm that I'll be over in five minutes. On a larger scale, it happens that (due mostly to longevity) I have a relation with no fewer than five different academic institutions—a smallish rather pretentious college, a very large private university (with its own sense of pride), an ordinary state university (with no particular claims to make), an independent graduate school for psychoanalysts, and an up-and-coming public

## 132 CHAPTER SIX

> university in Australia. All are very much wired, thus in principle part of a global network of educational institutions. Yet with no more than two exceptions (of which I am one), none has anything much to do with each other. They could, of course, but they don't. Just the same, and this may be a character flaw, I think of them as networks in which I and others of my age and position in life are suspended.

Informational technology is first among several causes of the radically new effects of networks in this world. Castells's thinking thus differs from Ohmae's (and certainly Friedman's) in large part because he is a serious scholar with a trained ability to think critically about new global realities.

One of the signs of Castells's scholarly aptitude is that he does not go overboard by suggesting, as some have, that information networks like the Internet and related social media are the be-all and end-all of globalization. Whether the metaphor of a global network sustains all the elements of a new global environment is open to question, but it does illustrate the extent to which Castells, without claiming the label for himself, is a globalist. Globalization is thus at once global across the world *and* a global process that is changing if not everything, everything that counts in ordinary life.

Other academic writers have made comparable, if not as ambitious, contributions to the globalist attitude. Peter Dicken, a now-retired geographer from Manchester University, for example, in *Global Shift: The Internationalization of Economic Activity* (1992) presents a version of Castells's general idea in a comprehensive study of the global effects of "the death of distance." The idea is that globalization alters how we think about geography. As a result, commodity production requires a complex melding of manufacturing and service sectors to provide, simultaneously, for local *and* global markets; hence, what Dicken calls a *geo-economy*.

There is a kind of irony in Dicken's view, which is made explicit by the Swedish anthropologist Ulf Hannerz in a 1996 book, *Transnational Connections: Culture, People, Places.* Hannerz revises Robert K. Merton's classic sociological theory of local/cosmopolitan social types, and revises it for a globalized world. Hannerz points out that, on the one hand, it is very, very difficult to remain a pure local. Even those who do not literally leave home allow themselves to be transported around the world by television and social media. At the same time, those who live in a global reality (today's cosmopolitans) share with all locals the necessity of keeping alive the cultural diversities that, for a number of reasons, impact small towns in Iowa as much as they do Queens in New York City. Even so apparently global a social reality as multicultural community life can be formed and maintained only in a locale. In effect, while we all may be cosmopolitan, so, too, must we be locals in the sense that without a home base, if not a home in the traditional sense, we are, in effect, nowhere. Even and especially the poor, who crowd from their original rural homes into Lagos and Mexico City, build a local life in these cities where thousands upon thousands are no more than squatters.

These examples merely hint at the variety of views that can be called, somewhat clumsily, globalist. Some are strangely over the top, like Friedman's writings. Others are very well thought through, like Castells's books on the subject. None seems capable of enjoying longevity. But all convey the idea that, one way or another, the world is globalized.

## ANTIGLOBALISTS

The antiglobalist view has always had the harder row to hoe. It is, as any teacher or trial lawyer knows, very difficult to demonstrate that something everyone believes is true is not. When a strong position like globalism is asserted, or even hinted at, its opponents are required to find evidence that what is claimed is not the case.

An early antiglobalist argument was made in a 1990 book, *Globalization in Question* by Paul Hirst and Grahame Thompson, who labeled globalization "the pathology of over-diminished expectations." In this sneering phrase they meant to say that most of the globalists, such as they were in 1990, ignored evidence to the contrary. Hirst and Thompson provided what at the time was a strong list of contrary empirical cases, including, for example, the OPEC oil crisis in the 1970s, which (they claim) destroyed the 1944 Bretton Woods accord on international economic cooperation. By 1990, nearly half a century after Bretton Woods established the dollar as the world's monetary standard, petroleum itself could be envisaged as a global currency. The price of petroleum more than once over many years has had deep effects on financial markets, thus appearing to demonstrate the instability of the dollar or any other currency as an unassailable standard of credit. Still, today, many decades after the oil crisis began, this antiglobalist argument seems weak against the evidence that, though the global system is increasingly multipolar, the dollar somehow holds its own. The dollar, perhaps not exactly unassailable, remains the global currency.

## 134 ✱ CHAPTER SIX

Yet other of Hirst and Thompson's points are well taken. At the least it is clear that the world's financial system has become more complex such that it is at least possible to imagine a circumstance in which the American dollar would give way, though now the Euro or China's renminbi doesn't seem capable of challenging it.

Then too, in some respects, deindustrialization in the United States and Britain has, in fact, left behind the ruins of the original and global heavy industrial system. Yet in the American Rust Belt, there has been a dramatic recovery in the renewal of modern, even postmodern, cities like Pittsburgh. Whether this sort of thing is in fact an antiglobalist argument remains to be seen. Hirst and Thompson also pointed to the new industrial cities in what then was called the Third World as a sign that industry remains a vital force in production. There is truth here. Cities like Puebla, Mexico, home of a major Volkswagen plant and other once–First World industries, are now part of the Mexico City megalopolis in a country of new wealth. Mexico, except for regions in the far south, is no longer part of the impoverished global periphery. It is obvious, to me at least, that today it is hard even to represent this sort of antiglobalist evidence without a contrary fact coming to mind. Still, a position like that of Hirst and Thompson's is an important reminder that there is something like a pathology of expectations attributable to the more overwrought globalist theories. At the least, Hirst and Thompson serve to warn of the easily forgotten reality that we can never be too cautious in claiming that the history of the present is fully discernible.

Another type of antiglobalist argument draws on the analysis of differences among global corporations. Alan Rugman and Richard Hodgetts in "The End of Global Strategy" (2001, 333–334) have said, tellingly,

> Globalization has been defined in business schools as the production and distribution of products and services of a homogeneous type and quality on a worldwide basis. Simply put—providing the same output to countries everywhere. And in recent years [before 2001, that is] it has become increasingly common to hear business executives, industry analysts, and even university professors talk about the emergence of globalization and the dominance of international business by giant multinational enterprises that are selling uniform products from Cairo, Illinois to Cairo, Egypt and from Lima, Ohio to Lima, Peru.

It is obvious that the authors, both business professors, are examining globalization from the point of view of the economic fate of corporations.

Rugman and Hodgetts go on to discuss the differing global destinies of major corporations. Coca-Cola, for example, has succeeded by selling a worldwide familiar product in strikingly local terms. On the other hand, The Walt Disney Company tried to sell Disneyland in standard Americanized terms in France. Yet Coca-Cola succeeded and Disney failed. The French were yawningly uninspired by the Disneyland near Paris. In effect, Rugman and Hodgetts argue, roughly, that when it comes to business, globalization demands different methods and products for different regions. As far as antiglobalist arguments go this is not a particularly strong one, but it is an excellent example of just how extreme Thomas Friedman's idea of globalization as a Golden Straitjacket is.

Rugman and Hodgetts, even granting their narrow focus on the business corporation, were clearly on to something. Today we know, for example, that Sony and IBM were once *the* global brands for televisions and personal computers. The companies still exist, but what they do is not what they were once famous for. Likewise, Nokia, the Finnish cell-phone maker, not long ago was the world's leader in its market. Today Nokia's cell-phone business is declining nearly as rapidly as has BlackBerry's, also a global favorite not so long ago. The conclusion is that globalization, when it comes to commodities, may incline for a while toward the standardization of product and selling methods. But few products, especially those that appeal to the young, keep anything like their original standardized form. Whether this in and of itself is a sufficient criticism of the globalist theory is unclear, but it is a cautionary note that simple, first-look theories of globalization require second and deeper looks over time.

There is another type of antiglobalist argument, one that is more overtly political than academic. Naomi Klein, an activist and writer, has long been an antiglobalization proponent and openly identified with the antiglobalization movement. Like many other social movements, this one is strictly decentralized, intentionally, without an obvious central authority, and thereby disciplined in its commitment to the local or regional effects of globalizing structures. For Klein and others, the most notorious instances of globalization gone very bad are free-trade agreements like NAFTA (the North American Free Trade Agreement), which in 1994 created a free-trade zone by opening markets among Mexico, the United States, and Canada. It would seem, from the name alone, that free trade is good for all. As the actual agreements turn out, they favor, by more than a little, capitalist investors who can buy and sell without tariff limits while squeezing out

136 CHAPTER SIX

workers and smaller businesses. For example, Starbucks is free to buy and sell its coffee products, while small-time coffee growers in Mexico cannot easily export their beans to the north. Naomi Klein's political argument favors a regional economy based more on social democratic participatory values than neoliberal market principles.

When antiglobalist theories are assessed in the long run, as hard as it is to generate convincing and enduring evidence that globalization is not real, Klein's political position is far and away the more important. Whatever globalization becomes in the long run, there is more than enough short-run evidence that there is much about globalization that is, if not evil, at least destructive for the global poor. Not only does endless capital accumulation in whatever form exclude those—now billions—who cannot serve the system, but, as anti–free trade activists make clear, global economic accords also work against hardworking but economically marginal people—coffee growers in Mexico, agricultural and construction workers the world over, small businesses that close down when Walmart destroys their local markets, and many others.

## TRANSFORMATIONALIST THEORIES

The third general type of globalization theory among the range of possibilities is called transformationalism by its proponents.

The principal proponent of transformationalism is David Held, who, with colleagues, published the book *Global Transformations: Politics, Economics, and Culture* (1999). The subtitle alone indicates the extent to which transformationalist theory compares well to the seriousness and thoroughness of a globalist like Manuel Castells. Held and his colleagues defined the major positions in the debate while lending considerable empirical and analytic weight to the transformationalist viewpoint.

In a scheme not entirely inconsistent with world-systems analysis, Held and his coauthors contend that globalization itself can be divided into three periods: early modern (1500–1850), modern (1850–1945), and contemporary (after 1945). Their way of stipulating the contemporary period is itself a clue to what transformationalists mean by their name. Rather than suggest that the post–World War II period marked a key transition, they soften the distinction between modern and contemporary, thereby giving no apparent importance to the post-1991 period. This may seem innocent enough, but it allows them to defend the idea that "globalization [is] a set of processes rather than a singular condition … [and] not a simple linear developmental logic [that] … refigures a world society or a world community" (Held et al. 1999, 27).

By the term "transformation," the theory grants that a great deal has changed in the modern world, especially in the half century before the twenty-first century. But (and it is a big *but*) those changes do not constitute the end of the modern era and its systems and the beginning of some possible new global form. Held describes the transformation of endemic pressures and strains in the late modern era this way: "Sovereignty, state power, and territoriality thus stand today in a more complex relationship than in the epoch during which the modern nation-state was being forged." In some ways, a statement like this is more or less straightforward. Transformationalists, for example, have little sympathy for the idea that the nation-state is disappearing in favor of new global forms of governance. What they think is that, indeed, even the nation-state is changed by globalization, in part because of the astonishing number of intergovernmental and nongovernmental organizations, from the United Nations and the Red Cross to Doctors without Borders, the International Monetary Fund, and thousands of others that have metastasized since the 1990s—changed, yes, but short of disappearing. The nation-state, they hold, however transformed it may be, remains just as salient in regard to sovereignty in general.

The nation-state may no longer be the supreme location of power and social control in the world. No state, even the most powerful, can on its own control or shape the global political economy as it was supposed the British did early in their imperial and colonizing history. Again, the idea is that the role of the state is transformed but still an important source of political power. Today China and the United States, the two largest economies by volume of capital wealth in the 2010s, are clearly not able to control their own populations, much less a major share of the world economy. China is beholden to American and European markets, as the United States and the European Union are in relatively less powerful financial positions due to China's control of the world currency, which may not control the world's capital but at least allows that capital to be traded in an orderly manner. Again, financial capitalism, like the global political economy in general, is different in the contemporary period. The global system is defined still by key participating nation-states—even in the case of the European Union, which bends to the wishes of its economic power brokers: notably Germany, but also at different times and to different degrees France and Great Britain.

## 138 ⊕ CHAPTER SIX

In certain respects, transformationalists may seem, to some, almost globalist in their ways of characterizing global distances or, as it is commonly put, territoriality. Space, and therefore distance and territory, has always been a key element in globalization, as it was among the ancient empires. Rabid globalists might say that global distances are shorter due to the sense of proximity created by all sorts of information technologies. There is much to be said for this idea.

Globalization changes our sense of distances, thus altering to a degree our sense of who and where we are. But in the end we still walk to school and work, fly to visit friends and relatives, and drive across our cities, many of which are so clogged with traffic as to prevent a car in the twenty-first century from covering urban spaces faster than a horse and buggy several centuries before.

Held, McGrew, and their colleagues offer lucid transformationalist theories to the effect that globalization involves "transnational interconnectedness" while being ubiquitous in the sense that no aspect of life seems to escape it (Held et al. 1999, 27). Then too, they add, globalization cuts

---

### BETWEEN FATHER AND DAUGHTER, GENERATIONS OF GLOBAL DISTANCES

When I was a boy in the 1950s, foreign places, even Europe, were remote. In those days only the very rich where I grew up ever dreamed of going to places we studied in geography lessons (except, of course, during the war, but that was hardly a dream). By contrast, my daughter had been to China (twice), Australia (once), and Europe (several times) before she left middle school. Her travels were somewhat due to the "shortening" of travel distances, but just as much to the fact that, even while watching her teenage television programs, she encountered stories from countries she was required to study in the school—and these, it appears, motivated her readiness to travel when opportunities arose. In my day, only children of the rich or missionary kids even thought to travel like that. Books remain basic in school, but the Web and other information technologies do, in fact, bring distant and strange places closer. This very local and personal story illustrates how globalization transforms the experience of global distances. The actual spatial distances are the same, but it matters how we experience those distances.

"through and across political frontiers" such that it "deterritorializes and reterritorializes" social, political, economic, and cultural activities. Put all too simply, the idea is that no aspect of life is unchanged. At the same time, as life's activities are transformed by globalization, people are left with the preexisting and modern instruments of state politics, economic markets, cultural fads, and social institutions in order to deal with these changes. My family today is transformed from my family as a child, but it is still called a family and still functions as modern American families, if there ever was a standard, long have.

It may be a little daring to say so, but, as a group, transformationalists may not be totally convincing though their leading theorists have long been recognized as among the world's most influential social theorists. If fame matters (which sometimes it does), the most justifiably famous among transformationalists is Lord Anthony Giddens—a sociologist, founder (with Held and John Thompson) of one of the world's most influential social scientific publishing groups (Polity Press), former director of the London School of Economics, advisor to former British prime minister Tony Blair, and (by Blair's appointment) member of the British House of Lords. Quite apart from all that, Giddens is first among equals in transformationalist theory.

Earlier, Giddens (1990) took a strong position on that day's fad, postmodernism. At a time when some were being swayed, or at least impressed, by the idea that the modern era was over, Giddens boldly defended what he called a radical modernist position. In effect, he said that while simplistic theoretical versions of modern social theory must be gotten over, the basic theoretical principles of late modern thought can and should be radicalized, not thrown out.

Giddens later added, in *Runaway World* (1999), that, ironically, "globalization is the reason for the revival of local cultural identities in different parts of the world." His reference here is to the global phenomenon that was especially acute in the 1990s: as nation-states lost a measure of control over their national populations, a considerable array of ethnic and other, more local movements rose to force their issues into the sphere of global recognition. After the Cold War, Russia struggled with rebellions in Chechnya, as the Chinese did with Tibet in its south and Turkic populations in its west. These and many others were, if not strictly local, at least ethnic, as opposed to national groups able to move against state powers by the relative openness of a global environment and the relative weakness of state regimes. Closer to the present, think of both the so-called Arab Spring after the Tunisian

## 140 ⊕ CHAPTER SIX

revolts late in 2010 and in Egypt in 2011, as well as subsequent antiregime rebellions in Libya, Syria, and Iraq. These were—and, it now seems, will be again—messy affairs in which the rebelling forces were not self-evidently on the side of modern democracy or able to sustain their revolutionary fervor—even, in the case of Egypt, after a legitimate election. External global forces of all kinds intrude on and aggravate already-destabilized and transforming regions. Above all, and this is Giddens's point, local traditions and practices, as well as ideologies, assert themselves where once-powerful state regimes held a firm grip.

There are other positions that do not claim any particular label but could be considered transformationalist. One of the most important of these is Aihwa Ong's 2006 book, *Neoliberalism as Exception*. Neoliberalism, simply put, is an essentially global revision of the older liberal economic theory that insists that markets are the principal and sole energizing force of economic growth. Since the 1990s, neoliberalism has been, to those on the left, an evil reincarnation of long-standing capitalist methods of accumulation. Ong, who surely is a culturally left thinker, takes up an idea that had been put into play by, among others, an Italian theorist.

In the 1990s, Giorgio Agamben revised a theory that had been previously held by theorists in prewar Germany. In simple terms, Agamben's point is that the modern state, as guarantor of the legal order, is endowed with the self-assumed right to make exceptions to its own laws. Agamben points to many examples; among them are war acts imposing restrictions on the rights of aliens and, most notoriously, Hitler's suspension of the Weimar Republic in order not only to exercise control over Germany but to exterminate the Jewish people. Agamben's short history of the modern state shows that no major modern state has failed to declare exceptions to it own civil-rights laws. This is an idea that has been chillingly emphasized by the South African social theorist and philosopher Achille Mbembe. He argues with uncommon finesse that modern politics are necropolitics, or the politics of death (Mbembe 2003). Where there is a sovereign there are exceptions to the rule of law, which, in effect, grant the sovereign the right to decide who lives and who dies.

Aihwa Ong applies the concept of sovereign exception, somewhat more gently, to the ways neoliberal states and others collude with market capitalism to declare exceptions where capitalist trade is significant. China's most striking example is Hong Kong. The condition under which Great Britain ceded control of Hong Kong to China was that it retain its long-settled free political economy. Whether China will respect this concession remains to be seen in light of the brutality with which it has dominated Tibet. Then too, Tibet is not a global economic force. If in the long run Hong Kong keeps hold of its relatively democratic system it will be because of its economic importance. Another Chinese exception is Taiwan, which, since the defeat of the nationalists in 1949, has claimed the right to be the true China. For years, the People's Republic in Beijing declared that it would fight to the end to regain control over Taiwan, but relatively early in the twenty-first century this resolve weakened such that today one hears little of the old saber-rattling. Instead there are daily flights from Shanghai to Taipei, a prospect once unthinkable. Why does it seem that China is willing to make these exceptions to its own political goals and authority? Simply because these small but vibrant nearby economies are good for China's own brand of neoliberal economics.

Among the three groups of theories of globalization—globalist, anti-globalist, and transformationalist—there are many variations within each and from each to the others. All three have their own logic and all appeal to evidence. That there is no clear way to resolve the differences goes to demonstrate the complexity of globalization and the necessary caution with which it should be thought through. Still, differences and problems notwithstanding, the prevailing theories of globalization reveal the extent to which something truly serious and global is going on this world. What it is or becomes remains to be seen.

CHAPTER SEVEN

# THE FUTURE OF GLOBALIZATION

## *THE UNKNOWN WORLDS TO COME*

Of all the world-important phenomena in human history, globalization may be, in its way, the most difficult to figure. It would be hard to imagine who on the planet has not, in some way, however small, been touched by globalization. Rich and poor, young and old, rural and urban, literate or not—everyone, it seems, has been affected by globalization. At the least, few are they who cannot readily figure out *that* it is. The difficulty is with *what* it is, *why* now, and *where* does it lead? Of these, the last is all but impossible to answer. Still, in this life, as it has come to be, we are always up against questions of the future.

In contrast to earlier world-changing phenomena (notably, modernization), globalization is one that not only disturbs local life but also impinges on the practical knowledge of all, however remote or impoverished their settlements may be. The often-isolated poor have at least occasional access to media, if only a telephone a long walk over to another village. In this respect, globalization is unlike any other world-important structure. None other has ever before come upon all everywhere at very nearly the same historical moment.

*The Future of Globalization*  143

> **PARTY LINES AND OPERATORS**
>
> When I was not long out of college and preternaturally immature, I took a summer job in a very small rural village in New Hampshire. I was housed that summer in a nearby, only somewhat larger town, at Mrs. Trow's Rooming House. She was kind enough to allow me use of her telephone. In those days, in those parts of the country, it was not unusual for people to share a party line. The party lay in the fact that it was possible to pick up the telephone and listen in on what others using the line might be saying. Stranger still, telephone connections were made by an actual operator—a person, somehow connected to a relay station, who answered the phone and to whom you gave the number you wished to call.
>
> My job that summer was to organize a small church that had been dormant for many years. My employer had but one name of a person known to have had something to do with the church in the old days. When I settled in my room at Mrs. Trow's, I used the telephone to call my contact. I did not have a reliable number, but that didn't matter. The operator asked the name of the party I was trying to reach. I told her, "Bea Smith." The operator said, "Well, she was up to Mary's earlier, but I think she's gone over to Kate's. I'll try for you." Sure enough, there she was. With her help we got the church going again.

People my age use the word "telephone" as though the word's meaning were perfectly evident. In a sense it is, since that particular instrument of communication has been around for well over a century. Today, however, the young, if they use the word at all, speak of phones—just as often of cells or mobiles—for which they are likely to use a commercial brand name (increasingly, at the moment, iPhones, usually with a model name like 5G or something of the sort). They are not wrong in this since, strictly speaking, a telephone broadcast over a distance is a "call," which is to say an actual voice passed along a series of wires. However that worked, today a "cell" passes along a series of encoded signals that are sent somehow into cyberspace then on to the recipient where, again somehow, the messages are decoded and made to sound like your voice. The mystery is greater yet. Still, it is apparent enough that, however inscrutable the descriptive nouns, context indicates what is meant by "telephone" is a globalized version of a tool that can still be found on the kitchen walls of a few older houses.

## 144 CHAPTER SEVEN

On the other hand, mention a computer, much less a personal one, and kids today have scant appreciation for the fact that this globalized thing is somehow new in recent years.

One of the consequences of this kind of change in the nature of things is a seldom recognized feature of globalization as we experience it today. It tends to erase everyday knowledge of the tools that may have been precursors of ones we use now. Already, the personal computer is disappearing in favor of notebooks, iPads, smartphones, and who knows what next. Between the time I write this and someone reads it, there will likely have been several newer generations of things of this sort. As things change, the tools themselves often cease to be what once they were. We might wonder, for example, if the typewriter is to the personal computer as the telephone is to the cell. Typewriters are, in fact, closer to handwriting than to word processing. Though the older version of a handwritten letter is fast fading away, handwritten texts in general are laborious, just as typewriters were. Typewriting, before the machines were fully mechanized (first with erasure functions, then with limited versions of saving and revising functions), was better than handwritten notes only in the sense that the writing produced was, on average, more likely to be legible than most handwritings are.

Soon enough, writing and typewriting will be completely replaced by word processing, which raises the question of what we are doing when we

---

### THE LAST TYPEWRITER

As it happens, the last typewriter repair shop in New England closed in 2013. Its owner and only repairman died shortly thereafter. He was ninety-six. Yet there are places where the typewriter is still used. For example, in Yangon, Myanmar (formerly Burma), where literacy rates are low, one can find on the city streets typewriters—not the machine alone, but people who, for a fee, will type on typewriters for people who cannot write (Fuller 2013). Yet even here, typewriters—the people and the machines—are at risk. Myanmar had suffered a long history of oppression under a military regime. In the past few years the regime has faded, making way for modernization. When, well into the twenty-first century, a nation modernizes, it is globalization and all its wondrous tools that rush in to push out the older ways—even in Yangon.

### The Future of Globalization

process words to one another. If, then, writing is not now what once it was, what today are we to make of *talking*? All too often, one hears people say they were "talking" to a friend the other day. What they were doing was probably texting. Talking to distant others has become an ambiguous activity. We may, of course, talk on the cell with friends in remote places. We can and do talk to them by other means like Skype and Snapchat (whatever that is or was), which are a little more like talking because social media often entail looking at. Still, few consider this strange fact that talking usually implies at least the possibility of *looking at*. I have a correspondent in Europe who, when she responds to an email, says nice to *read* you. She happens to be a psychoanalyst, so something deep may be going on there.

Globalization, we know very well, is not merely about social media or emailing or the like. But these new tools are at least metaphors. Their metaphoric truth may well point to a revolutionary fact of globalization. In some good degree, media are means by which meanings can come from anywhere without reason—and come they do, even when the means change with near blinding speed without rhyme or reason. What is happening today in Myanmar is what has already happened not that long ago in my town, and what will happen sooner or later on the steppes of Mongolia.

Globalization is changing our relations to material things while also changing our relations to others. It is unlikely that we will ever cease to have face-to-face relations with those about us. Yet if we can foresee the day when no one writes in the literal sense, then it may be that, soon after, we will no longer look at each other. Some people close their eyes at the crucial moment in lovemaking. Perhaps one day other forms of intercourse will fall into a similar blind climax. In fact, it is already common for people on fast joyrides to close their eyes when the speed exceeds what they are accustomed to. Life today may not be a roller coaster or some other fun-park ride, but it has become a ride in which the speed with which things change is so great that, in effect, we close the mind's eye so as not to notice the rush of feelings.

#### JUNK IN THE GLOBAL ATTIC?

In my house there is an attic full of stuff—old books, old TVs and computers, printers and other useless electronic junk, broken Ikea furniture, unused toys, and other trash of the family past. We may be bad

146 CHAPTER SEVEN

housekeepers, but our excuse for not throwing that stuff away is that there is so much of it that it seems an overwhelming job. We could, I suppose, hire someone to clean it out just as people in Yangon hire someone to write for them. If we might, we should do it soon because it won't be long before junk collectors will pass from the scene as the world changes again.

## FAST ACCUMULATION AND THE WASTING OF THE WORLD

Globalization, among much else, is about the accumulation of junk. Global culture has become, in the horrifying words of Zygmunt Bauman (2004, 94ff), a culture of waste. The world is becoming an attic filled with stuff no one wants and nearly no one knows how to get rid of. Where I live, and most other places around here, there is not a town or city without what is euphemistically called a landfill. Everyone knows that, whoever hauls away their weekly trash, a goodly part of what cannot be recycled is dumped in a space that is far enough from the daily run of things as to be somewhat out of sight. In cities of modest size, like mine, there is no hole deep enough to dump the junk. Landfill is a misnomer. In fact, the stuff is piled high then covered over with enough dirt to sustain grass or weeds, even trees. The result is that city junk becomes smallish hills that are meant to appear at a distance to be part of the natural landscape. No one seems to consider that, in time, the junk hills will become small mountains. Larger cities must ship their junk elsewhere. The problem they have is that no one wants it. New Jersey does not want New York City's junk, of which it already has too much.

The junk hardest to get rid of is electronic stuff. Guiyu is a city in Guangdong, China, that exists mainly to service one of the world's largest electronic junk dumps. The poor scavenge for marketable parts. The children play amid dangerous chemical and metallic remains. All but a few children suffer terrible diseases caused by the waste. Guiyu may be the extreme, but it warns us that, in due course, human junk of all kinds will make us all morbidly ill. It is seriously possible to consider the junk in our closets or attics as reminders of the true effect of capitalism on the world-system it has spawned and now is hell-bent on destroying.

Long ago Karl Marx, the first seriously scientific student of the capitalist system, said that capitalism is an endless series of heartless revolutions in and of the world it creates. His famous words in *The Manifesto of the Communist Party* (1848):

The bourgeoisie cannot exist without constantly revolutionizing the instruments of production, and thereby the relations of production, and with them the whole relations of society. Conservation of the old modes of production in unaltered form was, on the contrary, the first condition of existence for all earlier industrial classes. Constant revolutionizing of production, uninterrupted disturbance of all social conditions, everlasting uncertainty and agitation distinguish the bourgeois epoch from all earlier ones. All fixed, fast frozen relations, with their train of ancient and venerable prejudices and opinions, are swept away, all newly-formed ones become antiquated before they can ossify. All that is solid melts into air, all that is holy is profaned, and man is at last compelled to face with sober senses, his real conditions of life, and his relations with his kind.

There are few lines written in the modern era that are more elegant in their bitter denunciation of the world's worst faults. And here too, as only Marx could put it, is the deepest flaw of the modern world. No prior world was so systematically self-destructive. In fact (if you can take the term "industrial" as a figure of speech), these words from *The Manifesto* may best explain the difference between empires and world-systems: all earlier modes of economic and social order were concerned first and foremost with conserving themselves as they were. Thus, the Asian world economy grew not for profit but to maintain its ancient traditions; by contrast, capitalism is constantly changing.

Modernization and capitalism are commensurable. One cannot exist without the other. Bauman, more than a century after Marx, transformed

---

### THE PRODUCTION OF WASTED LIVES

The production of "human waste," or more correctly wasted humans (the excessive and redundant, that is the population of those who either could not or were not wished to be recognized or allowed to stay) is an inevitable outcome of modernization. It is an inescapable side-effect of *order-building* (each order casts some parts of the extant population as "out of place," "unfit," or "undesirable") and of *economic progress* (that cannot proceed without degrading and devaluing the previously effective modes of "making a living" and therefore cannot but deprive their practitioners of their livelihood"). (Bauman 2004, 4–5, emphases in original)

## 148 ⊕ CHAPTER SEVEN

the idea of capitalism as "melting all that is solid into air." Industrial capitalism was, and remains, nothing if not the issue of the hard-metal industry that so pervades global spaces as to make the wasting of human lives inevitable. For every job lost to deindustrialization in Ohio, workers in the Pearl River Delta are drawn to Shenzhen, built on the ruin of once-fertile soil. In time, the Pearl River having been depleted, what work there is will move to Vietnam or Bangladesh, and then, in due course, will reappear in the American rust belts where labor once again is cheap. Workers and their families, productive lands, nature's resource wealth, and much more are mined into bits and fed to the machine of capitalist production—from which surplus values are extracted out of the wreckage of human lives.

Capitalism, as Wallerstein reminds, is about the *endless* accumulation of capital. What Marx saw years ago was that the drive for accumulation is essentially destructive of the very economic (and social) order from which it extracts its profits. Marx was a genius at metaphoric language, but, as the lines from *The Manifesto* make clear, he could also mix metaphors to eerie effect— "everlasting uncertainty and agitation," "fixed fast frozen relations ... swept away," "all that is solid melts into air," "the new becomes antiquated before it ossifies," "what is holy is profaned," and "man is compelled soberly to face reality." To these, Marshall Berman (1982, 105–111), in *All That Is Solid Melts into Air,* adds nakedness. Some might complain at the mixing of figures, but the overall emotional effect is a creepy sense that, under capitalism, humanity is assaulted in every which possible way, stripped naked of all that matters.

Yet for all the terrible force of Marx's criticism of capitalism, in the end he held out for the promise of a better world in *The Eighteenth Brumaire of Louis Bonaparte* (1852):

> Bourgeois revolutions, like those in the eighteenth century, storm more swiftly from success to success; their dramatic effects outdo each other; men and things seem set in sparkling brilliants; ecstasy is the everyday spirit; but they are short lived; soon they have attained their zenith, and a long depression lays hold of society before it learns soberly to assimilate the results of its storm and stress period. Proletarian revolutions, on the other hand, like those of the nineteenth century, criticize themselves constantly, interrupt themselves continually in their own course, come back to the apparently accomplished in order to begin it afresh, deride with unmerciful thoroughness the inadequacies, weaknesses and paltriness of their first attempts, seem to throw down their adversary only in order that he may draw

new strength from the earth and rise again more gigantic before them, recoil ever and anon from the indefinite prodigiousness of their own aims, until the situation has been created which makes all turning back impossible.

With yet another stirring political elegy, Marx shows he believed that, yes, capitalism as embodied in the bourgeois revolution destroyed human prospects—but only to the point where the ideal of a proletarian revolution not only restored hope, but also came to the fore just when the capitalist system was shaken. In practical terms, capitalism's inherent contradictions make this a hard belief to hold and live by. Marshall Berman (1982, 348) sharpens the idea: "I believe that we and those who come after us will go on fighting to make ourselves at home in the world, even as the homes we have made, the modern street, the modern spirit, go on melting into air." Still, Marx and the many who trust him believe that the constant revolutionizing of bourgeois capitalism can be overcome. Even so, we may well be living in a time when globalization forces a deep reconsideration of the ideal of ultimate hope that stirs the soul of modernists.

## IS A GLOBAL REVOLUTION POSSIBLE?

The mostly modern word for a deep remaking of social hope is one seldom used seriously anymore—*revolution.* In an odd way, revolutionary hope, admirable though it may be, is often naive. The idea, at its best, is that when any global system—whether a state, or a generalized mode of production; an empire, or a world-system—is the object of structural change, there are only two major, general ways to account for the changes.

One general theory of revolutions trusts the ability of an aggrieved class to initiate a widespread movement that will put into play a rapidly expanding movement of movements. By their collective force, the ever-stronger force of social movements causes a decisive break in the reigning sovereign powers such that the prevailing system crumbles and a new one emerges. This theory of deep revolutions is based on the idea that social structures are inherently *fluid*—always moving with the flow of social history.

At the other metaphoric extreme is the second general idea of revolutionary structural change. Here, confidence is drawn from the assumption that there is an inherent structural flaw in any long-prevailing system—a flaw that can be expected to irrupt when structural time is ripe. Such a moment, often called a historical conjuncture, aggravates a system's structural

# 150   ⊕   CHAPTER SEVEN

contradictions, whereupon the structure either collapses or runs wild due to its inability to maintain itself. By consequence, this second theory must also bear a second, all-too-innocent belief that upon the breaking apart of a structure, some other system will take its place. This second view is that social structures are essentially *mechanical*—complex machines of many moving parts, each well oiled so as to work in harmony under constant pressure and ever-increasing speed. In the mechanical theory, structures can be sleek, even beautiful, as cars and planes or cells and laptops can be. Still, it takes only a fuel hose or an invisible circuit to wear out, and the structural weakness can cause the machine to crash.

Obviously, between the two general ideas there are many nuances. Still, both ideal types of social structures—fluid and mechanical—come up against the deepest of social structural tensions: inequalities. On one hand, those whose grievances are most serious are, by structural definition, politically weak and thus least able to force their will on the structures of inequality. For the marginal and otherwise impoverished, history does not flow toward the purifying waters of a revolution. On the other hand, those in the dominant position are actors who operate the machinery of inequality. They are possessors of nearly all the available power, ever more so now that, at long last, the basic facts of economic inequality are better known by virtue of Thomas Piketty's exhaustive and daring empirical research. In *Capital in the Twenty-First Century* (2014), Piketty provides the evidence that, over time, capital wealth almost always overwhelms the growth of income. Wealth belongs almost entirely to the dominant, while personal income is the slim hope of the less powerful and marginal. This reality has become so evident to all but the willfully ignorant that even those who have no particular affiliation with Marx know it is true.

---

## THOMAS PIKETTY: THE PAST DEVOURS THE FUTURE

The central contradiction of capitalism ... is that a market economy based on private property, if left to itself, contains powerful forces of convergence, associated in particular with the diffusion of knowledge and skills; but it also contains powerful forces of divergence, which are potentially threatening to democratic societies, and to the values of social justice on which they are based. ... The principal destabilizing force has to do with the fact that the private rate of return on capital, r, can be significantly higher for long periods of time than the rate of growth of income and output, g. The

> inequality r > g implies that wealth accumulated in the past grows more rapidly than output and wages. The inequality expresses a fundamental logical contradiction. The entrepreneur inevitably tends to become the rentier, more and more dominant over those who own nothing but their labor. Once constituted, capital reproduces itself faster than output. The past devours the future. (Piketty 2014, 571)

Those with the wealth can turn big structural things on or off, or fail to oil and maintain them, or otherwise run them to ruin. Even the most charitable theory of human nature gives little reason to trust the wealthy and powerful to give away either their wealth or their power. The most a few of the powerful and wealthy have done is to give enough away to encourage changes that come just short of driving them into a revolutionary wreck. Their resistance to changing the system they benefit from could well be, as Marx at least implied, the point at which, under historical pressure, their system comes apart.

To force the well-off to give up something to enhance the lives of the less well-off once was thought to be the proper outcome of revolutions. Yet be it 1789–1848 in Europe, 1911–1949 in China, 1917 in Russia, the world revolutions of 1968, or the triumph of capitalism in 1991, revolutions have not done what they promised. Not all were failures, but as things turned out, the more successful revolutions were not those that aimed to overturn the economic and social structures of a society, but ones directed more toward the liberation of a people, especially from a long colonial history. The conflict in India, for example, in 1947, though not a full-blown revolutionary war, did result in the removal of British colonial authorities, but at the cost of partitioning Hindu and Muslim populations. To this day, neither India nor Pakistan, both highly globalized and modernizing nations, is liberated (if the word applies here) from the agonies of their regional differences. In Africa, especially in the south, liberation struggles threw off colonial rule, which in time was often replaced by indigenous regimes that were, if anything, *more* brutal—in Congo and Uganda, for examples.

If revolutionary movements for deep structural change or liberation from colonial rule have so frequently failed, it seems fair to say that the many movements today actively seeking global relief from poverty or sane environmental restraint are only loosely models for eliminating the evils in the world made more real and acute by globalization. If there has been anything like a global structural change it has been the relative success of

152 CHAPTER SEVEN

curtailing the prospect of nuclear war. But the threat remains, and in a way it has become more, not less, dreadful. As the major nuclear powers have backed away from Cold War saber-rattling, globalization has led to the emergence of rogue states and movements developing nuclear weapon capacity. Iran today; who knows which tomorrow. Then too, the massive extent of underground arms sales the world over surely includes the prospect of a black market of nuclear weapons. This kind of thing is not limited to the movies that play on the threat of criminal nuclear attacks.

Yet even when one attempts to identify the good made possible by globalization, it is hard not to come upon still another of its evils. In some ways, the rejection of the good might be part of the human condition. The ancient Persian and early Christian Manicheans argued just this for thousands of years. Today, even in the most secular of societal sectors, one can hear idle talk of devils and evil empires and the like. Whatever one's religious or secular ideological outlook, belief in a global evil has the dispiriting effect of making believers look for solutions in another world. But when, as today, the global evils of poverty, environmental degradations, violence and war, and more are so apparently manmade, little good will come from dishonoring one's god by attributing them to him or her. Personally, I am a vaguely religious person who believes in various rather plastic versions of the Christian gods. But, aged though I am, I am also the father of a young daughter who will outlive me by decades. This, of course, is another age-old dilemma—obey the gods or care for the children? We are all, therefore, caught in Abraham's problem. Do we dare sacrifice our beloved children to win favor with the gods?

There is, of course, a fair amount of good that can be said of globalization's obvious human benefits. It is good that we live in a more cosmopolitan world where xenophobia tends, occasionally, to melt before the true-to-life virtues of living in multicultural communities. It is good, to be sure, that information technologies of all kinds are both affordable and technically accessible even to the technologically challenged. They are indeed tools that at least make it possible for the good of heart to appreciate cultural differences across very considerable geographic, as well as social, distances. At the other, more global end of the spectrum, whatever is to become of the nation-state, it is good that even the most powerful states are constrained by global forces. The long-lasting lessons of empires is that they don't last forever, but while they do last they can be terrifying in the horrors they too often visit on those under their fist. Hitler's was a pseudoempire that did

The Future of Globalization  153

not last much more than a decade in Germany. Still, no one would wish to revisit anything like the evil done by his Nazi regime, which, in fact, is about as close to an otherworldly evil as this world can get.

Then too, what is to be made of the unthinkably vast wealth globalization generates? Available wealth in a global system without any prospect of a single hegemonic power is wealth that, in principle, can be used for good. As economically corrupt as many, perhaps most, multinational corporations might be, there are many ways that corporate wealth has been used for the good of all. Robber barons of an earlier time—the Ford and Rockefeller families, among others—used, or caused their heirs to use, their extreme wealth for good and lasting purposes. So today, global philanthropists—Bill and Melinda Gates, George Soros, Warren Buffett, and others—are invaluable sources of funding for global health, education, and poverty reduction, as well as international understanding and cooperation, and much else. Plus, in the United States there is hardly a city, town, or region with a theatre company or an arts program that does not enjoy the support of a local bank or business.

Yet in the final analysis, globalization, whatever it turns out to be, has created a world of uncertainty. Hardly anyone enjoys uncertainty. But uncertainty is the coin of the global economic system. Whether or not there is a payoff, global uncertainty is far from the worst that can be had. In relative terms, comparing the state of the world-system such as it is in the twenty-first century with the more traditional modern one in the short twentieth century, the certitudes of the modern were in their way more dangerous. The cultural and political evil of the modern was its certainty that History (with a capital *H*) was headed toward a progressively better world that, as things turned out, never came close to the promise.

In the short run, from 1914 until at least 1968, then 1991, the modern world-system entered a period of global struggle that only appeared to have ended with the final defeat of Germany and Japan in 1945. But the period of economic affluence after World War II began to unravel in 1968 when the collective force of decolonization made more acute the crippling effect of the Cold War on global affairs, in which the United States was at the core.

> ### WHEN THE CRISIS HIT HOME
>
> Early in the 1970s, after a minicareer involved in the so-called revolutionary 1960s, I finished my graduate work, sought a teaching position,

## 154 CHAPTER SEVEN

> and went to work. The position I found was in a then-young university in the Midwest. At the time, it was thriving to the degree that when I came to its sociology department, I came with, as I remember it, ten new faculty—some were from Europe on visiting appointments; others, like me, in continuing positions. All were from what were considered elite schools. Though the pay was standard (thus, at the time, not so much), the university offered many opportunities, like support for research, including trips to Europe. Life was good. Even if the place was not ideal, it turned out to be a great place to start a career. Then, all of a sudden, the petroleum crisis struck home. No new colleagues. Less money for research. But, more to the point, interest rates soared, as did prices. In general, life slowed. Most of us in that small college town got through it, but many wondered what was happening. What happened, of course, was that all of a sudden the world supply of petroleum products—including fuel, hence energy—was globalized. OPEC (the Organization of the Petroleum Exporting Countries), which had been in existence since 1960, became a major force in the global oil market in 1973, when oil prices rose precipitously due to an embargo by Arab producers. OPEC sought to be not only a market force but also a player in the social and economic development of poorer countries. Then the global economy began to change in unexpected ways. For all but a few academic experts in the American Midwest, the very idea that fuel for cars, homes, and industry would be priced by forces outside local markets was a shock. Europe had long lived with high prices. But since World War II, the United States had gone on its merry economic way as if nothing in the world could alter its privileged status in the world. After 1973, even when prices stabilized and people adjusted to a new normal, all that had been was no longer. The crisis hit home, then became what one had to live with.

When the petroleum crisis became real, the economic vulnerability of the system's core state essentially revealed that capital accumulation measured by affluence for the few was coming to, in the expression of the day, the limits of growth. By 1989–1991, when the European communist bloc collapsed (and China's party under Deng Xiaoping had already been capitalizing through the 1980s), the so-called triumph of capitalism was in fact a bizarre confusion of the real and unreal.

By 1991, global rates of capital accumulation were rising to unheard-of levels. At the same time, it was just as true that levels of global poverty were as bad as before; 1991 was nearly fifty years after the 1944 Bretton Woods Conference establishing a global commitment to fight world poverty. Since 1944, the collective efforts of the globally wealthy acting through the International Monetary Fund, the World Bank, the United Nations, and countless other nongovernmental organizations did little to change the plight of the world's poor. Nations have modernized, to be sure. But their poor have been left out. According to the World Bank, though there has been some improvement, particularly in India and China, there remain 1.2 billion people in poverty, overwhelmingly in the countries with the lowest income:

> The objective of this note is to analyze some of the diverse characteristics of 1.2 billion poor people who are the focus of the poverty reduction efforts of governments and the international development community. Despite the impressive progress in the fight against poverty in the developing world as a whole, the progress has been much slower in Low Income Countries (LICs). Poverty for middle and high income countries fell by more than a half since 1981. For LICs, however, extreme poverty fell by less than a third.
>
> The depth of extreme poverty, that is, how far the average extremely poor person is from the $1.25 per day poverty line, has fallen by 25 percent in the past 30 years for the developing world as a whole. But most of this drop seems to have happened in China and India. For the rest of the developing world, individuals living in extreme poverty today appear to be as poor as those living in extreme poverty 30 years ago.
>
> The aggregate additional annual income needed to lift every individual in the developing world out of extreme poverty (the Aggregate Poverty Gap) has been reduced by more than half for the developing world. For LICs, it has increased by 33 percent between 1981 and 2010. This is due to an increase in the number of extremely poor individuals in LICs by more than 100 million, and the stagnant average income among the poor that remained almost as low in 2010 as it was back in 1981.
>
> As a share of the GDP of the developing world, the Aggregate Poverty Gap is now less than one tenth of what it was 30 years ago. For LICs, the share in 2010 was approximately 8 percent of their GDP, down from 24 percent in 1981. Notwithstanding this significant decline, the Aggregate Poverty Gap/GDP ratio in LICs is 16 times larger than the average for the developing world. (Olinto et al. 2013, 1)

156 &#x24E7; CHAPTER SEVEN

Nowhere was this contradiction more true than in the United States, which, in the course of the 1980s, fell from being the most egalitarian of the world's major economies to among the least. To make matters worse, the United States does less to reduce inequality than any other of the world's twenty-two richest countries. By the 2010s, after the economic crisis of 2008, the American stock market achieved record highs. Still, levels of unemployment remain high, especially when it is known that millions have given up looking for work and thus cannot be counted. The top 1 percent earned some 25 percent of US income, while the bottom 90 percent earned less than 50 percent (by 2010 estimates). Hence the driving concept of the Occupy Wall Street movement that began in 2011: the 99 percent and the 1 percent. American capitalism presides over obscene inequalities, both nationally and globally. Since the beginning of the short twentieth century, the overall trend has been a sharp decline of global income equality and, accordingly, of human well-being.

It may seem strange to describe 1914 to 1991 as a *short run* of modern time. But when referring to structural time, "short" can be very long when measured by the events of a lifetime. The twentieth century was, thus, short in two senses of the word: its span of time was far less than a 100-year century and its time was short structurally. What appeared in the aftermath of the wars early in that century to be a brilliant triumph turned out to be the first signs of ruin for the modern capitalist system. Such a claim that the capitalist system is headed toward ruin may seem preposterous in light of the fabulous amount of wealth it generates. But to assess the present situation, one must calculate the human costs that lie ahead—costs no amount of absolute wealth can prevent.

Put simply, the world faces a deadly shortage of the most basic of human needs for survival. Food, clean water, breathable air, and fuel of all kinds are headed toward critical shortages. According to UNICEF (2010), an estimated twenty-six million children in the developing world are, literally, wasting away for want of adequate nutrition.

## GLOBAL HUNGER

The United Nations Food and Agriculture Organization estimates that nearly 870 million people of the 7.1 billion people in the world, or one in eight, were suffering from chronic undernourishment in 2010–2012. Almost all the hungry people, 852 million, live in developing countries,

*The Future of Globalization*  157

representing 15 percent of the population of developing countries. There are 16 million people undernourished in developed countries (United Nations Food and Agricultural Organization, 2012).

The number of undernourished people decreased nearly 30 percent in Asia and the Pacific, from 739 million to 563 million, largely due to socio-economic progress in many countries in the region. The prevalence of undernourishment in the region decreased from 23.7 percent to 13.9 percent.

Latin America and the Caribbean also made progress, falling from 65 million hungry in 1990–1992 to 49 million in 2010–2012, while the prevalence of undernourishment dipped from 14.6 percent to 8.3 percent. But the rate of progress has slowed recently.

The number of hungry grew in Africa over the period, from 175 million to 239 million, with nearly 20 million added in the last few years. Nearly one in four are hungry. And in sub-Saharan Africa, the modest progress achieved in recent years up to 2007 was reversed, with hunger rising 2 percent per year since then.

Developed regions also saw the number of hungry rise, from 13 million in 2004–2006 to 16 million in 2010–2012, reversing a steady decrease in previous years from 20 million in 1990–1992. (World Hunger Education Service 2013)

To an even worse extent, the World Health Organization (2010) estimates that, worldwide, one in three persons suffers from the effects of a lack of clean water. Global climate change also threatens the supply of clean water. Life-threatening shortages like these could just as well be characterized as a global shortage of time—the time needed to change attitudes and policies defended by corporations and wealthy states concerning the coming crises of water, food, air, and fuel shortages.

Globalization, as noted, is about speed, technologies, changing relations, and fixed spaces. These four generic attributes of organized human life on this planet have together inclined over the millennia toward more and more global systems. The capitalist world-system after 1500 grew to dominate the world itself, in large part because its remarkable new technologies allowed for speed in shipping and transportation, which changed the relations among all people on earth. All the while, the ability of local peoples to live in isolation in their own traditionally fixed spaces was crippled. The system that resulted, and began to outrun its own capacity for growth in the short twentieth century, was based on endless accumulation. For a long while the illusion was that the endless accumulation of capital was, if not an unqualified good, a value-neutral process. In its most arrogant form, this idea was, all too simply, *The good get the goods; the lesser folk get what they deserve.* The extremes of inequality have, for all intents and purpose, made any type of global revolution, whether of the fluid or mechanical kind, virtually unthinkable.

Hence, the terrible prospect for the future of globalization. Capitalism has produced and accumulated more global wealth than once was beyond imagination. Its corollary effect is a comparable rise in the number of impoverished people the world over. This perverse proportion, if not an equation, is at least a real structural change in the relations among people, but also, and most terribly, of all people to the earth.

There can hardly be any doubt that the more serious crises facing the world as a whole are due to a global drive for more and more stuff. Food, water, fuel, and air are suffering shortages for one reason. Endless economic growth puts junk into the air and water, which in turn undermines food production—and these because, as capitalism has come to be since the short twentieth century, the global economy has become more, not less, dependent on fossil fuels. Movements to convert fuel sources to water, wind, and air power run up against the drive for economic growth. Endless all-consumption accumulation cannot help but fill the global attic with junk. All global waters, especially the fresh ones, are spoiled by chemical and material junk, by the detritus of human and industrial waste. As our garbage feeds hogs whose fecal waste poisons waters, so global industries spill chemicals and wasted fuel into the air and waters. Attics and junkyards are but odorless sewers for the disposal of the waste of mindless, unlimited growth. When all is well, we never think about the stuff we flush away, but there comes a time, which has come already to much of the world, when there is no place to rid ourselves of the stuff we expel.

Globalization, of course, is about the whole of this world. But it is also about how the moving parts of the whole are related to one another. In the days of Henry Ford, workers suffered, but still many thought the economic future was bright. In the days after Hitler killed himself, it was thought that a new world was before us. In the days after Mikhail Gorbachev turned off the lights of the Soviet system on Christmas day, 1991, it was thought that capitalism had won the day. Then in the days after September 11, 2001, and the years that followed, all the dreams of a new world have withered away in the fog of global uncertainty.

The Future of Globalization  159

## WHAT WILL BECOME OF GAIA?

New futures always, but especially in a time like ours, are hard, if not impossible, to predict. But they can be imagined—and imagined responsibly—with reference to the facts of current history as we understand them. When it comes to worlds that cannot be known, one must imagine them, which is not the same thing as making them up. Myths, for example, are sometimes wrongly thought to be sheer imagination with no basis in discernible reality. But even the well-known ancient Hebrew creation myth, clearly in some basic sense fiction, has proven to be factual in other ways.

---

### THE HEBREW MYTH OF THE ORIGINS OF ALL THINGS

**1** In the beginning, when God created the universe, **2** the earth was formless and desolate. The raging ocean that covered everything was engulfed in total darkness, and the Spirit of God was moving over the water. **3** Then God commanded, "Let there be light"—and light appeared. **4** God was pleased with what he saw. Then he separated the light from the darkness, **5** and he named the light "Day" and the darkness "Night." Evening passed and morning came—that was the first day.

**6–7** Then God commanded, "Let there be a dome to divide the water and to keep it in two separate places"—and it was done. So God made a dome, and it separated the water under it from the water above it. **8** He named the dome "Sky." Evening passed and morning came—that was the second day.

**9** Then God commanded, "Let the water below the sky come together in one place, so that the land will appear"—and it was done. **10** He named the land "Earth," and the water which had come together he named "Sea." And God was pleased with what he saw. **11** Then he commanded, "Let the earth produce all kinds of plants, those that bear grain and those that bear fruit"—and it was done. **12** So the earth produced all kinds of plants, and God was pleased with what he saw. **13** Evening passed and morning came—that was the third day.

**14** Then God commanded, "Let lights appear in the sky to separate day from night and to show the time when days, years, and religious festivals begin; **15** they will shine in the sky to give light to the earth"—and it was done. **16** So God made the two larger lights, the sun to rule over the day and the moon to rule over the night; he also made the stars. **17** He placed

## 160 CHAPTER SEVEN

the lights in the sky to shine on the earth, **18** to rule over the day and the night, and to separate light from darkness. And God was pleased with what he saw. **19** Evening passed and morning came—that was the fourth day.

**20** Then God commanded, "Let the water be filled with many kinds of living beings, and let the air be filled with birds." **21** So God created the great sea monsters, all kinds of creatures that live in the water, and all kinds of birds. And God was pleased with what he saw. **22** He blessed them all and told the creatures that live in the water to reproduce and to fill the sea, and he told the birds to increase in number. **23** Evening passed and morning came—that was the fifth day.

**24** Then God commanded, "Let the earth produce all kinds of animal life: domestic and wild, large and small"—and it was done. **25** So God made them all, and he was pleased with what he saw.

**26** Then God said, "And now we will make human beings; they will be like us and resemble us. They will have power over the fish, the birds, and all animals, domestic and wild, large and small." (Genesis 1)

Whether or not a god hovered over the creation, which took more than a few days, the general order of events is correct. The Big Bang took place in an incalculably distant past, but it was as a strike of light on gases that charged the original chemicals to make the waters and, in time, lands on which the living creatures came to be. One can hardly have missed the fact that the ancient Judeo-Christian story of creation still today is a subject of contention between Biblical literalists and serious science. Creationism and evolutionary theory are not, I don't mind saying (as a scientist of sorts who is also a practicing Christian), equal and equivalent theories of origins. Myths may contain and express truths, but, by their nature, they cannot be taken literally.

## HESIOD'S THEOGONY: THE BIRTH OF GAIA, MOTHER EARTH (CA. 700 BCE, GREEK)

Verily at the first Chaos came to be, but next wide-bosomed Earth, the ever-sure foundations of all the deathless ones who hold the peaks of snowy Olympus, and dim Tartarus in the depth of the wide-pathed Earth, and Eros (Love), fairest among the deathless gods, who unnerves the limbs and overcomes the mind and wise counsels of all gods and all men within them. From Chaos came forth Erebus and black Night; but of Night were

> born Aether and Day, whom she conceived and bare from union in love with Erebus. And Earth first bare starry Heaven, equal to herself, to cover her on every side, and to be an ever-sure abiding-place for the blessed gods. And she brought forth long Hills, graceful haunts of the goddess-Nymphs who dwell amongst the glens of the hills. She bare also the fruitless deep with his raging swell, Pontus, without sweet union of love. But afterwards she lay with Heaven and bare deep-swirling Oceanus, Coeus and Crius and Hyperion and Iapetus, Theia and Rhea, Themis and Mnemosyne and gold-crowned Phoebe and lovely Tethys. After them was born Cronos the wily, youngest and most terrible of her children, and he hated his lusty sire.

There is, however, a creation myth that expresses a now-familiar scientific principle called the Gaia hypothesis. The Gaia myth of the earth's origins was composed around 700 BCE by Hesiod, a Greek contemporary of Homer. The Gaia (or Earth) creation myth enjoys quite a few parallels to the Hebraic one—but with one difference. Gaia does not subdivide the things and creatures of the earth. The gods are one with man, as, by implication, are all organisms and material things. Gaia, in other words, is an organized whole.

The Gaia myth was picked up in 1972 by an English geophysicist, James Lovelock, and termed the Gaia theory of the earth (Lovelock 1989, 216):

> Like coevolution, Gaia reflects the apartheid of Victorian biology and geology, but it goes much further. Gaia theory is about the evolution of a tightly coupled system whose constituents are the biota and their material environment, which comprises the atmosphere, the oceans, and the surface rocks. Self-regulation of important properties, such as climate and chemical composition, is seen as a consequence of this evolutionary process. Like living organisms and many closed loop self-regulating systems, it would be expected to show emergent properties; that is, the whole will be more than the sum of the parts. This kind of system is notoriously difficult, if not impossible, to explain by cause and effect logic, as practicing inventors know to their cost. It is doubtful also if the fashionable and trendy use of Popperian falsification tests, so valuable for theories in physics, are really applicable to such systems. Consider, for example, the problem faced by someone unfamiliar with Earth-based life of designing a test to show that a Lombardy poplar tree was alive. These trees are all males and hence can be propagated only by cuttings, and 90 [percent] or more of a fully grown

## 162 CHAPTER SEVEN

tree is dead wood and dead bark with just a thin skin of living tissue around the circumference of the wood. Then there is the question, what does the word "alive" mean? Biologists studiously avoid trying to answer it.

The earth, says Lovelock, is a system comprising living and material things, organized without clear demarcation among the air, sea, and rocks provided by, in the word of the original myth, mother Gaia herself.

Recently, Gaia theory has entered the social science of globalization through the work of Bruno Latour, the French social scientist and theorist. Latour's stunningly original and unorthodox book, *An Inquiry into Modes of Existence: An Anthropology of the Moderns* (2013), pulls together work, both empirical and theoretical, he has been doing for a good quarter century. Over the years, Latour developed two important themes, both of which have disturbed the assumptions of more traditional theorists.

One of Latour's daring ideas was first put forth in *We Have Never Been Modern* (1991). Latour argues that moderns, culturally speaking, cast their lot with the massively wrong axiom that the social belongs to a different, and privileged, realm from the natural. Among other problems with this kind of thinking is that it is at odds with the practices of all proper sciences, wherein, to make it all too simple, whatever the object of investigation, it is studied as part of a field, or network, in which the human or social cannot be set apart. By contrast, modern liberal cultures, including academic fields like the humanities and social sciences, understand human thinking narrowly as a property of "Man," or the human being. As a corollary, social action is thought to be where the world's action is, and natural events are somehow lesser, more passive, and therefore less real. Put this way, the axiom of the modern is clearly nonsense to those who pay any serious attention to how the world actually works.

Latour's second important theme follows from the first. *Reassembling the Social: An Introduction to Actor-Network Theory* (2005) is his most systematic effort to redefine his own primary disciplines—social studies, including sociology. This must be done if one starts, as he does, with the rule that social things cannot be analytically distinguished from natural ones. Hence, Latour's twist on the theory of action as always and everywhere, organized in networks in which *actants* (his word)—whether humans, birds, rocks, or grains of sand—move together in discernible patterns. Rock slides, sand storms, and floods, like the migration of birds and humans, each and all (and more) are actants, without regard to their differences. Latour thus defines networks in a mildly comic manner by the phrases "surprise of association," "heterogeneous connections," "traverse domains," "networks of irreductions," and "extended associations" (Latour 2013, 488–489). Admittedly, the phrases are inscrutable. But the key concept, if there is but one, is *actant,* which is a play on the more usual sociological term *actor. Actant* is meant, among other effects, to dissolve the fixed connotation of *network*. Everything is what it is. Nothing cannot be reduced to anything else. Every connection is heterogeneous—a coming together of different things in surprising relations that can extend themselves in all directions (which is to say transversely). Hence, the remarkable statement in one of his earliest books: "everything happens only once, and at one place" (Latour 1988, 162). Plus, in all he says, there is the ghost of Lovelock's statement: "Gaia theory is about the evolution of a tightly coupled system whose constituents are the biota and their material environment." Everything happens once and everything is its own thing connected to other things living and material.

To be sure, Latour is a heavily complicated thinker whose ideas are hard going. At every level, he challenges the basic philosophical principles of the modern culture—that social things are somehow both separate from natural things and, in effect, superior. Complicated though it may be, Latour's theory is an expression of Gaia theory in a form that is, through and through, global. It means to account for the connection of all things on the earth by putting them on the same plane of existence—above all, no social/nature divide. Though a theory, it is a theory well enough certified by its ability to account for the fatal flaw in modern culture—its assumption that this one culture is the key to human progress. As such, Latour's ideas are a strong theory of globalization. If all things on the earth are connected without any one being reducible to any other, then all things face the risks and benefits of whatever might present itself before mother earth, Gaia. Still a theory, to be sure, but also a principle that, in its way, encourages an optimistic attitude toward unknown worlds to come.

Latour's revision of the Gaia principle raises the question any attempt to come to terms with globalization must address. Which as-yet-unknown worlds will come into being as our known world passes away?

## AMID THE UNCERTAINTIES: THREE POSSIBLE FUTURES

The uncertainty of the present situation is not entirely bad. When all the promises of endless growth, of better societies, of new worlds, of the end

164 CHAPTER SEVEN

of inequalities, collapse into the real world, where all grand promises are empty, then we must face the sober truth of the nature of things. This is the one good that can lead to honest change and realistic hope. Or, put more crudely, to embrace uncertainty is to smell the material and ideological waste that issues from the ruins of a system at its limits.

Once the deep stink of all that is rotten in the world is beyond any degree of normalizing deodorant, there is at least the possibility for a new kind of optimism. It would be wrong, for example, to assert that today's world early in the twenty-first century is not better than it was, say, in the mid-nineteenth century. Not better for all, not even better on average perhaps, but better at least in the sense that, inequalities notwithstanding, today's world exposes the promise of progress more honestly available to serious thought. Strange as it may seem to say, one of the hidden effects of globalization is that the very idea ultimately forces consideration less of the ideals than the realities. In practical terms, the real is what cannot be ignored—and therefore what has long been in force, even as false hopes, distorting ideologies, and evil promises serve to distract attention away from the harsh realities.

## *CLIMATE CHANGE: EVIDENCE & CAUSES*—AN OVERVIEW FROM THE ROYAL SOCIETY AND THE US NATIONAL ACADEMY OF SCIENCES

Since the mid-1800s, scientists have known that $CO_2$ is one of the main greenhouse gases of importance to Earth's energy balance. Direct measurements of $CO_2$ in the atmosphere and in air trapped in ice show that atmospheric $CO_2$ increased by about 40% from 1800 to 2012. Measurements of different forms of carbon reveal that this increase is due to human activities. Other greenhouse gases (notably methane and nitrous oxide) are also increasing as a consequence of human activities. The observed global surface temperature rise since 1900 is consistent with detailed calculations of the impacts of the observed increase in atmospheric $CO_2$ (and other human-induced changes) on Earth's energy balance.

Different influences on climate have different signatures in climate records. These unique fingerprints are easier to see by probing beyond a single number (such as the average temperature of Earth's surface), and looking instead at the geographical and seasonal patterns of climate change. The observed patterns of surface warming, temperature changes through

> the atmosphere, increases in ocean heat content, increases in atmospheric moisture, sea level rise, and increased melting of land and sea ice also match the patterns scientists expect to see due to rising levels of $CO_2$ and other human-induced changes.
>
> The expected changes in climate are based on our understanding of how greenhouse gases trap heat. Both this fundamental understanding of the physics of greenhouse gases and fingerprint studies show that natural causes alone are inadequate to explain the recent observed changes in climate. Natural causes include variations in the Sun's output and in Earth's orbit around the Sun, volcanic eruptions, and internal fluctuations in the climate system (such as El Niño and La Niña). Calculations using climate models have been used to simulate what would have happened to global temperatures if only natural factors were influencing the climate system. These simulations yield little warming, or even a slight cooling, over the 20th century. Only when models include human influences on the composition of the atmosphere are the resulting temperature changes consistent with observed changes. (Royal Society 2014, 5)

If today there is one global reality that cannot much longer be ignored, Latour's version of the Gaia principle helps put it front and center. Climate change is real. It cannot be explained without considering the human causes. While climate change is not by any means the only Gaia effect at work in the world, it is surely the most serious and immediate. Its familiar causal chain threatens us all: *overreliance on carbon fuels > atmospheric warming > melting ice caps > warming seas > dying sea life and rising seas > flooding coast lines and natural disasters > human settlements at risk.* To make matters worse, each of the causal links is (in Latour's word) transverse, moving up and through many layers and networks of earthly life and things. The reality of it all, very well documented by serious science, is what allows for a degree of optimism about the global future. The causes of the crisis are a known world. Powerful economic interests want nothing to do with alternatives to fossil fuels on which they have long staked their global bets. Yet technologies exist that are capable of changing the relations of social beings to each other and, in turn, to the earth. Solar, wind, water, and nuclear power are slowly but deliberately moving into the energy sector of human communities. Most are renewable. Some, like nuclear power, carry their own risks. Others, like the sun and the winds it stirs, are just there for the taking. All entail costs, to be sure. But none involves the terrible consequences of fossil fuels.

## 166 CHAPTER SEVEN

Will the economic interests vested in petroleum yield to necessity? Will alternative sources of power become as able to accumulate capital wealth? Will the common sense of political and cultural leaders force the hand of the capitalists? The answers are unknown, but there are signs that change is at least on the table, and some changes, like wind-generated power, appear to be a winning hand. The human animal is as stupid as any other. We follow habits, if not instincts. We fear and flee violent change. Just the same, there is more than a little evidence from times of terrible human disasters that we are willing to face up to certain realities. If attacked, people will fight back. If neighbors are at risk of flood and fire, we pitch in to do what can be done. If others are dying of disease or famine, many will put themselves at risk to help.

Yet overoptimism is not a solution. Nor is overly confident trust in human good. Yet there is a degree of confidence that could be inspired if we were to consider that, in the order of all things, human beings are not inherently so superior to natural things that they can live without or escape them. To capture the basic truth of nature, in all its aspects, could lead us to help save the world by accepting the Gaia principle that all things are swept along by the sands of time. When it comes to being and surviving, humility is always the better attitude.

If *optimism* is a primary attitude toward the unknown worlds, then the second, perhaps more realistic, approach to the future would be *cautious optimism*. While the more optimistic attitude begins with the dire nature of global forces, a more cautious approach would be one that takes serious account of the economic realities. When it comes to human economies, caution is always the more prudent approach.

Capitalism remains the dominant force in the global economy. So far as can be seen, it will always rely on endless capital accumulation. Capitalist greed has caused terrible human waste and violence. At the same time, capitalism, especially as it has evolved in our day, has been a force for change. The quest for endless accumulation is also an impetus for growth—which, for better or worse, is also a force for change. Capitalism is rapacious, to be sure, but its obsession with change also makes it capacious. Capitalism has always altered and expanded global capacity for new technologies, new relations, speed, and, by consequence, an occasional promise of better ways to overcome the conflicts arising from fixed spaces. Gold, like fossil fuels, is stored deep in the earth. To get at buried wealth, the earth must be mined. By contrast, wind and solar power, like water and even nuclear power, can be farmed. Farming can have its risks, to be sure, but even the greediest farmer realizes that he cannot finally destroy the source of his wealth. Zygmunt Bauman reminds that mining steals from the earth, while farming promotes its growth. Capitalism does both, but the cautious promise it holds out is that it, too, has an interest in growth of all kinds. Wealth may be capitalism's reason for being, but to accumulate capital wealth it must invent technologies that cannot help but change the relations of humans to the earth as to one another.

The hard plow and the stirrup made large-scale farming possible, which in turn forced peasants off their land to the factory towns. Factories make rapid, industrial production possible, for which workers suffered dreadful working conditions. Industrial products made cheap, useful products available to the masses, which in turn standardized not only the products but the work lives of industrial workers. When, in time, industries became larger, more visible work places, the ability of workers to organize for better working conditions grew. That, however, made them vulnerable to capital greed, which succeeded, to a degree, in undermining the rights of workers to organize. Organized, large-scale industry eventually outgrew the assembly line as technologies automated production, which, in another turn, put the older industrial factories out of business, which left once-thriving towns poor and decrepit. Then new industrial technologies grew the world over as capital sought the cheapest possible labor costs by deploying near-miraculous instruments of informational technologies to automate production. And so on. Nothing is ever simple, least of all capitalism. It mines and wastes. It invents and grows new links, many of them transverse and all of them networked.

## WORLD'S RURAL SETTLEMENTS DISAPPEARING

Africa's urban population will increase from 414 million to over 1.2 billion by 2050, while that of Asia will soar from 1.9 billion to 3.3 billion. Both regions together will account for 86 per cent of all increase in the world's urban population. . . . This unprecedented increase in urban population will provide new opportunities to improve education and public services in Africa and Asia, as more concentrated populations become easier to reach. However, this will also pose new challenges of providing urban jobs, housing, energy and infrastructure to mitigate urban poverty, expansion of slums and a deterioration of the urban environment.

## 168  CHAPTER SEVEN

> With half of humanity living in cities today, urbanization is a critical issue. . . . Cities are where the pressures of migration, globalization, economic development, social inequality, environmental pollution and climate change are most directly felt. Yet at the same time they are the engines of the world economy and centers of innovation where many solutions to global problems are being piloted. . . .
>
> The largest increases in urban population are expected in the following countries: India, China, Nigeria, the United States of America and Indonesia. Over the next four decades (2010 to 2050), India will add another 497 million to its urban population; China—341 million, Nigeria—200 million, the United States—103 million and Indonesia—92 million.
>
> The projected increase in urban population in India and Nigeria between 2010 and 2050 will be higher than that of the past 40 years. This trend is particularly prominent in Nigeria, where its urban population grew by only 65 million between 1970 and 2010, and yet it is now projected to increase more than three times between 2010 and 2050, thus by 200 million. (United Nations Population Division 2012)

Capitalism is growth. Growth creates problems, some of them impossible to solve. Growth creates opportunities, many of them good. The rural farm fades away, the urban metropolis dominates. People are networked more closely. They get in each other's way. They suffer and gain from what capitalism does to all things around.

Nevertheless, capitalism is not a free-standing network. Quite apart from Latour's strong theory of networks and actants, Wallerstein's work on the history of the capitalist world-system introduces an element that straightforward Gaia theory cannot. Whether of social or natural origins, all things have a history. This was, at least, one of the basic principles of French historian Fernand Braudel. There are three kinds of history, Wallerstein thinks (following Braudel): of events, of structural conjunctures, and of the long-enduring relations where the human must contend with nature's more durable material realities. For every individual who must leave her village, babe in arms, there are deserts or mountains to traverse or seas to cross—after, that is, she finds a way to hide from the armed militia or customs agents that serve the will of revolutionary or civil officials. Migrating individuals, structural changes, and long-barren deserts are all and each part and parcel of the capitalist world-system. And that system in its own way has a history, which means that it is vulnerable to change—to beginnings and endings.

When the modern and capitalist world-system begins to falter, as it seems to have, there are but two ways things can go: "one that results in a non-capitalist system that retains all the worst features of capitalism (hierarchy, exploitation, and polarization); or one that lays the basis for a system that is based on relative democratization and relative egalitarianism, a kind of system that has never yet existed" (Wallerstein 2013b). There could not be a clearer illustration of the cautiously optimistic attitude toward future worlds. Either the capitalist system gives way to some other that fails in much the same way or another, more democratic and fair system takes its place. The one is not so good; the other good and hopeful. The caution of the former is qualified by the optimism of the latter.

There is, however, a good, if insufficient, argument for caution that is not optimistic that capitalism will ever give way to a seriously democratic system unlike any its deep market philosophy has ever considered. Capitalism, as it has become, has always been modern, and the modern has always professed democracy as its necessary political form.

The modern idea of democracy was always a liberal bourgeois democracy bound up from the beginning with capitalism. Hobsbawm, not by any means an optimist, was right on this. The question, of course, is whether

---

## THE GREAT REVOLUTION OF 1789–1848

The revolution which broke out between 1789 and 1848 ... forms the greatest transformation in human history since the ancient times when men invented agriculture and metallurgy, writing, the city and the state. This revolution has transformed, and contributed to transform, the entire world. But in considering it we must distinguish carefully between its long-range results, which cannot be confined to any social framework, political organization, or distribution of international power and resources, and its early and decisive phase, which was closely tied to a specific social and international situation. The great revolution of 1789–1848 was the triumph not of "industry" as such, but of *capitalist* industry; not of liberty and equality in general, but of middle class or "*bourgeois*" liberal society; not of "the modern economy" nor "the modern state," but the economies and states of a particular region (part of Europe and a few patches of North America), whose center was neighboring and rival states of Great Britain and France. The transformation of 1789–1848 is essentially the twin upheaval which took place in these two countries, and was propagated thence across the entire world. (Hobsbawm 1962, 17)

## 170 CHAPTER SEVEN

such a world-transforming change as the one that produced this imperfect form of democracy and modern capitalism could fall away in favor of some new, more democratic and egalitarian system. Capitalism both is and is not democratic.

Yet capitalism is also a global system that, as few consider, is both human and natural. Without workers and entrepreneurs, it would be nothing. Without material resources to mine or farm, it would have nothing tangible to produce. Good and bad, social and natural—capitalism stands athwart the world it aims to conquer and remake. Just the same, the fact remains that capitalism was, from its beginning, not just global but also systematic. The essence of capital enterprise is, as Weber taught, a culture of rational calculation that adjusts means to ends for the sake of endless accumulation.

Still, the system that began to find its global structure in the long sixteenth century is today no longer what it had been for a good half millennium. For one thing, what remains of the classic world-system does so without a core state; or, put more generally, none of the dominant global economies today enjoy enough political authority to control global affairs. As soon as the United States rose to unrivaled global prominence after World War II, it immediately became embroiled in a Cold War neither it nor any other power could win without destroying the whole. When all that ended, more or less around 1990, neither Russia nor China, not the United States nor the rising European Union was in a position to control global affairs by itself—as Great Britain once did, and as the Dutch and Iberians did in their times.

Capitalism remains and, in an important sense, reigns where once powerful states did. The peripheral, impoverished regions of the global economy are, in relative terms, as poor and as much exploited as they were through the tenure of the world-system. It is, in fact, fair to say that it is the global force of international business corporations that determines the world's political order. When labor markets, financial centers, consumer markets, and all else that makes capitalism work are dispersed around the globe, no one state or region has a free hand. Neither East Asia nor South Asia; not the European superstate nor the North Atlantic alliance is free to do as it pleases. Each has its strengths, but each and all are dependent on the markets and labor, technical genius, and purchasing power for whatever degree of global influence it may have. Some say that China is slipping as Japan did not long ago, and that India is the rising Asian giant. But India has a massive problem with its rural and urban poor. For a long while, the European Union was considered the world's most original and global political form, but now, as its population ages and its currency falters, Europe, still powerful, is no longer on an upward trajectory. The North Americans enjoy a considerable military and economic authority, but Brazil and Mexico, in particular, are global economies that limit America's onetime hemispheric dominance, as Russia limits Europe by virtue of its fuel resources, as the empty and melting Arctic emerges out of the cold to become a global pathway and a now-open source of minerals and fuel.

Many consider today's global structures multipolar, with many vectors of economic and political force. Though capitalism, for better or worse, remains the one constant power, capitalism itself is being transformed. The wealth it generates is weirdly out of proportion to the good it does. National or global wealth, however great it may be, means nothing to the millions upon millions it excludes, to say nothing of the added millions who get by on hard work but cannot get ahead.

Thomas Piketty, in *Capital in the Twenty-First Century* (2014), has made it clear that wealth seems destined always to outrun the growth of income, which is to say that capital accumulation has redounded, as it still does, to the well-off few. Yet Piketty (2014, 572) concludes with the remarkably simple solution of a progressive annual tax on capital—a tax so small in its effect on wealth that it would not discourage capitalism, but would yield enough surplus to encourage global income growth. Could this happen? Is Piketty right? For the time being, all that matters is that pessimistic as one might be about the ability of capitalism to change or to yield its way to a better system, Piketty's idea is so simple, even obvious, that it suggests that someone out there will find a politically viable solution that turns global capitalism back on its head.

After *optimism* and *caution,* a third possible way of imagining a future world is, it hardly need be said, *pessimism.* One might at first suppose pessimism imagines a world headed nowhere good. But that clearly is not true. Pessimism is not nihilism. People, through the ages, have lived in worlds so one-dimensional and unchanging that anything like optimism was not in their vocabularies. In the West, generation upon generation endured a Dark Age of a near millennium, a mostly monotonic world of medieval slumber. Globally, it is hard to identify any civilization, ancient or premodern, without a medieval age of its own. Yet all these—even the most resistant to change—eventually gave way less to revolutions than to some prospect of a better world.

## 172 CHAPTER SEVEN

Pessimism, whatever else it is, is basically a deeply inbred cultural sensibility—one that persists in compliance with dominating systems that impose and enforce a narrowly bleak attitude toward a world they control. Very often, these have been systems where religions or their functional equivalents point common cultures toward some distant or transcendent other world. But religion is far from the only hegemonic culture. Modern cultures think of themselves as free-thinking and progressive. Just the same, they too are stubborn in their commitment to an exaggerated idea that history is moving ever forward to some future fulfillment of a better world. Even capitalism, to some the hope for a future, is medieval in its own way—in particular the way its wealth justifies the exclusion of the poor as somehow their failure to thrive.

Pessimism, or skepticism, toward a future world is far from being utterly negative. In fact, it would seem that studied uncertainty, so valued in modern science, is at least as promising a cultural attitude for the invention of or facing up to a new world. At the least, pessimism, as a moral attitude, avoids the false certainty of overwrought optimism, which cannot help but incline in the long run toward despair. Pessimism shares a good bit with the caution of the cautiously optimistic. If one wonders what evidence a thorough pessimism toward the future might offer, one only need take the arguments for caution as serious, if not sufficient, on their own terms. In this world, perhaps all worlds, there is no limit of good reasons to doubt where things are going.

In a global situation such as the one prevailing still early in the twenty-first century, when the end of our known worlds seems quite at hand, it may well be that a healthy dose of pessimism is in order. Or, better, we might call it skepticism. While the difference is small, sheer pessimism can encourage if not nihilism, a kind of historical gloom, which is hardly what is needed to face whatever comes next. On the other hand, skepticism, as it is used in common parlance, tends to retain an element of, to be a bit glib, "getting things done." Pessimism can trail off into futility. Skepticism can clarify action. Either way, radical doubt as to what comes with the new dawn is not all that different from the attitude the early explorers in the sixteenth century must have had. Columbus, Magellan, and the others surely had good reason to trust that they were not going to fall into an abyss at the end of the world. They also had a clear vision of what lay out there beyond their known world—some version of the wealth of Asia that Marco Polo had been the first to bring back. Yet if not pessimistic, they had to have

## The Future of Globalization  173

been at least skeptical as to where they were going and what they would find. Otherwise, Columbus would not have so radically misjudged how far he had sailed, and where he was, when first he came to land. Nor, clearly, would Magellan have gotten himself killed in the Philippines had he not suffered a naively false attitude as to what the locals would do when he presumed the superiority of his powers. Overconfidence in one's own ways is the flip side of a dysfunctional pessimism toward a new, unknown world. This may not amount to an honest skepticism, but it does suggest the extent to which radical doubt is never far away from innocence.

If there is a serious proponent of skepticism in respect to social theory and global futures, it would be Zygmunt Bauman. Not many intellectuals have experiences with failed worlds and the suffering they bring. Bruno Latour is from a family of privilege in France. Immanuel Wallerstein is from a family in which both brothers became world leaders in their fields after enjoying the accessibility to culture and education available in New York City, which also provided inspiration for his early study of South Asian and African struggles for independence from domination and poverty. Manuel Castells came of age during Franco's totalitarian regime in Spain but fled first to France, then the United States. Such is the range of normal backgrounds of critical theorists of the world. Bauman's early life in his native Poland, on the other hand, was fraught with the horrors of the Nazi invasions, and then Soviet domination. Always a political leftist, Bauman was recognized for his role in resistance movements against his country's militaristic invaders.

It is a mistake to assume that an intellectual's way of thinking owes to his or her personal background. Yet when it comes to a robust pessimism, it is sometimes likely that those who are skeptics very often have seen worlds fail, as Bauman did. He ties in with his later writings on wasted lives and liquid modernity by drawing on a figure of speech Marx and Engels used (in *The Manifesto of the Communist Party*): the melting away of the world under industrial capitalism. While some of Marx's political ideas held out the hope that a worker's revolution could install a new world of radical democracy led by the people, those who adopted a version of his state socialism of the people in the early Soviet Union and in Mao's cultural revolution in China created the unspeakable horrors of gulags and reeducation exiles. Bauman, to be sure, never inclined toward blind appropriation of dangerous ideas like these. If anything, he fought against them, both on the ground in Poland and in his writings after 1971 in England. Still, of all the major interpreters of global realities, Bauman's core ideas usually return to the conviction that the modern world is deadly, wasting away both human and material things. He favors farming as a figure for life in this world, but he recognizes that capitalism mines the biotic and material things from which it extracts its profits.

To allow oneself the benefits of a rigorous pessimism as to the future is to live honestly with the pervasive reality of life itself. All life is sailing toward death. There is no ship that can get around or beyond that. If there is a serious weakness of optimisms of all kinds—and of Gaia optimism in particular—it would be that it so accentuates possibilities, including those brought into view by leveling of all things in the world, that the reality of death is occluded. This may seem to be a statement that steps over the negative limit of pessimism as a way of looking at worlds to come. Yet given that any particular general attitude gets sloppy at its edges, any attempt to estimate a radically different future is, at best, a way of suggesting possibilities, not stipulating outcomes. A suggestion, thus, is an informed guess.

---

## THE GLOBAL FUTURE AT SEA

One thing which even the most seasoned and discerning masters of the art of choice do not and cannot choose, is the society to be born into—and so we are all in travel, whether we like it or not. We have not been asked about our feelings anyway. Thrown into a vast open sea with no navigation charts and all the marker buoys sunk and barely visible, we have only two choices left: we may rejoice in the breath-taking vistas of new discoveries—or we may tremble out of fear of drowning. One option not really realistic is to claim sanctuary in a safe harbour; one could bet that what seems to be a tranquil haven today will be soon modernized, and a theme park, amusement promenade or crowded marina will replace the sedate boat sheds. The third option not thus being available, which of the two other options will be chosen or become the lot of the sailor depends in no small measure on the ship's quality and the navigation skills of the sailors. Not all ships are seaworthy, however. And so the larger the expanse of free sailing, the more the sailor's fate tends to be polarized and the deeper the chasm between the poles. A pleasurable adventure for the well-equipped yacht may prove a dangerous trap for a tattered dinghy. In the last account, the difference between the two is that between life and death. (Bauman 1998)

## The Future of Globalization

Thus, to consider life for what it is in relation to death is to consider the reality of the limits of all things. Even mountains are not forever. Among living creatures, only the cockroach seems to have had not more than a practical immortality. For all the remainder of things on earth, there are limits, which is to say limits to times and spaces, to tools and technologies, and, above all, to the relations any and all have to each other. To take seriously limits is not sheer morbidity and certainly not nihilism. Healthy pessimism, when it comes to futures, is in its way at least mature. Unknown worlds, by definition, cannot be known. In respect to the future, what seems to be driven by skepticism, if not pessimism, may be the only realistic atitude. No one knows. Any effort to know the unknown would seem to be a fool's errand. Yet in times like these, when there are compelling reasons to think the world is changing beyond what was a sure thing not that long ago, we humans are all on an errand into the wilderness (as Perry Miller [1956] famously characterized the early English settlements in the North American wilds). To be modern is, more often than not, to consider practical life a series of errands—shorter, sometimes longer, efforts to get things done in order to make a future more or less better. We come to a global future with cultural baggage in hand. We can only think as we have been taught to think, which means that if the future is actually unknown and unknowable, then we face it ill-equipped. Then too, all who venture over the seas beyond known worlds are less well equipped than they would like to be.

To thus venture forth may well be the one quality of human being that surpasses lesser things. We face the winds of life in small boats with crude maps. That we do is a matter that modern, globalizing cultures have pressed upon us for at least a half millennium. If we continue to delude ourselves that we can spoil the seas and lands while colonizing the world, we will lapse into a fatal ignorance. Ignorance may be part of human nature, but whatever the unknown worlds may become, from what we know of the actual present, they are unlikely *not* to turn on us. Storms, floods, droughts, and rising seas are already normal. They may be the revenge of nature. We may not ever know. But our children's children will. That should be enough to take the future more seriously than so far we have.

# REFERENCES

Agamben, G. (1998) *Homo Sacer: Sovereign Power and Bare Life*. Stanford, CA: Stanford University Press.

———. (2000) *Means with Ends: Notes on Politics*. Minneapolis and London: University of Minnesota Press.

Arrighi, G. (1994) *The Long Twentieth Century: Money, Power, and the Origins of Our Times*. London: Verso Books.

Attali, J. (2014) "The Last Chance for Israel and Palestine." *Huffington Post*, July 15. www.huffingtonpost.com/jacques-attali/the-last-chance-for-israe_b_5586936.html. Accessed August 28, 2014.

Bauman, Z. (1998) *Globalization: The Human Consequences*. Cambridge, UK: Polity Press.

———. (2000) *Liquid Modernity*. Cambridge, UK: Polity Press.

———. (2004) *Wasted Lives: Modernity and Its Outcasts*. Cambridge, UK: Polity Press.

Berman, M. (1982) *All That Is Solid Melts into Air: The Experience of Modernity*. New York: Penguin Books.

Braudel, F. (1969*) Écrits sur l'histoire*. Paris: Flammarion.

———. (1972 [1949]). *The Mediterranean and the Mediterranean World in the Age of Philip II*. New York: Harper and Row.

Castells, M. (2006) "The Network Society: From Knowledge to Policy," in Castells, M., and Gustavo, C., eds., *The Network Society*. Washington, DC: Johns Hopkins Center for Transatlantic Relations.

Diamond, J. (1997) *Guns, Germs, and Steel: The Fates of Human Societies*. New York: W. W. Norton.

## R-2 References

Dicken, P. (1992) *Global Shift: The Internationalization of Economic Activity.* London: Paul, Chapman.

Du Bois, W. E. B. (1935) *Black Reconstruction.* New York: Russell and Russell.

Foucault, M. (1978) *History of Sexuality, Volume 1: An Introduction.* New York: Pantheon Books.

Frank, A. G. (1992) "The Centrality of Central Asia Studies." *Studies in History* 8, 1 (February): 43–97. Also in *Bulletin of Concerned Asian Scholars* 24, 2 (April–June): 50–74.

———. (1998) *ReOrient: Economy in the Asian Age.* Berkeley, CA: University of California Press.

Friedman, T. (2000) *The Lexus and the Olive Tree: Understanding Globalization.* London and New York: HarperCollins Publishers.

Fuller, T. (2013) "Yangon Journal: As Myanmar Modernizes." *New York Times,* November 20: A6–8.

Fukuyama, F. (1992) *The End of History and the Last Man.* New York: The Free Press.

Fussell, P. (1975) *The Great War and Modern Memory.* Oxford, UK: Oxford University Press.

Gibbon, E. (1952 [1776–1789]; six volumes) *The History of the Decline and Fall of the Roman Empire.* London and New York: Penguin Books.

Giddens, A. (1990) *The Consequences of Modernity.* Stanford, CA: Stanford University Press.

———. (1999) *Runaway World.* Cambridge, UK: Polity Press.

Hannerz, U. (1996) *Transnational Connections: Culture, People, Places.* London and New York: Taylor Francis/Routledge.

Harvey, D. (1989) *The Condition of Postmodernity.* Oxford, UK: Blackwell Press.

Held, D., McGrew, A., Goldblatt, D., and Perraton, J. (1999) *Global Transformations: Politics, Economics, and Culture.* Cambridge, UK: Polity Press.

Hirst, P., and Thompson, G. (1990) *Globalization in Question.* Cambridge, UK: Polity Press.

Hobsbawm, E. (1962) *The Age of Revolution: 1789–1848.* New York: Penguin Books.

———. (1994) *The Age of Extremes: A History of the World, 1914–1991.* New York: Vintage Books.

Hoffman, S. (2002) "Clash of Globalizations: A New Paradigm?" *Foreign Affairs* (July/August). www.foreignaffairs.com/articles/58044/stanley-hoffmann/clash-of-globalizations. Accessed October 15, 2014.

Huntington, S. (1996) *Clash of Civilizations.* New York: Simon and Schuster.

Klein, N. (2004) "Reclaiming the Commons." In Mertes, T., ed., *A Movement of Movements.* London: Verso Books.

Kristof, N. (2014) "'Jane' Didn't Get the Help She Needed." *New York Times,* June 28. www.nytimes.com/2014/06/29/opinion/sunday/nicholas

-kristof-when-the-juvenile-justice-system-isnt-the-answer.html?_r=1. Accessed August 28, 2014.

Latour, B. (1988) *The Pasteurization of France*. Cambridge, MA: Harvard University Press.

———. (1991) *We Have Never Been Modern*. Cambridge, MA: Harvard University Press.

———. (2005) *Reassembling the Social: An Introduction to Actor-Network Theory*. Oxford, UK: Oxford University Press.

———. (2013) *An Inquiry into Modes of Existence: An Anthropology of the Moderns*. Cambridge, MA: Harvard University Press.

Lemert, C., Elliott, A., Chaffee, D., and Hsu, E., eds. (2010) *Globalization: A Reader*. London and New York: Routledge/Taylor and Francis.

Lovelock, J. A. (1989) "Geophysiology, the Science of Gaia." *Reviews of Geophysics* 17: 215–222.

Marx, Karl. (1976 [1867]; 3 volumes) *Capital*. Vintage Books Edition. New York: Random House.

Mbembe, A. (2003) "Necropolitics." *Public Culture* 15(1): 11–40.

Miller, P. (1956) *Errand into the Wilderness*. Cambridge, MA: Harvard University Press.

Ohmae, K. (1995) *The End of the Nation-State: The Rise of Regional Economies*. New York: Free Press.

Olinto, P., Beegle, K., Sobrado, C., and Uematsu, H. (2013) "The State of the Poor." *The World Bank: Poverty Reduction and Economic Management Network,* Number 125. www.worldbank.org/economicpremise. Accessed September 3, 2014.

Ong, A. (2006) *Neoliberalism as Exception: Mutations in Citizenship and Sovereignty*. Durham, NC: Duke University Press.

Piketty, T. (2014) *Capital in the Twenty-First Century*. Cambridge, MA: Harvard University Press.

Rostow, W. W. (1960) *Stages of Economic Growth: A Non-Communist Manifesto*. Cambridge, UK: Cambridge University Press.

Royal Society and US National Academy of Sciences. (2014) *Climate Change: Evidence and Causes*. http://nas-sites.org/americasclimatechoices/events/a-discussion-on-climate-change-evidence-and-causes/. Accessed September 3, 2014.

Rugman, A., and Hodgetts, R. (2001) "The End of Global Strategy." *European Management Journal* 19(4).

Scott, James C. (1998) *Seeing Like a State: How Certain Schemes to Improve the Human Condition Have Failed*. New Haven, CT: Yale University Press.

Sobel, D. (1995) *Longitude: The True Story of a Lone Genius Who Solved the Greatest Scientific Problem of His Times*. New York: Walker and Company.

## R-4 References

Suroor, H. (2013) "British Peer Reveals MI6 Role in Lumumba Killing." *Hindu.* Updated April 1. www.thehindu.com/news/international/world /british-peer-reveals-mi6-role-in-lumumba-killing/article4567513.ece. Accessed August 29, 2014.

Taylor, F. (2013) *The Downfall of Money: Germany's Hyperinflation and the Destruction of the Middle Class.* London and New York: Bloomsbury Press.

Taylor, F. W. (1911) *The Principles of Scientific Management.* New York: Harper and Row.

Toynbee, A. (1961 [1934–1961]; 12 volumes) *A Study of History.* Oxford, UK: Oxford University Press.

Turkle, S. (2011) *Alone Together.* New York: Basic Books.

United Nations Population Division. (2012) *World Urbanization Prospects.* New York: United Nations (press release, April 5).

United Nations Population Division. (2013) *World Urbanization Prospects.* New York: United Nations.

Wallerstein, I. (1974) *The Modern World-System I: Capitalist Agriculture and the Origins of the European World-Economy in the Sixteenth Century.* New York: Academic Press.

———. (2006) *World-Systems Analysis: An Introduction.* Durham, NC: Duke University Press.

———. (2013a, unpublished) "China, Africa, and the World-System Since 1945." November 19. New Haven: Yale University, Council on African Studies.

———. (2013b) "The Structural Crisis: Middle-Run Imponderables." *Commentary* 358 (January 15). www.iwallerstein.com/structural-crisis-middlerun -imponderables/. Accessed September 3, 2014.

Wallerstein, I., Lemert, C., and Rojas, C. (2012) *Uncertain Worlds: World-Systems Analysis in Changing Times.* Boulder, CO: Paradigm Publishers.

Weber, M. (1992 [1904–1905]) *The Protestant Ethic and the Spirit of Capitalism.* Translated by Talcott Parsons. New York and London: Routledge.

World Hunger Education Service. (2013) "2013 World Hunger and Poverty Facts and Statistics." Hunger Notes. www.worldhunger.org/articles/Learn /world%20hunger%20facts%202002.htm. Accessed October 17, 2014.

# INDEX

accumulation, 82–85, 116–121, 145–149, 154
actant, term, 163
actor-network theory, Latour on, 162–163
Africa: decolonization in, 151; hunger in, 157; urbanization in, 167–168
Agamben, Giorgio, 140
agriculture, 167; Latour on, 174; medieval, 39–40, 64, 71
Alexander the Great, 45–46
Alex Supertramp, 65
Al Jazeera, 130
American Century, 102–103
antiglobalists, 126, 133–136
Arab Spring, 139–140
Arrighi, Giovanni, 126–127
asceticism, worldly, 78
Asia, world-systems analysis on, 43–44
assembly line, 105, 107–108
astrolabe, 72
Australia, 123
automobiles, 105, 113
*axis mundi,* 33
Aztecs, 85

Bauman, Zygmunt, 83, 146–147, 167, 173–174; background of, 173
beginnings: of globalization, 36–64; importance of, 38
Beijing, 118
Bentham, Jeremy, 80–81
Berlin Wall, 110
Berman, Marshall, 148
Bessemer, Henry, 77, 112–113
Beyoncé, xiii
Big Bang, 160
bin Laden Osama, 3
Bitcoin, 114
Blair, Tony, 139
Boyle, Robert, 77
Braudel, Fernand, 98–99, 168
Brazil, 122
Bretton Woods Agreement, 73–74, 89, 133
BRIC nations, 122
Britain, 3–4, 27, 48, 57, 85; and assassination, 60; and colonialism, 68; and imperialism, 50; and measurement, 73; and sea power, 72; and Spanish Armada, 68

I-1

I-2 Index

Calvinism, 70, 77–78
Canada, 123
cannibalism, 6
capital accumulation, 82–85, 116–121, 145–149, 154
capitalism: versus empire, 59; ethic of, 53–56; future of, 166–175; new type of, 116–121; Piketty on, 150–151; and poverty, 101–102. *See also* fast capitalism
capitalist world system, 50–51, 54–62, 85–92; 1914–1991, 93–121; post–Cold War, 123
Castells, Manuel, 131–132; background of, 173
Catholicism, 78–79
cell phones, 14
Central Asia, world-systems analysis on, 43–44
Chaplin, Charlie, 105
China, 41, 88, 101, 112, 122; and assembly line, 107–108; and flexible accumulation, 117–118; and globalization, 41–43, 59; and imperialism, 49–50; and revolution, 151; and sovereign exception, 140–141; and state, 129–130, 137
Churchill, Winston, 51–52, 56, 110–112
Civil War, 104, 126–127
clash of civilizations theory, 19, 26, 127–128
climate change, xiv, 30–31; and crisis, 90–91; and floods, 37; future of, 164–166
CNN, 130
coal, 41–42
Cold War, 99, 102–103, 110–116
colonialism, 3–4, 57–58, 68
Columbus, Christopher, xi, 31, 67
commodities, 62–63; market in, 115–116
communication: globalization and, 7–8, 16–18. *See also* information technology
communism: Chinese, 112; Cold War

and, 110–116; collapse of, 18–19, 56
conflict: globalization and, 26–29; imperial disposition and, 40–41. *See also* violence
consumption, 62; new patterns of, 116–121; and waste, 145–149
Copernicus, Nicolaus, xi, 70
core, 86–87, 122–123
corporations, 10, 58; antiglobalists and, 133–134; and imperialism, 50; multinational, 130, 153; and world-systems, 61
credit crisis, 119–120
crises: credit, 119–120; oil, 133–134, 153–154; world-system and, 90–92
cultural globalization, 31–32; importance of, 62; theory and, 124–126
cyberspace: and cultural globalization, 31–32; life in, 20–25
Cyrus the Great, 45–46

da Gama, Vasco, 68
Darwin, Charles, 82
Dayal, Rajeshwar, 60
decolonization, 4, 34, 102, 153; effects of, 151
deconstruction, 20
Delambre, Jean-Baptiste, 73
Deng Xiaoping, 101, 154
Descartes, René, 79
Detroit, 108
developed nations, 87
developing nations, 87
Diamond, Jared, 66
Dicken, Peter, 132
Dinklage, Peter, xiii
disease, and crisis, 90–91
distance, globalization and, 20–23, 132, 138
Dutch, 58, 85

Earth, future of, 159–163
economic globalization, 32–33; importance of, 61–62; world-systems analysis and, 49–50

Index 🌐 I-3

Elizabeth I, queen of England, 63
email, 145
empire: versus capitalist world-system, 59; and development of world system, 45–56; ethic of, 55; Toynbee on, 47–48; World War I and, 102
Engels, Friedrich, 83
Enlightenment, 73, 80
environment, globalization and, 7
Europe: 1848 and, 127; and colonialism, 57, 68; World War I and, 103–104, 108–109
European Economic Community, 18
European Union, 121
event history, 98
evil, 26, 152–153
evolution, 82

Facebook, 20–21
farming. *See* agriculture
fast capitalism, 118
flexible accumulation, 116–121
floods, 36–38
Ford, Henry, 105
Fordism, 105–108, 112
France, 57–58, 85; and colonialism, 68; and measurement, 73; and religion, 79
Frank, Andre Gunder, 43–44, 50
Franklin, John, 5–6, 43
French Revolution, 58
Friedman, Thomas, 130–131
Fukuyama, Francis, 19, 127
Fussell, Paul, 104

Gaia: future of, 159–163; hypothesis of, 161–163; myth of, 160–161
Genghis Khan, 43, 55
geography, globalization and, 132
Germany, 74, 108–110, 121
Gibbons, Edward, 47
Giddens, Anthony, 139–140
Gilgamesh, 36–37
global economic system. *See* capitalist world system

globalists, 125–133
globalization: 1500–1914, 65–92; 1914–1991, 93–121; 1991–present, 122–141; beginning of, 36–64; capitalism and, 56–62; dark side of, 1–15, 92, 133–136; future of, 126, 142–175; nature of, xii–xiv, 16–35; stances on, 125–126; and standardization, 72–76; term, xii, 14, 18–20; types of, 29–30
Golding, William, 1–2
gold standard, 73, 113–114
good, 152–153
Great Depression, 107
Greece, 46, 48, 51–52
Greenwich Mean Time, 72
growth: effects of, 158; future of, 166–168; necessity of, 59, 84–85; stages of, 88
Guiyu, 146
Gutenberg, Johannes, 70

Han Dynasty, 41–43
Hannerz, Ulf, 132–133
Harvey, David, 116
Held, David, 136–139
Herodotus, 51
Hesiod, 160–161
Higgs boson, 125
Hindenburg, Paul von, 110
Hirst, Paul, 133–134
historical conjuncture, 149
history, 97–99, 153; ancient versus modern conceptions of, 51–55; types of, 168
Hitler, Adolf, 3, 55–56, 109–110
Hobsbawm, Eric, 99–100, 169
Hodgetts, Richard, 133–134
Hoffman, Stanley, 29–30, 34, 61–62, 128
homelessness, 8, 10
Hong Kong, 140–141
hope, 149
human relations: changes in, 29–35; globalization and, 145; technology and, 18, 20–25

## I-4 · Index

human rights, sovereign exception and, 140–141
hunger, 156–157
Huntington, Samuel, 19, 127–128

imperial disposition, 40–41; economic motives and, 49–50. *See also* empire
India, 4, 101, 122, 151
individualism: Descartes and, 79; and technological development, 77–82
industrial production, 105, 107–108, 112–113; new forms of, 116–121
inequality, 12–13, 102, 155–158; flexible accumulation and, 120; and revolution, 150
information, globalization and, 31
information technology: and globalization, 62–63; and networks, 131–132. *See also* technology
International Monetary Fund, 74, 89
Iron Curtain, 110–111
Israel, 27–28, 45

Japan, 128–129
Jay-Z, xii

Kant, Immanuel, 80
Kennedy, John F., 110
Klein, Naomi, 134–135
Kristof, Nicholas, 8

labor, 83
labor power, Marx on, 75–76
Lakota, 26
latitude, 70, 72
Latour, Bruno, 162–163; background of, 173; actor-network theory of, 162–163
Lea, David Edward, 60
Leibniz, Gottfried, 80
Leif Ericson, 67
Levy, David, xiii
local issues, and globalization, 124, 132–133, 139

Locke, John, 67
longitude, 70–72
*Lord of the Flies* (Golding), 1–2
Lovelock, James, 161–162
Luce, Henry, 102–103
Lumumba, Patrice, 60
Luther, Martin, 70–71

Magellan, Ferdinand, 67–70
malnutrition, 156–157
Manichean dualism, 45, 152–153
manners, 5
Mao Zedong, 101, 112
Marx, Karl, 74–76, 81, 83, 146–149; on structure, 99–100; on surplus value, 114–115
mass culture, 63
Mbembe, Achille, 140
McCandles, Chris, 65
Méchain, Pierre, 73
media, globalization and, 13
Mencius, 41
Merton, Robert K., 132–133
migration, 9–11, 65–69
military, scientific management and, 120
Miller, Perry, 175
mining, 167
mobile phones, 143
modernization: limits of, 93–95; term, 93; theory of, 87–88, 127
modern world: beginning of, 38–40, 55; and history, 51–54; Latour on, 162; world-systems analysis and, 48–49, 55
monad, term, 80
monetary value, 113–116, 133; standard measure of, 72–76
multinational corporations, 130, 153. *See also* corporations
myths, 124, 159–161

NAFTA, 134–135
Napoleon Bonaparte, 81, 104
nation-state. *See* state
natural selection, 82
navigation, 68–69. *See also* sea power

*Index*  I-5

neoliberalism, 140–141
networks, 131–132; Latour on, 162–163
Nigeria, 101–102
Noah, 37, 40
Northwest Passage, 5, 43, 59
nuclear weapons, 152; and crisis, 90–91
nutrition, 156–157

obsolescence, planned, 83–84, 142–145; and waste, 145–149
Occupy movement, 156
Ohmae, Kenichi, 128–129
oil crisis, 133–134, 153–154
Ong, Aihwa, 140–141
optimism, 166; cautious, 166–169
organic food, 76
original position, 35

Pakistan, 151
Palestine, 27–28
pandemics, and crisis, 90–91
Park, Daphne, 60
Parsons, Talcott, 32
party line, 143
Pericles, 51–52
periphery, 86–87
pessimism, 171–175
Piketty, Thomas, 150–151, 171
politics: globalization and, 18–19, 33–35, 62. *See also* state
Polo, Marco, 31, 41–43
Portugal, 57, 68, 85
post-developed nations, 87
postglobalists, 126
postmodernism, 19–20, 93–95, 139
poverty, 9, 12–13, 32, 155–158; capitalism and, 101–102; globalization and, 14–15; and hunger, 156–157; and migration, 66
printing press, 70
Protestant Ethic, 78
Protestant Reformation, 70

Raleigh, Walter, 68
Rawls, John, 35

Reagan, Ronald, 18, 48
reality: cyberspace and, 20–25; evil and, 26
Reconstruction, 94
remittances, 117
revolution: effects of, 151; global, possibility of, 149–158; Hobsbawm on, 169; Marx on, 146–149
Rihanna, xii
Roanoke colony, 2
Rome, 2–3, 27, 48, 50, 61
Roosevelt, Franklin D., 112
Rostow, W. W., 88
Rugman, Alan, 133–134
rural areas, future of, 167–168
Russia, 122; and imperialism, 49; revolution in, 151. *See also* Soviet Union

science. *See* technology
scientific management, 105–107, 110; and military, 120
Scott, James, 74
sea power, 68–72; future of, 174
semiperiphery, 86–87, 123
September 11, 2001, 3, 19
service-sector employment, 116–121
Shackleton, Ernest, 43
Shakespeare, William, 63
Shenzhen, 117–118
siege, 2–5
Silk Road, 13, 41–43
skepticism, 171–175
slave trade, 85–86
Sobel, Dava, 72
social action, Latour on, 162
social media, 131–132, 145
social structures: global, 95–99; nature of, 95–96; and revolution, 149–150
Society for Creative Anachronism, xv
South Africa, 123
sovereign exception, 140–141
sovereignty, 57, 137–138
Soviet Union, 58, 100–101; and Cold War, 99, 102–103, 110–116. *See also* Russia

spaces, globalization and, 29–35, 95–99
Spain, 58, 85; Armada, 68; and colonialism, 68
speed: globalization and, 16–18, 23; standard measure of, 72–76
Stalin, Joseph, 111
standardization: extreme of, 130–131; and globalization, 72–76
state, 33; Agamben on, 140; China and, 129–130; corporations and, 61; Held on, 137; Mencius on, 41; Ohmae on, 128–129; Peace of Westphalia and, 57; World War I and, 102. See also politics
stock market crash, 107–108
Sumer, 45
surplus value, 114–115

Taiwan, 141
Taylor, F. W., 105–106
Taylor, Frederick, 108–109
technology: and capital accumulation, 82–85; development of, 142–145; globalization and, 16–18; individualism and, 77–82; innovation and, 116–121; medieval, 39–40, 64, 71; military, 34–35; and navigation, 69–72; Turkle on, 23–25. See also information technology
telephone, 143
texting, 145
theory: and global cultures, 124–126; nature of, 125
Thompson, Grahame, 133–134
Thompson, John, 139
Thucydides, 51–52
Tibet, 141
time: ancient versus modern conceptions of, 51–53; globalization and, 20–23; navigation and, 69–72; present, nature of, 97
Tordesillas, Treaty of, 68
Toynbee, Arnold, 47–48
trade, free, 76; critiques of, 134–135; global, 113

transformation, term, 137
transformationalists, 126, 136–141
travel, globalization and, 138
triangle trade, 85–86
Turkle, Sherry, 23–25, 131–132
twentieth century: globalization in, 93–121; as long, 126–127; as short, 99–102, 156
Twitter, 108
typewriters, 144–145

ugliness, 26
uncertainty, 153, 158, 163
underdeveloped nations, 87
unemployment, 12, 156
United States: and Cold War, 99, 102–103, 110–116; as global leader, 85, 108; inequality in, 156; Luce on, 102–103; military, 120–121; and monetary standard, 73, 118, 133; postwar, 58–59; and state, 137
urbanization, 46, 167–168
utilitarianism, 80–81

Versailles, Treaty of, 108–109
violence: empire and, 45; globalization and, 26–29; world systems and, 61. See also conflict

Wallerstein, Immanuel, 43, 48–51, 55, 64, 84, 90–92; background of, 173; on future, 168–169
Walton, Calder, 60
waste, 145–149
water issues, 157
Watt, James, 77
Weber, Max, 51, 53–54, 78
weight, standard measure of, 72–76
West, Kanye, xiii
Westphalia, Peace of, 56–57
White, Lynn, 38–39
World Bank, 74, 89, 155
worldly asceticism, 78
world-systems: development of, 45–56; and structural crisis, 90–92; World War I and, 102–110

**Index**   I-7

world-systems analysis, 43–44, 48–51,
55, 89, 94, 127
World War I, 99; and world-system,
102–110
World War II, 103; end of, 110, 112
Wotjobaluk, xii
writing, technology and, 144–145

xenophobia, 124

Yalta Conference, 112

Zarathustra, 40, 45

# ABOUT THE AUTHOR

**Charles Lemert** is Senior Fellow in the Center for Comparative Research, Yale University, and Vice Chancellor's Professorial Fellow, University of South Australia, Adelaide. He is the author or editor of numerous books including *Uncertain Worlds* (with Immanuel Wallerstein and Carlos Rojas), *Thinking the Unthinkable,* and *Globalization: A Reader* (with Anthony Elliott, Daniel Chaffee, and Eric Hsu).

CPSIA information can be obtained at www.ICGtesting.com
Printed in the USA
BVOW06*2034121115
426603BV00004B/6/P